The Macroeconomic Debate

To my Mother and the memory of my Father

THE MACROECONOMIC DEBATE

Models of the Closed and Open Economy

Brian Hillier

BLACKWELL Publishers

First edition published as *Macroeconomics: Models, Debates and Developments* 1986
Second edition published 1991
Reprinted 1992, 1993, 1995, 1996, 1997, 1998

Blackwell Publishers Ltd
108 Cowley Road
Oxford OX4 1JF, UK

Blackwell Publishers Inc
350 Main Street
Malden, Massachusetts 02148, USA

British Library Cataloguing in Publication Data
A CIP catalogue record for this book is available from the British Library

Library of Congress Cataloging in Publication Data
Hillier, Brian
The Macroeconomic debates : models of the closed and open economy/
Brian Hillier.
p. cm.
Includes bibliographical references and index.
ISBN 0–631–17084–7 — ISBN 0–631–17758–2 (pbk)
1. Macroeconomics. 2. Keynesian economics. 3. Classical school of economics. 4. Neoclassical school of economics.
I. Title.
HB172.5.H54   1991   90–37553
339—dc20   CIP

Typeset in 11 on 12pt Times by Photo-graphics, Honiton, Devon
Printed and bound in Great Britain
by Athenæum Press Ltd, Gateshead, Tyne & Wear

This book is printed on acid-free paper

Contents

Preface

Macroeconomics is the study of the behaviour of broad economic aggregates such as output, unemployment, inflation, the balance of payments and so on. It is an interesting subject not only because it deals with such important topics, but also because it is marked by controversy and debate. There are strong differences of opinion between leading macroeconomists and correspondingly different policy recommendations made by them. This book explores the issues at stake by examining the major theoretical debates that have taken place in macroeconomics since the publication in 1936 of Keynes's *General Theory of Employment, Interest and Money*. Looking at the issues in this way enables the reader to see both the initial sources of the controversies and how the debates have led to the development of macroeconomic analysis. It is hoped that this process provides a clear and non-partisan picture of the state of macroeconomic theory.

The text begins with a thorough examination of Keynes's *General Theory* and its relationship to the Classical Model, followed by an analysis of the Neoclassical Synthesis and of the constrained equilibrium interpretation of the *General Theory*. Specific macroeconomic topics and their policy implications are then examined to provide a broadly based theoretical view of modern macroeconomic issues. The topics examined are wealth effects and the government budget constraint; inflation and unemployment; the New Classical Macroeconomics and the responses to it; and some aspects of open-economy macroeconomic modelling. It should be noted, however, that this book does not present a detailed analysis of the component parts of macroeconomic models; and it uses highly simplified forms of the consumption function and so on, in order to focus upon the underlying methodology of the models.

To capture the issues at stake in the important controversies, this book employs the types of models currently presented in intermediate-level textbooks, rather than presenting the debates exactly as they emerged, although many references to the original works are made and many quotations are used to illustrate the views of the important contributors to the debates. It is hoped that students will be familiar with elementary macroeconomic concepts and models. It is not, however, assumed that they have thoroughly absorbed the material from their introductory courses, so this book is self-contained and may be used as a textbook in its own right or as a useful complement to a more standard text. The models are developed as the discussion proceeds, using a mixture of verbal, geometric and algebraic analysis. The level of technical expertise required of the reader should not be beyond anyone who has studied elementary algebra and geometry. Terminology and techniques are introduced gradually, and the technical analysis is always backed up by verbal discussion. The reader is advised to read the appendices to the early chapters of the book before proceeding on to the later chapters.

The book is aimed at the second- and third-year undergraduate level, although large parts may be understood by beginning students. It is also hoped that graduate students and others looking for a concise overview of the state of macroeconomic theory will find the book useful. On the other hand, since each part of the book is relatively self-contained, it could prove helpful as a reference or revision source for specific topics.

The above paragraphs are taken from the first edition of this book, *Macroeconomics: Models, Debates and Developments*. The title has been changed for this new edition at the instigation of Mark Allin of Basil Blackwell. The new title more clearly indicates the focus upon the debate in macroeconomics which provides the theme of the first five sections of the book, and the new sub-title explicitly mentions the open economy, the treatment of which has been substantially revised and given more weight in the current edition. The new title does, therefore, seem to be appropriate.

The first eight chapters bear a very close resemblance to the original versions. The interpretation of Keynes's views on macroeconomic policy in chapter 2 has, however, been changed significantly and a new section on targeting policies has been added to that chapter. A new appendix has been added to chapter 4 to show how the aggregate supply curve may be derived under the assumption of downward rigidity in both prices and money wages, thus allowing a little more formal treatment of modelling under quantity constraints. These are the only major changes to the first eight chapters; although I have added a note or two here and there, rephrased the odd section and added some references to some recent work in the concluding section of chapter 8. I deliberately chose not to make wholesale changes, since I was happy with the way the book worked to put across the points which I wished to make; a view based in part upon the response of students using the book, several of whom said that they found it to be the most readable textbook they had ever come across. Since the book was written for students, such a response was indeed music to my ears. There are many topics that I could have introduced into the book, but I did not wish to harm the flow of ideas throughout the text, or attempt to turn it into an encyclopaedia of macroeconomics.

I was, however, not nearly as happy with the open-economy chapters of the first edition. I have, therefore, totally rewritten the section on the open economy and extended the treatment from two to four chapters. The new chapters cover more material, more slowly, and in a less technical manner (the phase diagrams of the first edition do not reappear here). The reason for this change is partly in response to comments that the open-economy section of the first edition did not work as well as the earlier chapters on the closed economy, but mainly because I am convinced that since we live in open economies it is important to give more weight to the treatment of open-economy issues than I did before. This change mirrors a change in my teaching, which involved substituting more lectures on the open economy in place of lectures on the component parts of the models. I hope that the result of this change to the book is to make the treatment of the open economy more consistent with the treatment of the closed economy in the earlier part, and also to improve the balance of the book.

I wish to thank several people for help in preparation of this book. My colleagues at the University of York, David Gowland and Bill Gerrard, and Teresa Lunati, a former graduate student, have influenced my ideas as well as listened patiently as I have rehearsed them. Students at both York and Trent University in Ontario have also influenced my exposition of ideas and deserve my gratitude. The current edition owes much to the first edition, and, therefore, to those thanked in the original preface and not yet thanked here: my colleagues John Bone and John Hey; Bob Jones of the University of Melbourne; Sue Corbett, then the Economics Editor at Blackwell Publishers; and students at Sunderland Polytechnic. I thank Christopher Long for copy-editing and my wife Ann for typing.

Introduction

Overview

Two issues underlie the major recurrent controversies in macro-economics. The first is whether or not a competitive monetary economy has sufficiently powerful built-in mechanisms to maintain acceptable levels of employment via automatic adjustment; the second concerns the role of the government within such an economy.

Debate on these issues was especially intense following the publication of Keynes's *General Theory of Employment, Interest and Money* (Keynes, 1936). Keynes denied, in contradiction to the then-prevailing orthodoxy, that the existence of wage and price flexibility within an economic system would guarantee full employment. On the contrary, he claimed that the system could settle at an equilibrium with unacceptably high levels of unemployment – unacceptably high in the sense that there was something that the government could and should do to improve the situation by means of demand management policies (whose usefulness the then-prevailing orthodoxy denied). It is with such issues that Part I of this book is concerned. In it, we shall examine the Classical model as a representation of the orthodoxy that Keynes set out to attack, his reasons for denying the validity of the Classical model, and the famous *IS–LM* model put forward by Hicks (1937) as an interpretation of some of Keynes's ideas and as a tool for policy analysis.

Readers should take care to note the importance of expectations in Keynes's *General Theory*. The careful reader will see from the discussion in Part I that volatile expectations about an uncertain future have a key role to play in Keynes's explanation of the business cycle (the movements in output and employment levels). However, despite his emphasis upon the importance of the future, the formal model developed by Keynes appears to neglect expectations, and the *IS–LM* model developed below does not explicitly contain them, although they are mentioned in the accompanying discussion. According to Begg, the answer to this seeming paradox is that

> Keynes decided to treat expectations as exogenous. The basic strategy is to solve the model for the current equilibrium conditional on a particular set of expectations about the future. . . . the *General Theory* confronts . . . intertemporal questions, but greatly simplifies them by adopting a particular expectations assumption, which is uniformly and consistently applied throughout, namely that expectations are exogenous, temporarily fixed, and are not systematically revised as current endogenous variables change. (Begg, 1982a, p. 25)

Begg goes so far as to say that he 'can find no other interpretation of the expectations assumption which renders the *General Theory* coherent' (1982a, p. 25). But in spite of this, and in spite of the fact that, on this interpretation, Keynes's approach greatly simplifies the analysis, it is surely rather disconcerting. If expectations are so important, a theory which simply takes them as given offers little or no explanation of one of the factors to which it gives prime importance. This could be because, as Keynes probably believed (see note 6 of chapter 4 below), expectations are based on incomplete information, and are subject to sudden revision in a way which is incapable of formal modelling. If this is so, it deals a devastating blow to macroeconomic modelling and empirical work. As Begg puts it, 'If expectations are arbitrary, and unobservable, we can never identify separately the influence of expectations and the influence of underlying economic relations; we can never test intertemporal economic theories empirically; and we can never forecast' (1982a, pp. 26–7).

Readers should bear the above interpretation of the *General Theory* in mind as they progress through Parts I, II and III of this book; it will help in understanding Keynes's methodology, and even in understanding why the *General Theory* was misinterpreted in the Neoclassical Synthesis (see below). Readers should also note that expectations, although discussed in the early parts of the book, do not formally enter centre stage until the latter pages of Part IV and, especially, in Part V. This is in accordance with the strategy of showing how debates developed over time in the economics profession. It was not until relatively late in the debate that formal modelling of expectations attracted the limelight.

The Neoclassical Synthesis is developed in Part II. It is shown that the *IS–LM* model is a model of aggregate demand only, and neglects the supply side of the economy and the determination of the price level. It is also a comparative-static model, and we will see how it can be appended to the supply side of the economy to produce a comparative-static model of the economy that makes it appear as though Keynes's *General Theory* were not really general, but rather a special case of the Classical model dependent upon the assumption of money-wage rigidity. A broad agreement was reached in the 1950s and early 1960s that this view, known as the Neoclassical Synthesis, was correct. Keynes was held to have developed nothing but a special case of the Classical model and to have added little to macroeconomic theory, even though some of his (or his disciples') policy recommendations were worthwhile.

Part II also examines the response to the Neoclassical Synthesis, led by Clower and Leijonhufvud, which offered a re-interpretation of Keynes. According to this re-interpretation, which is consistent with the discussion offered in Part I of Keynes's points of departure from the Classical model, the Neoclassical Synthesis seriously mis-represents the issues at stake between Keynes and the Classics.

The discussion in Parts I and II makes it clear that technical issues about wealth effects and interest elasticities in component parts of the models have been important in various stages of the debate. Although we do not dwell on a detailed analysis of the component parts of the models, Part III focuses upon the roles of wealth effects and the government budget constraint in the 'crowd-ing-out' debate, which concerned the relevance of fiscal policy in explaining the level of aggregate demand and led to a much improved understanding of the relationship between different government policies.

Alongside the controversies examined in Parts II and III, there has been a debate about the relationship between inflation and unemployment: about whether or not such a relationship exists, and, if it does, what form it takes and whether governments can engineer a preferred mix of the two evils. This debate forms the subject of Part IV, which shows how the explicit formal modelling of expectations at last began to assume central importance, and led to major developments. It will also be obvious that the key issues between Keynes and the Classics remain unresolved at the heart of the debate – the strength of the automatic stabilizing properties of a competitive monetary economy, and the role of government.

One way of modelling expectations is to use the assumption of rational expectations, and this assumption, allied with an assump-tion of market clearing, has produced the New Classical Macroecon-omics, which, as the name suggests, has much in common with the

Classical model. Part V deals with the New Classical Macroeconomics, and examines the claim that a predictable, deterministic monetary policy can have no effect on real magnitudes in the economy. This view suggests that an activist monetary policy (that is, one which responds to events in the economy in a predictable way) should not be used. The concluding section of chapter 8 draws together some of the ideas from earlier in the book on the competing schools in macroeconomics, and also briefly introduces the reader to some more recent developments.

The material in the first five parts of the book is presented so as to show how one debate led to another and how controversy has bred further controversy, and also, how this process has led to improvements in the techniques of analysis and the level of debate. This perspective will be best gained by reading each part of the book in turn, and it may even be useful to return occasionally for a glimpse at this Introduction to help place ideas in their proper context.

The earlier parts of the book deal with the closed economy (that is one with no links with the rest of the world); finally Part VI deals with the open economy. This part of the book, unlike the earlier parts, does not emphasise the role of debate and controversy in the development of the models to be presented. After first introducing the reader to the necessary new terminology, and describing different exchange rate systems, the analysis is developed in a step-by-step fashion using open-economy versions of the models developed earlier in the book. The implications for policy of recognizing open-economy issues are stressed, and it is shown how they depend upon the type of exchange rate system in use.

Some Preliminaries on Macroeconomic Modelling

In model-building, the relationships between variables are specified rigorously and their policy implications are examined. These relationships may be definitional – for example, total output may be defined to be equal to the sum of consumption and investment – or behavioural – for example, consumption may be assumed to depend upon total output. Definitional relationships are called 'identities', as opposed to behavioural equations or assumptions about behaviour. Models are used to simplify and present, in an abstract form, the most important elements of the complex real world. This abstraction is undertaken to reduce the complicated details of the economy in order to allow the analysis to focus upon important economic phenomena, and make it easier to predict and explain the behaviour of important variables. Indeed, for our purposes it will suffice to look at highly simplified forms of the component parts of the models. Detailed examination of the component parts, and of the controversies concerning them, is not undertaken in this book.

The decision to study aggregate variables rather than disaggregated data may also be viewed as a simplifying abstraction. For example, 'the price level' is an index formed from the individual prices of many different commodities, and it veils relative price changes such as the relative prices of apples, pears and oranges. Nevertheless, it is useful to abstract from the complications of relative price changes.

It is important to recognize that, although macroeconomics is concerned with broad aggregates, this does not mean that it is totally divorced from microeconomics; there are, in fact, a number of important linkages between the two. First, much work in macroeconomics has been concerned with making the aggregate behavioural relationships used in models consistent with theories of decision-making by individual economic agents. However, the advantages of basing macroeconomic relationships upon microeconomic foundations have been questioned by economists, noting the severe difficulties of inferring macroeconomic relationships from microeconomic ones (see for example Debreu, 1974). Second, while macroeconomics is distinct from the partial equilibrium microeconomic analysis concerned with the determinants of the price and quantity sold on the market of one commodity, say potatoes, taking all other prices and quantities as given, it is much more closely related to general equilibrium microeconomic analysis, which examines all markets simultaneously. Indeed, the Classical macroeconomic model to be analysed below will be seen to be the macroeconomic analogue of a special general equilibrium microeconomic model known as the 'Walrasian general equilibrium model'. Third, aggregation up to the industrial or sectoral level is common in microeconomics, and some degree of disaggregation is common in macroeconomics too. Thus, it may be difficult to decide whether some model is a sectoral microeconomic general equilibrium model or a disaggregated macroeconomic model.

The models to be discussed below are used for both comparative-static and dynamic analysis. The former consists of the study of the equilibrium properties of the model, and of how they change in response to changes in various factors. The latter consists of the study of the evolution of the values of the variables in the model over time, and of the stability of the model, which concerns whether or not the variables in the model will move from one set of equilibrium values towards some other set in response to changes in various factors.

The success of a model is usually measured by the degree of consistency between its predictions and real-world observations (see Friedman, 1953); but other desirable properties of models are simplicity in use and intuitive acceptability to the model-user. It should be noted that theory and evidence are closely linked by a two-way process. Models are developed in order to explain important empirical observations, are tested by confrontation with empirical observations, and are accepted, rejected or reformulated as a result of such confrontations; while at times new theories force researchers to examine and collect observations on variables previously ignored. Thus, although this book is concerned with macroeconomic theory, it is important to recognize at the outset the interplay between theory and evidence.

Part I

Keynes versus the Classics: Will Money–Wage Cuts Remove Unemployment?

1

The Classical Model

We will begin our study of macroeconomics by examining the great debate between Keynes and the Classics.[1] This task will be accomplished using stylized models to express the ideas under contention. The reader is, however, recommended to read the preface and first three chapters of Keynes's *General Theory of Employment, Interest and Money* to gain some flavour of the intensity of the debate and some measure of the task that Keynes believed he was undertaking in challenging the then-prevailing orthodoxy.

Keynes began chapter 1 of the *General Theory* by arguing that

> the postulates of the classical theory are applicable to a special case only and not to the general case. . . . Moreover, the characteristics of the special case assumed by the classical theory happen not to be those of the economic society in which we actually live, with the result that its teaching is misleading and disastrous if we attempt to apply it to the facts of experience. (Keynes, 1936, p. 3)

[handwritten margin note: class special case only]

It is useful to proceed by examining a version of the Classical model and showing how such a model implies that involuntary unemployment does not exist unless rigidities prevent market clearing. It should be noted at the outset, however, that the Classical model presented here may be said to be closer to 'a convenient strawman of Keynes's invention' (Blaug, 1978, p. 691) than a fair representation of the thinking of Keynes's predecessors, and it will be necessary, therefore, to offer some remarks later to try to balance the overall picture.

1.1 A Geometric Version of the Classical Model

The model to be outlined in this section (and in algebraic form in appendix 1.1) may be viewed as the macroeconomic analogue of the Walrasian general equilibrium microeconomic system. This system consists of a series of simultaneous supply and demand equations describing all markets throughout the economy. It is assumed that individuals and firms decide how much to buy and how much to sell of the factors and commodities in which they are interested on the basis of a given set of prices, at which they consider they can buy or sell as much as they like of these factors or commodities, constrained only by their initial endowments of factors and other assets. A crucial assumption is made that all market participants have perfect knowledge and know the values of all prices in all markets before they actually engage in any buying or selling. Furthermore, it is assumed that no trade takes place until the set of prices established in all markets is that set at which supply and demand is equated in each and every market. In order to ensure that the market-clearing set of prices is achieved, the Classical economists relied on the idea of tâtonnement or re-contracting, that is, offers to buy and sell being made but not carried out until a set of prices was found at which all markets cleared, or on the Walrasian auctioneer who was imagined to call out prices until the market-clearing set was found, at which point – and only then – trade took place.

Thus, the Classical theory is essentially a theory of continuous competitive exchange equilibrium in which prices and quantities adjust perfectly and all markets always clear. It is, therefore, a system in which involuntary unemployment of labour, which implies that the labour market is failing to clear, does not exist. Any unemployment in the real world must, according to the Classical view, be due to real wages being too high, owing to either downwards rigid real or money wages. The policy to remove unemployment would then be to adjust minimum wage regulations, curb trade union powers or, in the case of nominal wage rigidity, increase the money supply to pull up the price level, and thereby reduce the real wage towards the market-clearing level.

It ought to be clear to the reader already that the Classical view still persists today and, in its original or modern forms, continues to emerge in economic policy discussions. Similarly, it will soon be seen that Keynes's attack on the Classical model remains influential.

The variables of interest in the Classical model of this section are real output, employment, real and nominal wages, the price level, and the rate of interest. The model is of a closed economy, that is, one which does not have links with the rest of the world.

'Real wage' refers to the nominal or money wage divided by the price level; that is, if the money wage is £100 per week and consumer output costs £1 per unit, the real wage is 100 units of output, but if output costs £2 per unit the real wage is correspondingly lower, at 50 units of output, since that is all that the money wage of £100 is then worth in terms of output. Thus, real wages increase as nominal wages increase with a given price level, but decrease as the price level increases with a given nominal wage. This is why wage bargains, which set nominal wages, take into account the price level, and why wage-earners may push for nominal wage increases to try to maintain their real wages when the price level rises in inflationary times.

The Classical model may be illustrated using the figures 1.1, 1.2, 1.3, 1.4 and 1.5, which represent the separate parts of the model. These parts are put together in figure 1.6.

Figure 1.1 represents the production function, which illustrates the assumption that, with technology, capital stock and skills of the labour force all given, real output, represented by the symbol y on the horizontal axis, is determined by the level of employment, represented by the symbol N on the vertical axis. In other words, y is a function of N.[2] The slope of the function in the figure shows that output rises as employment is increased, but at a diminishing rate. That is, as employment increases from N_1 to N_2, output rises from y_1 to y_2; but for a similar increase in employment from N_2 to N_3 output rises by a smaller amount, from y_2 to y_3. Thus, successive additions to employment generate smaller and smaller increases in

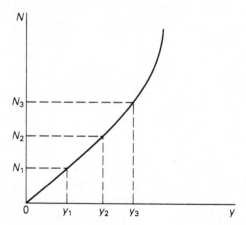

Figure 1.1 The production function

output; or, in other words, the model assumes diminishing marginal productivity of labour.

Notice that output, y, is measured in terms of units produced per period, and employment, N, is measured in terms of the number of workers employed in a given period, on the assumption that all workers are equally good at working and that they all work a constant number of hours per period. The latter two assumptions are obviously 'unrealistic' – workers are not all the same, or homogeneous, and do not all work similar hours – but these assumptions are examples of the type of abstraction, discussed in the Introduction, which is undertaken to simplify the analysis and allow it to focus more clearly on essential points. In so far as assumptions 'assume away' complications, they are useful, but of course it is possible to argue that, in some cases, relaxing assumptions and adding complications may be worthwhile if doing so allows the model to take into account or explain important phenomena which it could not do otherwise. Whether a model is considered to be acceptable must then depend, to some extent, upon the use to which it is to be put.

It should also be noted that, in the long run, positive net investment – that is, investment over and above that necessary to offset depreciation of the capital stock – will add to the size of the capital stock, while technical progress will change the state of technology, and the workforce will change in size and acquire, or lose, skills. The assumptions of a constant size of capital stock, state of technology and labour force skills and size, therefore, mean that the model is useful for short-run analysis rather than long-run analysis. The 'short run' refers to that period of time in which employment levels can change, but in which the size of capital stock, state of technology and labour force skills and size may be assumed to be fixed. The models analysed in this book are short-run in this sense.

To summarize, the production function in figure 1.1 shows the relationship between output and employment in the short run. This figure cannot, on its own, determine the level of output or the level of employment, but it can help to determine these things when used in conjunction with the other parts of the model, as will be shown.

Figure 1.2 represents the labour market.[3] The real wage, w, is plotted on the horizontal axis and employment, N, on the vertical. The supply of labour, or the number of people willing to work, is assumed to depend upon the real-wage level in such a way that, as the real wage rises, so does the number of people willing to work out of a population of a given size. The labour supply function is

(employment)

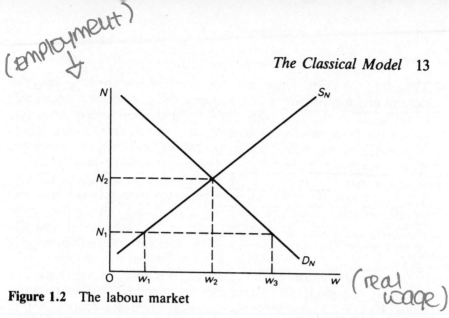

(real wage)

Figure 1.2 The labour market

plotted as the upward-sloping line S_N, which shows that N_1 people are willing to work for the real wage w_1, but N_2 are willing to work for the higher real wage w_2. The assumption about the slope of S_N would seem to be reasonable, but the reader may like to try altering it to see what happens to the conclusions reached.

The demand for labour, shown in figure 1.2 by the line D_N, also depends upon the real wage, but in such a fashion that as the real wage falls the demand for labour rises. At real wage w_3, the demand for labour is N_1, while at the lower real wage w_2 the demand for labour is higher at N_2.

The demand-for-labour curve D_N may be derived in several ways. One possible way is to assume perfect competition in both the labour and product markets. Under such circumstances profit-maximizing employers will be willing to pay workers a real wage equal to their marginal product (since this implies that the money wage is equated to the marginal revenue product of labour, that is, the market value of the marginal product of labour). Given diminishing returns to labour in the production function, employers will need a lower real wage to induce them to demand more labour; hence the D_N curve slopes downwards, as shown. Notice that in this model the demand for labour depends only upon the production function and not at all upon the level of demand that employers expect to receive for their output. The precise position and slope of D_N should, therefore, depend upon the production function drawn in figure 1.1.

The Classical model assumes that real wages are perfectly flexible and will adjust instantly to that level which clears the labour market.

Therefore, the real wage and the level of employment may be determined from figure 1.2; the supply and demand for labour will be equated at the real wage level w_2 and employment level N_2. Given the level of employment N_2 determined from figure 1.2, it is possible to use figure 1.1 to determine that output will be y_2. Thus, employment, real output and the real wage may be determined in the real sector of the model, that is, in figures 1.1 and 1.2, independently of any knowledge of the monetary sector of the model, which, given the level of real output, determines only monetary or nominal variables such as the price level and the money wage. This determination of the real variables independently of the money sector is known as the 'Classical dichotomy'.[4]

In order to determine the remaining variables of the model, or complete the model, it is necessary to introduce further relationships. Figure 1.3 represents the Classical aggregate demand curve, showing the relationship between real aggregate demand for output y, which is plotted on the horizontal axis, and the price level P, which is plotted on the vertical axis. Real aggregate demand represents the sum of the demands for output of all the individuals in the economy.

The Classical aggregate demand curve, AD, is derived from the quantity theory of money, which assumes that money is used exclusively as a means of exchange and as such is passed from individual to individual at a constant income velocity of circulation, V. The income velocity of circulation is a measure of the average number of times the money stock is exchanged in income-generating transactions during the period of analysis, so that, when V is multiplied by the nominal stock of money M, it must yield the

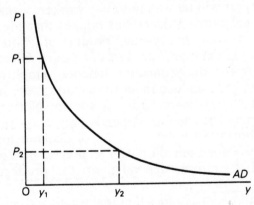

Figure 1.3   The classical aggregate demand curve

nominal value of income, Py. Thus, MV equals Py. Given that V is assumed to be constant, at least in the short run, a given nominal money stock M will yield a relationship between P and y, since manipulation of MV equals Py yields y equals MV/P. The nominal money stock M is the currency value of the money stock, for example £X, whereas the real money stock, M/P, measures the number of units of output which could be bought in one transaction using the entire nominal money stock. The curve plotted in figure 1.3 is a rectangular hyperbola determined by MV, and shows that, for given M and V, the level of aggregate demand will be y_2 if the price level is P_2, and y_1 if the price level is P_1.

Since output has already been determined to be y_2, then, given M and V, figure 1.3 indicates that the price level will be P_2. It is assumed that the government, via the central bank, can control the quantity of money in circulation, and hence can control the position of the Classical aggregate demand curve. However, since output and other real variables are determined independently of the monetary sector, such control allows the government control only over the price level and other nominal variables, but not over any real variables.

The model is completed by considering money-wage determination in figure 1.4 and interest rate determination in figure 1.5. In figure 1.4 the real wage, w, is defined as the money wage, W, divided by the price level, P. Hence, w equals W/P or W equals Pw; and for any real wage, w, there is a relationship between money wages and the price level which yields a straight line through the origin in figure 1.4. The line drawn corresponds to the real wage w_2. It shows that such a real wage could be achieved with a

Figure 1.4   Money-wage determination

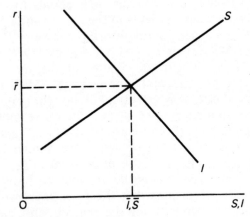

Figure 1.5 Interest rate determination

money wage W_2 and price level P_2, or with a money wage W_1 and price level P_1, or with any such combination along the line drawn. The higher the price level, the higher the money wage necessary to maintain any given real wage.

Interest Rate Determination

The interest rate, r, is determined in figure 1.5, where it is expressed as a percentage per period, and depends upon the interaction of the savings and investment functions.[5] In some circumstances it is necessary to distinguish between real and nominal rates of interest, where the real rate is, to a close approximation, the nominal rate minus the rate of inflation of the price level. For instance, if the annual nominal interest rate is 10 per cent and the inflation rate is 10 per cent, then the real rate of interest is zero. This is because £100 invested at the beginning of the year would show a nominal increase in value of £10 to £110 by the end of the year, but in real terms the £110 at the end of the year would purchase only as many goods as would the £100 at the beginning of the year, so it is sensible to say that in real terms the investment had not increased in value, or that the real interest rate was zero. However, since it is assumed here that the inflation rate in equilibrium is zero, then the real and nominal interest rates are equal in equilibrium and it is possible to talk unambiguously of the interest rate.

It will suffice, for our purposes, to use a very simple theory of investment. It is assumed that the amount of investment undertaken per perid, I, depends inversely on the rate of interest, r. This relationship is based on the idea that, for given expectations about the future net returns or profits from an investment, the higher the rate of interest, the greater is the cost of borrowing to finance investment (or the more attractive is the alternative use of funds), and hence, the lower the profitability of investment, and therefore the lower the amount of investment. Thus, the investment function is plotted as the downward-sloping line *I* in figure 1.5, which shows that, the lower the rate of interest, the higher the amount of investment. It should be noted, if it is not already clear, that 'investment' refers to investment in gross new capital formation and in inventories or stocks of finished or partly finished goods, but not to the purchase or sale of existing assets, either physical (e.g., second-hand plant and machinery) or financial (e.g. stocks, shares, building society deposits), which might in everyday usage be termed 'investment'.

It will also suffice to use a very simple theory of saving. It is assumed that the amount of saving undertaken per period, *S*, depends positively on the rate of interest, such that more will be saved the higher the rate of interest. The savings function is plotted as the line *S* in figure 1.5.

The Classical model assumes that the rate of interest adjusts to equate the supply of loanable funds created by the act of saving to the demand for such funds generated by investment. The rate of interest would, therefore, adjust to $\bar{r}$ in figure 1.5. Since this is the real (and nominal) rate of interest and can be determined independently of the level of the money supply, then this too is part of the Classical dichotomy between real and nominal variables. Since saving is just that part of income which is not consumed, and investment is just that part of output which is not consumed, then the role of figure 1.5 is really merely to show the breakdown of the demand for output, or the use of income, between expenditure on consumption and new capital goods.

It is convenient, at this point, to introduce the distinction between stock and flow variables. Flow variables are those which must be measured in terms of so many units per period. Investment is, therefore, an example of a flow variable. Stock variables, on the other hand, are those which must be measured in terms of so many units at a point in time, say the beginning of the period. An example of a stock variable is the capital stock. Stocks and flows may be related; for example, the capital stock at the end of period t is equal to the capital stock at the beginning of the period t, plus the amount of investment which was carried out during period t, minus the amount of depreciation, or wearing out of capital, which took place during period t. Since our concern is with short-run models, we neglect the effects of positive net investment on the size of the capital stock, although this neglect could be rectified to turn the model into an economic growth model. (For a discussion of such models see Haache, 1979.) Readers ought to be able to work out which of the variables discussed so far should be categorized as stocks and which as flows. Some variables, however, are best categorized as ratios rather than as stocks or flows; for example, the price level may be interpreted as the ratio of the flow of cash to the flow of goods.

The Complete Classical Model

Having discussed the separate parts of the Classical model, it is now useful to put those parts together in a way which facilitates comparative-static analysis. This is done in figure 1.6, which draws together figures 1.1–1.5.

Figure 1.6 may be interpreted as follows. The labour market in part (i) determines the real wage and employment levels, $\bar{w}$ and $\bar{N}$, at which, given the S_N and D_N curves, the labour market clears. Following the broken horizontal line from N in part (i) across into part (ii), it is possible to determine from the production function that the corresponding level of output will be $\bar{y}$. The vertical broken line drawn below $\bar{y}$ in part (ii) leads to the AS line in part (iii). The AS line represents the Classical aggregate supply function, which shows that, whatever the price level, the level of aggregate supply or output will be $\bar{y}$. In other words, output is independent of the price level in the Classical model, since changes in the price level will be matched by corresponding changes in the money wage to maintain the labour market-clearing level of employment, $\bar{N}$, and output, $\bar{y}$. Part (iii) also contains two Classical aggregate demand curves, AD_1 and AD_2, drawn for two different levels of the money stock, M_1 and the higher level M_2, respectively. For the moment consider only the curve AD_1. The intersection of the AD_1 and AS curves determines that the price level will be given by $\bar{P}_1$. Reading across from $\bar{P}_1$ to part (iv), it is possible to determine the money wage by noting that at the price level $\bar{P}_1$ the market-clearing real wage, $\bar{w}$, will be given if the money wage is given by $\bar{W}_1$. Notice, too, that it is not possible to read up from part (iv) to part (i) since the variables on the horizontal axes are different in each case. Finally, part (v) determines the level of the interest rate and of saving and investment.

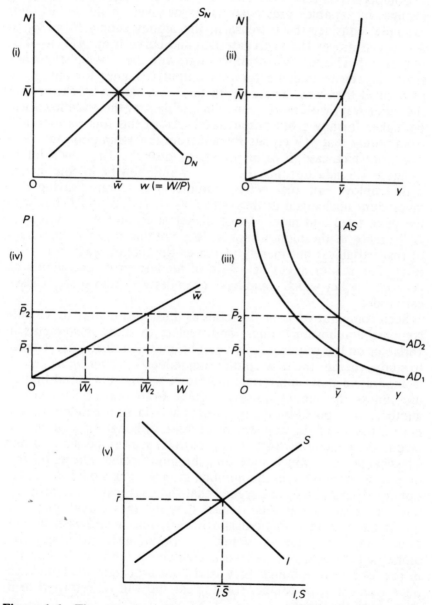

Figure 1.6 The complete Classical model. (i) The labour market. (ii) The production function. (iii) The AS–AD curves. (iv) Money-wage determination. (v) Interest rate determination

Comparative-static exercises are carried out by considering changes in variables previously taken as given in the model. For example, consider the increase in the money supply from M_1 to M_2, which moves the aggregate demand curve from AD_1 to AD_2 in part (iii). This movement shows that, with the new higher money stock, aggregate demand for real output is higher for any given price level than was the case with the lower money stock; or, put the other way, with more money in circulation, the price level will be higher for any given output level. All of this follows naturally from noting that MV equals Py and from the assumption that V is fixed, in which case, if M increases, so must Py. The new solution in figure 1.6 indicates that the model would now be in equilibrium with employment, real wage, output, interest rate, saving and investment unchanged at the values $\bar{N}$, $\bar{w}$, $\bar{y}$, $\bar{r}$, $\bar{S}$ and $\bar{I}$, but with the price level and money wage higher at P_2 and W_2. Therefore, an increase in the money supply does nothing to alter the values of real variables, but merely increases the money wage and price level. The reader might be aware of modern pronouncements on economic policy which could have been derived from such a Classical model.

Such comparative-static exercises as those carried out above only compare equilibrium values, and neglect to study movements in variables on the way from one equilibrium to another – or, indeed, to study whether the new equilibrium values will ever be achieved. Comparative-static analysis is, therefore, worthwhile but of limited use unless the model quickly adjusts from one equilibrium to another. It is possible to argue that the Classical economists did have a theory of the adjustment process, although they tended to favour the comparative-static approach. It is even possible to find Classical writings which state that the intermediate effects on real output of an increase in the nominal money stock would be expansionary. Hicks (1967) has argued that the Classical economists did not emphasize such points because they felt they would 'play into the hands of crude inflationists' (p. 260), who would wish to continue stimulating the economy by continuously increasing the money supply, which the Classical economists felt must be harmful in the long run, although they could not articulate their feelings. Such issues are, of course, still topical and will be returned to in Part IV of this book.

1.2 The Classical Model and Unemployment

The Classical model in its purest form assumes that the labour market clears via real-wage adjustment, and that the demand for labour depends only on the properties of the production function. This gives rise to the Classical dichotomy, or the property of the values of the real variables in the model being determined independently of the value of the nominal money stock. Hence government control of the money stock allows it to control only nominal variables.

Implicit in the Classical model is the view that the price system works, so that price adjustment ensures that all markets clear, including, of course, the labour market, where the real wage may be viewed as the price of labour. Acceptance of this view implies little role for government in macroeconomic management of the economy, though it may be assigned the role of ensuring that laws are established and obeyed which permit the price system to operate successfully. Any unemployment which occurs in the economy is seen as being caused by rigidities in the way of the price system's success; for example, trade union pressures or minimum wage legislation may prevent the real wage from falling to its market-clearing level.

Pigou, whose work was used by Keynes to illustrate the Classical view, summed up the position as follows:

> There will always be at work a strong tendency for wage-rates to be so related to demand that everybody is employed. Hence, in stable conditions everyone will actually be employed. The implication is that such unemployment as exists at any time is due wholly to the fact that changes in demand conditions are continually taking place and that frictional resistances prevent the appropriate wage adjustments from being made instantaneously. (Pigou, 1933, p. 252)

It is worthwhile examining how rigidities create unemployment in the Classical model. Figure 1.7 deals with real-wage rigidity and figure 1.8 with money-wage rigidity. For the sake of simplicity, both figures neglect the determination of the rate of interest and the levels of savings and investment.

In figure 1.7, part (i) represents the labour market, and shows that the market-clearing real-wage and employment levels are given by $\bar{w}$ and $\bar{N}$, respectively. However, it is now assumed that for some reason the real wage does not adjust to $\bar{w}$, but instead is rigid at the higher level of w_1. At this level of the real wage the demand for labour, N_1, falls short of the willing supply of labour, N_3.

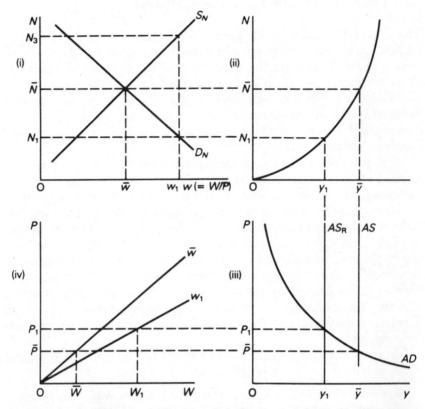

Figure 1.7   Real-wage rigidity in the Classical model. (i) The labour market. (ii) The production function. (iii) The *AS–AD* curves. (iv) Money-wage determination

Assuming that employers are not forced involuntarily to hire people, they will hire N_1 employees, leaving $(N_3 - N_1)$ people willing to work at the going real wage, w_1, but unable to find employment. Given the level of employment, N_1, it is possible to see from the production function in part (ii) that the corresponding output level would be y_1. Since the levels of employment and output can be determined independently of the money supply or the price level, the assumption of real-wage rigidity leaves this part of the Classical dichotomy intact. (We neglect to consider a determination of the real interest rate.) The relevant aggregate supply function in part (iii) is still, therefore, a vertical line, but now it is the line AS_R for the output level y_1. The market-clearing or full-employment output

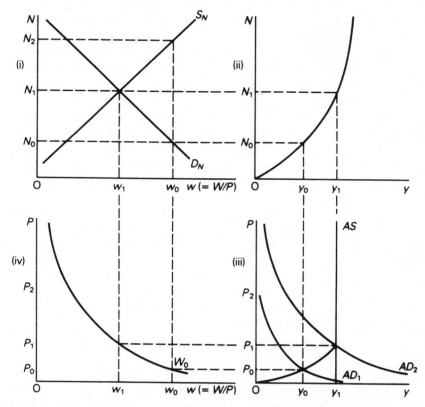

Figure 1.8 Money-wage rigidity in the Classical model. (i) The labour market. (ii) The production function. (iii) The $AS–AD$ curves. (iv) Real-wage determination

level $\bar{y}$ and the corresponding AS curve are shown in parts (ii) and (iii) to allow comparison between the rigid real-wage case and the market-clearing case. Given the level of output y_1, the price level is determined at P_1 by the intersection of the AS_R and AD curves in part (iii); compared with $\bar{P}$ for the market-clearing case. Finally, part (iv) shows the rigid real-wage line, w_1, as well as the market-clearing real-wage line, $\bar{w}$. Notice that the w_1 line lies below the $\bar{w}$ line, even though w_1 is the higher real wage. This is because, for any money-wage level, the w_1 line shows a lower price level, and therefore a higher real wage. To determine the money wage when the price level is P_1 and the real wage is w_1, it is necessary to read along the broken line from P_1 to the w_1 line and then down to the money wage W_1 in part (iv). the market-clearing money wage, $\bar{W}$, found by reading along the broken line from $\bar{P}$ to the $\bar{w}$ line, is shown for comparison.

If unemployment is due to real-wage rigidity, the government can do nothing to reduce it by adjusting its spending, taxing or monetary policies, but, according to the Classical view, can only urge wage-bargainers to settle for lower real wages via money-wage cuts, or forcibly curb union powers or change minimum wage legislation to the same end.[6] If unemployment is due to money-wage rigidity, then the Classical view may still be said to support money-wage cuts as a remedy for curing unemployment, but it could also recommend adjustment of the money supply, as figure 1.8 will demonstrate.

In figure 1.8, the money wage is treated as downward-rigid, and, furthermore, too high to allow full employment to be reached. Parts (i) and (ii) of the figure are identical to their counterparts in figure 1.7. However, it is now assumed that the money wage is exogenously determined at the level W_0, and is downward-rigid. There is, therefore, a relationship between real wages and the price level for the given money wage. This is shown in part (iv) of the figure, which determines the real wage for any price level, as opposed to part (iv) of figure 1.7, which determined the money wage.

Figure 1.8 may be interpreted as follows. Begin in part (iv) and consider the price level P_0, which yields the real wage $w_0 (= W_0/P_0)$. Reading the broken line up from w_0 in part (iv) to part (i) (which can now be done since the horizontal axes are the same in each case) shows the demand for labour at that real wage to be N_0 while the supply is N_2. Thus, at price level P_0 there will be $(N_2 - N_0)$ people unemployed. Notice that it is assumed that when supply exceeds demand the employers are not forced to hire more labour than they wish, while if demand exceeds supply people are not forced to work. These assumptions about the determination of employment when the labour market fails to clear are known as 'the short-side rule', since it is the short side of the market which determines employment (the short side being the demand side if D_N is less than S_N, and vice versa). Thus, at price level P_0 employment will be N_0, which, from the production function in part (ii), will yield output of y_0. Hence the point P_0y_0 in part (iii) is a point on the aggregate supply curve. Other points on the aggregate supply curve can be derived in a similar fashion, with the general result that, for the given money wage W_0, as the price level rises, the real wage falls so that employment and output rise with the price level up to full employment. At full employment the aggregate supply curve becomes vertical. At the price level P_1, the real wage w_1 clears the labour market for the money wage W_0. If the price level were to rise beyond P_1, to P_2 say, then the real wage, given the money wage W_0, would become so low that the demand for labour would exceed the supply of labour, but such conditions would not persist. Instead, the money wage would be bid up higher than W_0 until the real wage once again cleared the labour market.

Since the money wage is assumed to be flexible upwards, the aggregate supply curve becomes vertical, once full employment is reached, but if the money wage rises above W_0, as it would if the price level rose above P_1, then part (iv) of the diagram would need redrawing and the upward-sloping part of the AS schedule in part (iii) would shift as a result.

Finally, two different Classical aggregate demand curves are drawn in part (iii) of figure 1.8. The AD_1 curve is drawn for a level of money supply M_1, and the AD_2 curve for the higher money supply, M_2. Consider first the AD_1 curve. Its intersection with the AS curve at the price level P_0 and the level of output y_0 shows that, with the money supply M_1 and the money wage W_0, the real wage would be too high to clear the labour market; unemployment would result, and output would lie below its full-employment level of y_1. On the other hand, consideration of the intersection of the AD_2 curve with the AS curve shows that, with the money supply M_2 and the money wage W_0, the price level would be higher, at P_1, and the real wage correspondingly lower, at w_1. In this case the labour market clears, there is no unemployment, and output is at its full-employment level, y_1.

The importance of the comparison of the results for the two alternative money supplies, and the corresponding aggregate demand curves, is that it makes clear that in the face of money-wage rigidity the Classical economists could not only recommend policies to induce money-wage cuts, but could also recommend increases in the money supply to move the aggregate demand curve, increase the price level, reduce the real wage and, hence, increase employment. Also, notice that the Classical dichotomy no longer holds once money-wage rigidities are recognized; as the price level changes, it changes the real wage, employment and output.

Thus, the Classical model can be made to account for unemployment by introducing rigidities in the way of market clearing. In the case of either real- or money-wage rigidities, one policy recommendation to remove unemployment would be to remove the rigidity and bring about money-wage cuts; only in the case of money-wage rigidity would monetary policy or aggregate demand management offer any alternative, but such a policy would not be necessary if the rigidity were removed.

Keynes did not accept that the Classical model provided a reasonable understanding of the real economy, nor did he accept the policy recommendations put forward by the Classical economists. First, and possibly foremost, he argued that removing rigidities and introducing flexibility into wage bargaining would not necessarily improve the situation, and that money-wage cuts could, instead, even make matters worse and increase unemployment. In this, Keynes was questioning the stability of the economy and raising questions of dynamics. To formalize such questions requires the use of difficult techniques, and although many of Keynes's arguments in the *General Theory* concern dynamics, most of the formal modelling is, like that of the Classical model, comparative-static. This, partly at least, explains why the *General Theory* is such a difficult book to read. Keynes was grappling with difficult dynamic issues, but with only comparative-static apparatus at hand.

Thus, Keynes did not agree with the Classical view about the cause of unemployment, or with the view that money-wage cuts could help to remove it. Instead, he insisted on the need to manage the level of aggregate demand and put forward a theoretical case for the use of fiscal as well as monetary policies for that purpose. Before examining Keynes's ideas in the next chapter, it is worthwhile concluding this chapter by comparing what Keynes's predecessors actually said with the views attributed to them by Keynes and illustrated here using the Classical model.

According to Keynes, the Classical economists had no answer to unemployment other than monetary policy and the reduction of money wages. Blaug, however, has criticized this as an inaccurate description. He commented:

> That Keynes's predecessors placed much faith in monetary policy is not open to question. But it is not true that they ignored the need for compensatory public works expenditures. Nor is it true that they generally advocated wage cutting as a practical cure for unemployment. The influence of Keynes on attitudes to these policy questions was one of degree, not of kind: the upshot of Keynesian economics was to strengthen the case for public works and to place the burden of proof on anyone who would seek to remedy unemployment by depressing the wage rate. (Blaug, 1978, p. 683)

In support of this view, Blaug goes on to argue that Pigou, in *Unemployment* (1914), was putting forward a case for tax-financed increases in public expenditure as a means to reduce unemployment. Indeed, Blaug says that 'Economists before Keynes generally disapproved of unbalanced budgets. But the idea that this necessarily prevented them from advocating fiscal policy to eliminate unemployment is not supported by the evidence' (1978, p. 685).

Similarly, not all economists prior to publication of the *General Theory* favoured wage-cutting as a policy to remove unemployment. Pigou did so in his *Theory of Unemployment* (1933), but he had been less optimistic about such a policy in earlier writings; while other important writers, such as D. H. Robertson (1915), had favoured public works proposals over wage-cutting. Even those who did favour wage-cutting were probably reacting to special circumstances in Britain. The return in 1925 to the prewar exchange rate of $4.86 to £1 was widely viewed as requiring a reduction in the price level to maintain it. It is not surprising, therefore, that in such circumstances some economists also wished to see money wages fall.

It is possible, then, to view the Classical model as a distortion of the orthodox opinion really prevailing before publication of the *General Theory*. However, a more balanced view might be reached if we remember that Keynes himself was a respected Classical economist, and that in order to put his ideas across he needed a simplified version of the orthodoxy with which to contrast his views. Perhaps we should provide an understanding response to the request Keynes made in the preface of the *General Theory*, where he wrote: '. . . I must ask forgiveness if, in the pursuit of sharp distinctions, my controversy is itself too keen' (1936, p. v). After all, Keynes did improve the modelling of aggregate demand to provide a theoretical rationale to support the claim for fiscal policies, even if others had supported such policies, and he also offered some penetrating insights to explain the failure of the self-regulating properties of the monetary economy. That these insights are still controversial, and are still providing inspiration for economists attempting to provide rigorous theoretical foundations for Keynesian economics, is surely a measure of the fact that Keynes raised important questions and offered some forceful answers, even if not everyone is convinced by those answers or the policy recommendations to which they gave rise in the hands of Keynes and his followers.

Appendix 1.1
An Algebraic Version of the Classical Model

The Classical model represented in the diagrams of this chapter may be represented algebraically using the following equations, where, as before, y equals real output, N equals employment and so on. The reader who is uncomfortable with algebra is urged to attempt this section, but not to worry if it seems difficult. Wherever possible in the text, verbal and geometric analysis will be used as well as algebraic treatment.

$$y = y(N) \qquad\qquad dy/dN > 0, \; d^2y/dn^2 < 0 \qquad (1.1)$$

$$\frac{dy}{dN} = w \qquad\qquad\qquad\qquad\qquad\qquad\qquad (1.2)$$

$$D_N = D_N(w) \qquad\qquad dD_N/dw < 0 \qquad\qquad (1.2a)$$

$$S_{N_t} = S_N(w) \qquad\qquad dS_N/dw > 0 \qquad\qquad (1.3)$$

$$MV \equiv Py \qquad\qquad\qquad\qquad\qquad\qquad\qquad (1.4)$$

$$M\dot{V} = Py \qquad\qquad\qquad\qquad\qquad\qquad\qquad (1.4a)$$

$$W \equiv Pw \qquad\qquad\qquad\qquad\qquad\qquad\qquad (1.5)$$

$$I = I(r) \qquad\qquad dI/dr < 0 \qquad\qquad\qquad (1.6)$$

$$S = S(r) \qquad\qquad dS/dr > 0 \qquad\qquad\qquad (1.7)$$

Equation (1.1) simply states that y depends upon N, where $dy/dN > 0$ implies that y rises as N rises ($dy/dN < 0$ would have implied that y falls as N rises). dy/dN is, in fact, the first-order derivative of y with respect to N. Readers unfamiliar with calculus are urged not to worry about this terminology but to notice that dy/dN represents the marginal product of labour, that is, the amount by which output rises as a marginal extra labourer is employed. $d^2y/dN^2 < 0$ implies that dy/dN falls as N rises ($d^2y/dN^2 > 0$ would have implied that dy/dN rises as N rises); that is, it states that successive additions to employment generate smaller and smaller increases in output. Equation (1.1) is then the algebraic analogue to the production function drawn in the geometric analysis and is just another way of saying the same thing.

Equation (1.2) states that the marginal product of labour, dy/dN, equals the real wage, w, which, as discussed in the text, may be used to derive the demand-for-labour schedule, which is given in equation (1.2a). Equation (1.2a) states the demand for labour, D_N, depends upon the real wage in such a way that as w rises D_N

falls, as implied by $dD_N/dw < 0$. The labour market is completed by equation (1.3), which states that the supply of labour, S_N, depends upon the real wage, w. $dS_N/dw > 0$ implies, as in the geometric version above, that the supply of labour rises as the real wage rises.

Equation (1.4) is, in fact, an identity, which is represented by the symbol $\equiv$. That is to say, equation (1.4) must always hold by definition of V, which, it will be recalled, is the income velocity of circulation of money. It is impossible to predict, for example, the effect on Py of an increase in M using equation (1.4), since the effect will depend on whether V remains constant, rises or falls. Equation (1.4) is known as the 'equation of exchange'.

The Classical model goes beyond the statement of a definitional relationship such as the equation of exchange, however, and assumes that, in the short run at least, V is constant. This is shown by the use of the bar over the V in equation (1.4a), which again uses the = symbol since it is not an identity. Unlike equation (1.4), (1.4a) yields definite predictions about the effects on Py of changes in M. According to equation (1.4a), as M rises so must Py, and this is the fundamental equation of the quantity theory of money; (1.4a) is, unlike (1.4), testable, since it is possible to observe data on M and Py to see if they are in fact related in the way stated. Equation (1.4a) is just the algebraic equivalent to the Classical aggregate demand curve drawn in the geometric presentation in the text.

Note that equation (1.5), like equation (1.4), is an identity, since by the definition of the real wage, the money wage, W, must always equal the multiple of the price level and the real wage, Pw. However, for given values of P and w, equation (1.5) can be used to solve for W, and so serves a similar role to figure 1.4 in the geometric version.

Finally, equations (1.6) and (1.7) represent investment, I, and saving, S, as functions of the rate of interest, r.

Equations (1.1), (1.2), (1.3), (1.4a), (1.5), (1.6) and (1.7) may be used to solve for the values of the levels of real output, employment, prices, real wages and nominal wages in a similar way to the geometric analysis. Of course, to yield specific numerical solutions would require specific numerical versions of the equations, but the technique may be explained by the following discussion.

Equations (1.2a) and (1.3) represent the demand and supply of labour, each as functions of the real wage. They therefore represent the labour market of figure 1.2, and under the Classical assumption that the labour market clears (which, strictly, ought to be represented by a separate equation, $D_N = S_N$), may be used to determine the real wage and level of employment. The level of employment so determined may then be used in the production function equation (1.1) to determine the level of output. Thus, once more it is shown that the Classical model solves for the values of real variables independently of the quantity of money. Knowing now the level of output, it is possible to use this value in equation (1.4a), where, with further knowledge of the values of $\bar{V}$ and M, it is possible to determine the price level. All that then remains is to use the solution values for the price level and real wage in equation (1.5) to determine the solution for the money wage, and to use equations (1.6) and (1.7) to determine the interest rate, saving and investment under the Classical assumption that the interest rate adjusts to equate saving and investment (which, strictly, ought to be represented by a separate equation $S = I$). It is clear that this discussion using the equations is analogous to the discussion based upon figure 1.6 above.

Some Useful Terminology

'Exogenous' or 'autonomous' variables are variables whose values are not determined within a given model. Examples from the Classical model are the money stock, M, and the income velocity of circulation, V, whose values are said to be exogenous to the model. On the other hand, 'endogenous' variables are variables whose values are determined within a given model, examples from the Classical model being the real and money wages, w and W, whose values are said to be endogenous to the model.

While variables are classed as exogenous or endogenous in relation to a given model, they are classified as 'independent' or 'dependent' in relation to a given equation. For example, in the production function equation (1.1) the level of employment, N, is the independent variable, its value being determined outside equation (1.1); and the level of output, y, is the dependent variable, its value being determined by equation (1.1) given a value for N. y is said to be dependent upon N.

The 'parameters' of a model are the constants which, along with the values of the exogenous variables, would need to be known precisely in order to solve the model numerically, or to draw accurately the curves in the geometric representation.

An 'exogenous shock' is a change in the value of an exogenous variable or parameter, and comparative-static analysis examines the effects of such a shock on the values of the endogenous variables.

Notes

1 It may be noted that Keynes included what would now probably be called Neoclassical economics within the heading of Classical economics. See Keynes (1936, p. 3) and Blaug (1978, p. 162 and ch. 8) for a discussion of the terminology.
2 Readers may be used, in other contexts, to the dependent variable, in this case output y, being placed on the vertical axis rather than on the horizontal axis as here. There is nothing significant in choosing not to follow the usual convention here, the choice being based on the geometrical arrangement of later diagrams.
3 Straight-line functions are plotted in figure 1.2 for the sake of simplicity and neatness, although there is no requirement, in terms of the economic argument, that the functions plotted be linear. In general, throughout the remainder of the book, straight-line functions are used wherever convenient as long as the economic argument does not specifically require a curved function.
4 The Classical dichotomy occurs in this way because market-clearing real-wage adjustment fixes the level of employment and, hence, output. It will be shown below that a rigid real wage would, similarly, produce a dichotomy, while a rigid money wage would not do so; nor would a flexible money wage and market clearing if labour supply were a function of money rather than real wages.
5 Of course, in the real world there is more than one rate of interest. The rate of interest may, therefore, be assumed to be a representative rate of interest, applicable to a representative borrower or lender.
6 If it is the after-tax real wage that is downward-rigid, the government might be able to reduce the before-tax real wage paid by employers by reducing income taxation, although this may necessitate cutting government expenditure.

2

Keynes's *General Theory*

Having outlined the Classical model in the previous chapter, we now examine Keynes's reasons for rejecting that model and its associated policy prescriptions, and look at the theory and policies he offered in its stead. The first of these two tasks will be accomplished mainly by reviewing the arguments presented by Keynes in the first three chapters of the *General Theory*, but the latter task will make use of a stylized presentation of some of Keynes's ideas, especially those that can be put foward within the *IS–LM* model. This chapter also offers a brief comparison of the ideas of Keynes, the Keynesians and the Monetarists, and the final section shows how the *IS–LM* model may be used to analyse the choice between two simple proposals for stabilizing the economy – fixing the interest rate as Keynes suggested, or fixing the money supply as Friedman suggested.

2.1 Keynes's Rejection of the Classical Model

The previous chapter noted that Keynes was unwilling to accept either the Classical explanation of unemployment or the policy prescription of reducing money wages. Keynes objected to the Classical view that money-wage and price flexibility would ensure a reasonably stable dynamic system with strong forces working to keep the economy close to full employment.

According to Keynes, the fundamental basis of the Classical model may be represented by two postulates:

I   The wage is equal to the marginal product of labour . . .
II The utility of the wage when a given volume of labour is employed is equal to the marginal disutility of that amount of employment.

(Keynes, 1936, p. 5)

These postulates both relate to the labour market of the Classical model and are entirely consistent with the analysis in the previous chapter. Keynes was quite willing to accept the first postulate, which relates to the analysis of the demand for labour in the Classical model. He rejected the second.

In terms of figure 2.1, the first postulate implies that employment and real-wage levels will be given by some point on the demand-for-labour curve, D_N. The second postulate implies that 'the real wage of an employed person is that which is just sufficient (in the estimation of the employed persons themselves) to induce the volume of labour actually employed to be forthcoming' (Keynes, 1936, p. 5). In other words, the second postulate implies that labour supply depends upon the real wage, and that employment and real-wage levels will be given by some point on the labour supply curve, S_N, in figure 2.1. Taken together, the first and second postulates imply that the levels of employment and real wages will be those at the intersection of the supply and demand-for-labour schedules, shown at $\bar{w}$, $\bar{N}$ in figure 2.1, or that the labour market clears by a process of real-wage adjustment. In rejecting the second postulate, Keynes rejected the Classical view that the price system worked successfully to clear the labour market.

Keynes expressed two objections to the second Classical postulate. The first concerned 'the actual behaviour of labour' (1936, p. 12), which he believed did not, as a rule, for a given money wage, reduce the supply of labour in response to a rise in the price level. Such behaviour, he felt, was not consistent with the Classical model.

Figure 2.1 The labour market

But the other, more fundamental, objection . . . flows from disputing the assumption that the general level of real wages is directly determined by the character of the wage bargain. In assuming that, . . . the classical school have slipt in an illicit assumption . . . There may exist no expedient by which labour as a whole can reduce its *real* wage to a given figure by making revised *money* bargains with the entrepreneurs. This will be our contention. We shall endeavour to show that primarily it is certain other forces which determine the general level of real wages. . . . We shall argue that there has been a fundamental misunderstanding of how in this respect the economy in which we live actually works. (Keynes, 1936, p. 13; italics in original)

Clearly, in this passage Keynes was raising questions about the dynamic stability of the economy and dealing with more difficult issues than those of comparative statics. He is often criticized for using primarily comparative-static techniques in the *General Theory*, even though he raised dynamic questions. On the other hand, the comparative-static *IS–LM* model is criticized as a misrepresentation of Keynes because it neglect dynamics. It is not necessary to dwell on these points now, for they will form the basis of Part II of this book. It is, however, worth noting that Keynes did raise dynamic questions, but this did not preclude him from dealing with some comparative-static issues too, and the *IS–LM* model may well illustrate some of his ideas and yet neglect others. What is generally agreed is that the *General Theory* is a difficult book to understand, but whether this is because it 'is simply an untidy and badly written book' (Blaug, 1978, p. 682) or because Keynes was breaking new ground and tackling difficult problems for the first time is another question.

To return to the issue of dynamic stability, Keynes believed that the economy would not, of its own accord, maintain reasonably full levels of employment. Part II of this book will show that some writers gained the impression that Keynes's case rested on the assumption of fixed money wages, 'an impression which was false but not preposterous on a careless reading of the *General Theory*' (Hahn, 1984, p. 10). Rather, Keynes argued that 'There is, therefore, no ground for the belief that a flexible wage policy is capable of maintaining a state of continuous full employment. . . . The economic system cannot be made self-adjusting along these lines' (1936, p. 267). His reasons behind this claim depended on arguments that distribution and expectations effects may destabilize the adjustment of the economy and render wage and price flexibility useless, or even harmful.

First, consider distribution effects. Falling money wages and prices mean that the real value of debts will rise, increasing the real wealth of lenders and the real indebtedness of borrowers. It cannot be assumed that these two effects will cancel one another out. On the contrary, as Keynes put it, 'the embarrassment of entrepreneurs who are heavily indebted may soon reach the point of insolvency – with severely adverse effects on investment' (1936, p. 264). Second, the fall in money wages and prices may create expectations of further falls, leading to households and firms post-poning purchases. Both these effects may cause the demand for output to fall as the price level falls, and not, as in the case of the Classical aggregate demand curve of the last chapter, to rise as the price level falls. Aggregate demand (and hence, as we shall soon see, supply) may move away from its full-employment level as the price level falls. In the light of such considerations, Keynes even favoured money-wage rigidity over flexibility (1936, p. 270). He did not, therefore, rest his case on the assumption of rigid money wages. Had he done so, the *General Theory* would have been little more than a special case of the Classical model, and little different to the analysis discussed using figure 1.8, with money-wage rigidity imposed upon the Classical model.

Keynes did, however, argue that workers would resist money-wage cuts, while they might not resist cuts in real wages brought about by increases in the price level. Such behaviour on the part of workers may appear, at first sight, to depend on irrational money-wage illusion, the worker being concerned about money wages rather than about the real value of those wages. This is not, however, necessarily so. Keynes argued that workers cared about their position in the wage distribution, or their wage relative to other workers' wages, as well as about absolute real wages. There is nothing necessarily irrational in this; it all depends on what provides utility for workers. If workers are concerned about relative wages, then they may, quite rationally, resist money-wage cuts imposed on one industry, or even one firm, at a time, since this would imply a reduction in their real wages relative to the general level. On the other hand, they may not resist real-wage cuts brought about by increases in the price level, which affect all workers simultaneously and do not affect relative positions.[1] Keynes, there-fore, recognized the difficulty of imposing money-wage cuts on a piecemeal basis, but did not rely on this for his case against Classical economics.

Keynes agreed with the Classical economists in recognizing that some frictions or rigidities in the real world must be the cause of some unemployment. Like the Classical economists, he too defined full employment to be consistent with both frictional and voluntary unemployment – frictional unemployment being due to 'various inexactnesses of adjustment which stand in the way of continuous full employment', such as 'the fact that the change-over from one employment to another cannot be effected without a certain delay'; voluntary unemployment being due to 'the refusal or inability of a unit of labour, as a result of legislation or social practices or of combination for collective bargaining . . ., to accept a reward corresponding to the value of the product attributable to its marginal productivity' (Keynes, 1936, p. 6).

Thus, like the Classical economists, Keynes accepted that some unemployment may be due to rigidities in the way of market clearing. However, he went further than this and added a third category of unemployment called 'involuntary unemployment', defined as follows: 'Men are involuntarily unemployed if, in the event of a small rise in the price of wage-goods relative to the money-wage, both the aggregate supply of labour willing to work for the current money-wage and the aggregate demand for it at that wage would be greater than the existing volume of employment' (Keynes, 1936, p. 15). In other words, involuntary unemployment exists if men are unemployed who, in the face of a rise in the price level, would be offered and would accept jobs at a lower real wage than that prevailing in the labour market.

In terms of figure 2.1, involuntary unemployment exists if the real wage is set at w_1 above the market-clearing level $\bar{w}$, with employment set by the demand for labour at N_1 below the market-clearing level of $\bar{N}$, and with N_3 people willing to work at the wage w_1. Involuntary unemployment is measured by $(\bar{N} - N_1)$ rather than $(N_3 - N_1)$; if the real wage fell to $\bar{w}$ and employment rose to $\bar{N}$, then involuntary unemployment would disappear. Involuntary unemployment is then, according to Keynes, just that part of the number of unemployed people which can be removed by reducing the real wage. The trouble with this definition is that it would seem to apply equally well to unemployment caused by a minimum wage law, in which case a rise in the price level would help to reduce the real wage and, possibly, increase the demand for labour, although Keynes clearly wished to describe such unemployment as voluntary. The point is that Keynes's classification of unemployment depends upon the *causes* of unemployment, even if the *effects* of various causes appear to be similar. The policy implications may depend more upon the cause of unemployment than upon the effects; for example, unemployment due to an excessive minimum wage might be reduced by a cut in the legal minimum wage, but unemployment due to a lack of aggregate demand might not be reduced, and could feasibly be increased, by such a policy.

Involuntary unemployment is caused by the failure of the real wage to adjust to clear the labour market, which Keynes believed to be due to the inability of labour, as a whole, to reduce the real wage by making money-wage bargains with employers. It is also clear that involuntary unemployment is inconsistent with the second Classical postulate since that postulate implies the absence of unemployed people willing to work for a real wage below the prevailing real wage; that is, the second postulate implies that employment and real wages will be given by some point on the labour supply curve and not by some point off it like w_1N_1. It is equally clear that, according to Keynes, involuntary unemployment is due to an excessively high real wage. But Keynes, unlike the Classical economists, believed that unemployment was not necessarily due to labour demanding too high a real wage, nor would acceptance of lower money wages necessarily prove to be a remedy for unemployment; instead, a rise in the price level would be a better way to bring about a fall in real wages and increase employment. Keynes was, in this sense, possibly playing into the hands of the crude inflationists.

To summarize, Keynes's main objection to the Classical model concerned the second Classical postulate and the idea that the real wage would adjust to clear the labour market. In the *General Theory*, therefore, he attempted to work out the behaviour of a system which did not assume labour market clearing, and which allowed for the possibility of involuntary unemployment. He, therefore, argued that his was the more general theory, since the Classical theory was applicable only to the special case of labour market clearing, or full employment.

The *General Theory* is, however, a difficult text, and so economists following Keynes attempted to set out the main ideas using relatively simple frameworks, the most important of which became a standard tool for macroeconomists under the name 'the *IS–LM* model'. The next section turns to such simplified expressions of Keynes's ideas.

2.2   Keynesian Models of Income Determination

The previous section has shown that Keynes's most fundamental objection to the Classical model concerned the assumption that money-wage and price flexibility would ensure full employment. This is a dynamic issue, and Keynes offered persuasive reasons depending upon distribution and expectations effects to support his views.[2] However, he was unable to offer a formal dynamic model in place of the Classical model. Instead, he illustrated the effect of the failure of the price mechanism by treating expectations, money wages and prices as given within a comparative-static model, and he showed that in such circumstances involuntary unemployment could occur. This part of his argument is, indeed, at first sight, little different from the Classical model with the assumption of money-wage rigidity added. The difference lies not so much in the model Keynes offered at this stage, which can be viewed as just a more complicated model of aggregate demand than that provided by the quantity theory, as in Keynes's reason for assuming given money wages, prices and expectations, and in his contrary opinion as to what would happen if money wages and prices were flexible in the real world.

Keynes's comparative-static analysis will be examined using stylized models which have been developed to simplify his ideas. These models, like the Classical model of the previous chapter, deal with a closed economy; it will also be useful to add the new assumption that the price level and money wage are fixed. It should be noted that, as in the *General Theory*, this assumption is made for simplicity and convenience and is not meant to be a description of reality.[3] Under this assumption, therefore, all changes in aggregate demand result in changes in real income or output at a constant price level.

The Keynesian Multiplier Model

This is the simplest Keynesian model available and is usually covered in introductory macroeconomics courses. It is, however, worth reviewing here.

Having rejected the second Classical postulate and the assumption of full employment, Keynes had to provide an explanation of the forces which actually determined the levels of output, employment and real wages. His central answer was that they all depend upon the level of 'effective demand' in the economy. The government, therefore, has a potential role in Keynes's system, since by adjusting its policies it can hope to adjust effective demand. This role is similar to that allowed for monetary policy in the Classical model with money-wage rigidity, but Keynes also offered a role for fiscal policy, and, as has been said above, he denied the usefulness of money-wage cuts.

Keynes defined 'effective demand' as the total of the consumption and investment demand which businessmen expect to experience given the amount of employment they currently undertake. Business expectations are not explained within the model, but it is clear that, for the economy to be in a position of rest (with no forces making for changes in the value of economic variables), effective demand expected by businessmen must equal actual aggregate demand, and businessmen must provide just enough output to meet aggregate demand. Thus, in a position of rest, aggregate demand determines real output or income, but since consumption demand may be assumed to depend upon income, then both aggregate demand and income simultaneously determine one another. According to Keynes, there is no reason why the level of effective demand at a position of rest or equilibrium ought to coincide with the level of real income necessary for full employment. For Keynes, equilibrium simply meant a state of affairs at which expectations were being fulfilled and businessmen had no reason to revise either their expectations or their employment and output levels, while for the Classical economists, equilibrium also implied market clearing. Keynesian unemployment equilibrium, therefore, is sometimes referred to as a disequilibrium state, since unemployment implies that the labour market does not clear.

The effective demand idea may be illustrated using the following, very simple, system of equations:

$$E \equiv C + \bar{I} \tag{2.1}$$

$$C = a + by \qquad a > 0, 1 > b > 0 \tag{2.2}$$

$$y = E. \tag{2.3}$$

Equation (2.1) is a definitional relationship defining effective demand, E, to be equal to the sum of consumption demand, C, and investment demand, $\bar{I}$. It can be assumed that, in equilibrium, effective demand equals actual demand. The bar over the I term in equation (2.1) indicates that it is given exogenously; C, however, is determined within the model by equation (2.2). Remember that 'investment' refers to investment in gross new capital formation and also includes any change in inventories, but excludes the purchase or sale of existing assets either physical (e.g. plant and machinery) or financial (e.g. stocks and shares), since such sales do not directly add to the demand for current output. Equation (2.2) is a behavioural relationship which expresses the assumption that consumption is determined by a constant, *a*, and some proportion, *b*, of the current level of real income, *y*. 'Consumption' refers to expenditure by the personal sector on new goods and services. The parameter, *b*, is known as 'the marginal propensity to consume', and represents that proportion of any increment in income which will be spent on consumption; following Keynes, it is assumed that *b* is greater than nought but less than one, so that part, but not all, of any increment in income will be consumed. The parameter *a* is often assumed to represent the minimum consumption requirements necessary to sustain life, but is best seen as a mathematical artefact used to allow a nonlinear real-world relationship to be approximated by a straight line, and in a statistical estimation of the consumption function it is certainly not an estimate of minimum consumption requirements. Equation (2.3) is the equilibrium condition that output, *y*, equals effective demand, *E*.

Equations (2.1)–(2.3) are known as the 'structural' equations of the model, since along with the parameters or coefficients of the equations, such as *a* or *b*, they define the structure of the model. Manipulation of the equations (2.1)–(2.3) to yield solutions for the endogenous variables of the model, such as *C* and *y*, in terms only of the exogenous variables and parameters, yields 'reduced-form' equations. For example, to find the reduced form for *y* substitute (2.2) into (2.1) to yield (2.4) and then substitute (2.4) into (2.3) to yield (2.5), which, on taking all the *y* terms to one side and rewriting, yields (2.6) as follows:

$$E = a + by + \bar{I} \tag{2.4}$$

$$y = a + by + \bar{I} \tag{2.5}$$

$$y = \frac{a + \bar{I}}{1 - b} \tag{2.6}$$

Equation (2.6) is the reduced form for *y*. Similarly, it is possible to derive the reduced form for *C*, which yields (2.7), by substituting (2.6) into (2.2):

$$C = a + b \left(\frac{a + \bar{I}}{1 + b} \right). \tag{2.7}$$

If government spending on real goods and services, G, is introduced into the model and assumed to be given by government decision, then structural equation (2.1) in the above model may be replaced by equation (2.8):

$$E \equiv C + I + G. \tag{2.8}$$

Solving equations (2.8), (2.2) and (2.3) for the reduced forms for y and C yields equations (2.9) and (2.10):

$$y = \frac{a + I + G}{1 - b} \tag{2.9}$$

$$C = a + b \left(\frac{a + I + G}{1 - b} \right). \tag{2.10}$$

As equation (2.9) shows, the government may adjust y by adjusting G. Specifically, a change in G by the amount ΔG will change y by the amount Δy equals $\Delta G/(1 - b)$, as may be seen by comparing equations (2.9) and (2.11). The Δ symbol is used to represent changes in variables:

$$y + \Delta y = \frac{a + I + G + \Delta G}{1 - b}. \tag{2.11}$$

Thus, in this model changes in G have multiple effects on y of $\Delta G/(1 - b)$ where $1/(1 - b)$ is greater than unity since b is less than unity and greater than nought. The term $1/(1 - b)$ is known as the 'multiplier'.[4] If the economy were represented by some set of equations such as those above, and the government knew the value of the multiplier, then it could achieve a level of y consistent with full employment by manipulating the level of its spending, G.

The above model may be illustrated diagrammatically using figure 2.2, with E plotted on the vertical axis and y on the horizontal axis. The dotted line drawn at 45° to the horizontal and vertical axes plots all points at which y equals E. The $C + I + G$ line cuts the vertical axis at $a + I + G$ when $y = 0$ and has a slope of b, which relates increases in C to increases in y. The point at which the $C + I + G$ line cuts the 45° line gives the solution to the system. The solution shown of y_0, E_0 is assumed to be below the level of full-employment income, y_{fc}, which could, however, be

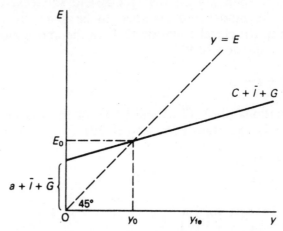

Figure 2.2   Effective demand and income in a simple Keynesian model

achieved if the government increased G to raise the $C + \bar{I} + G$ line to the point of intersection with the 45° line vertically above y_{fc}.

This simple model takes as an assumption Keynes's idea that the economic system does not necessarily yield a full-employment equilibrium, and illustrates the roles of aggregate demand and fiscal policy in determining equilibrium in non-market-clearing models.[5] However, it is a very simple model and omits several important factors discussed by Keynes in the *General Theory*. Therefore, it is worthwhile dealing with a more complete, and complicated, model which captures more of Keynes's ideas. Such a model is the *IS–LM* model which is presented next.

The IS–LM Model

The *IS–LM* model captures more of Keynes's ideas than the multiplier model by introducing the money market as well as the product, or goods, market and also by dealing with endogenous investment. The terminology *IS–LM* was popularized by Hansen (1949), but the actual technique stems from an article published by Hicks (1937) a few months after the publication of the *General Theory*, of which it has now become the standard summary. Indeed, Keynes himself wrote to Hicks that he 'found it very interesting and really [had] next to nothing to say by way of criticism' (Moggridge, 1973, p. 79).

It will be useful first of all to examine the goods market, or *IS* part, of the model, then to examine the money market, or *LM* part, before the two are put together to complete the model.

The IS *Function: Goods Market Equilibrium in a Closed Economy Without Government* Unlike the multiplier model, the *IS–LM* model does not assume that investment is exogenous; rather, it is assumed to depend upon expectations, the price of capital goods, the price of other inputs and the rate of interest. All the determinants of investments other than the rate of interest will be treated as exogenously given, the rate of interest being determined within the model by the interaction of the goods and money markets. It will suffice to assume that investment depends inversely on the rate of interest, *r*, as in the Classical model. Thus, investment and the interest rate are related as follows.[6]

$$I = I(r) \qquad \frac{dI}{dr} < 0 \qquad\qquad (2.12)$$

Equilibrium in the goods market requires effective demand to equal output, as in the multiplier model above, or, equivalently, planned savings to equal planned investment. There is a distinction between planned (or desired or *ex ante*) measures of variables and actual (or realized or *ex post*) measures.[7] Actual savings are defined to equal actual investment, since in the simplest system output equals consumption plus investment and output equals income, which is either consumed or saved. However, plans need not always be fulfilled. Firms may plan to sell more output than they actually sell, and may then add the difference to inventories; this will represent unplanned investment. Actual investment will, therefore, consist of a planned and an unplanned component. Only in equilibrium will all plans be fulfilled and planned savings equal planned investment. Dynamic models need to specify carefully what happens when all plans are not consistent with one another and to specify which, if any, are fulfilled. The present discussion is concerned with Keynesian unemployment equilibrium modelling and need not discuss dynamic issues further. Clearly, the notation *I* and *S* stand for planned values of those variables in the present context.

Planned investment is an inverse function of the rate of interest, but for Keynes, and unlike the Classical model, planned savings are assumed to vary positively with income. This follows naturally from the assumption that consumption depends on income. If consumption rises with income but the marginal propensity to consume is less than unity, then savings must rise with income too. Keynes did, in fact, recognize the influence of several factors other than income on both consumption and savings, and among these he included the interest rate. However, explicit inclusion of these other factors in the analysis complicates matters, so the simpler functions are used here. It will be seen in Part II of the book that recognition of the role of wealth in these functions has important consequences on the arguments, but recognizing a role for the interest rate would not have such profound effects.

Now, if, starting from an initial equilibrium, planned savings rise with income, it will be necessary for the interest rate to fall in order to induce greater planned investment to maintain equilibrium with planned savings equal to planned investment. The *IS* curve is the locus of all combinations of income and interest rate values at which planned savings would equal planned investment, and it slopes downwards from left to right in figure 2.3. The *IS* curve in figure 2.3 represents points of equilibrium in the goods market; if the rate of interest is r_0 and the level of income is y_0, then planned investment will equal planned savings; but so too, if the rate of interest is r_1, then, although planned investment would be higher than at r_0 and equilibrium would require higher planned savings also, these would be forthcoming if income were y_1. Any point on the *IS* curve represents a potential equilibrium point for the economy as a whole; which equilibrium point will prevail will be shown to depend upon the interaction of the goods market with the money market. Notice that equilibrium in the goods market in this context means that, if a certain level of output, say y_0, were to be produced,

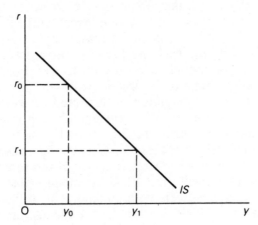

Figure 2.3 The *IS* curve

then it would also be demanded if the rate of interest were at a certain level, r_0 in this case.[8] This notion of goods market equilibrium does not, therefore, closely parallel the usual microeconomic notion of the intersection of supply and demand curves. Indeed, it will be shown in the next chapter that the *IS–LM* model is really only a demand side model.

The IS *Function: With Government Spending and Taxation*   It is useful now to extend the *IS* curve analysis to include government spending, G, as an extra element of demand, and taxation, T, as a drain on people's spending power. In this case, the equilibrium condition is no longer that planned savings equal planned investment, but rather that planned withdrawals from income, that is savings plus taxes, equal planned injections into demand, that is government spending plus investment, so that, once again, in equilibrium what is produced is demanded. This yields

$$S + T = I + G \qquad\qquad (2.13)$$

as the equilibrium condition. That this is the correct equilibrium condition can be seen by considering that output now equals C plus I plus G, that output equals income, and that the part of income which it is not planned to consume must be planned to be used to pay taxes or save. Hence when (2.13) holds, all plans will be fulfilled and all output will be demanded without any involuntary savings or investment taking place.

Under the simplifying assumption that government expenditure and tax receipts are independent of the level of income, it is quite easy to show that the position of the *IS* curve depends upon the levels of government expenditure and taxation. Increasing (reducing) G moves the *IS* curve rightwards away from the origin (leftwards towards the origin), since it increases (reduces) planned injections at any interest rate and requires correspondingly higher (lower) income levels to maintain equality between planned injections and withdrawals. The reader ought to be able to understand why reducing (increasing) taxes shifts the *IS* curve rightwards (leftwards), that points off the *IS* curve to the right represent points of excess supply of goods (planned withdrawals exceed planned injections), and that points off the *IS* curve to the left represent points of excess demand for goods (planned injections exceed planned withdrawals). Also, the reader ought to be able to work out the effects of a standard rate income tax on the *IS* curve.

Appendix 2.1 presents a diagrammatic derivation of the *IS* curve with government spending and taxation, and the reader may find that it helps to clarify the above discussion.

To summarize, the *IS* curve provides a locus of combinations of *y* and *r*, any of which could equilibrate the goods market; it does not show which of those combinations would yield overall equilibrium in the economy. In order to solve for the overall equilibrium *y* and *r* values it is necessary to consider also the money market. Unlike the pure Classical model, there is no dichotomy between the goods and money markets. In the Keynesian *IS–LM* model the values of real variables, such as income, depend upon the money supply.

The LM *Function: Money Market Equilibrium in a Closed Economy*   Equilibrium in the money market requires that the demand for money, *L*, equal the supply of money, *M* (hence, *LM* for *L* = *M*), and, as for the goods market, this depends upon specific combinations of *y* and *r*. The supply of money may be considered to be determined exogenously by government decision.[9] The demand for money is determined within the model.

Following Keynes, the demand for money may be analysed according to the motives which induce people to hold money. Keynes identified three such motives:

(1)   the transactions motive, i.e., the desire to hold money to carry out personal and business transactions;
(2)   the precautionary motive, i.e., the desire to hold money for security to cover unforeseen expenditures;
(3)   the speculative motive, i.e., the desire to hold money with the object of making a profit by reacting to expected changes in the interest rate.

Since all three are motives for holding wealth in the form of money rather than other assets, and since money is the most liquid of all assets, where liquidity is a measure of the certainty of the money value of an asset and the ease with which it may be used to acquire other assets, then Keynes's demand for money has come to be called the liquidity preference theory.

The amount of money necessary to satisfy the transactions and precautionary motives is assumed to depend positively upon the level of income both for individuals and for society as a whole. Let the sum of the demand for money to satisfy these two motives be known as the 'demand for active balances', and denoted by the symbol L_1. It is then possible to write

$$L_1 = l_1(y) \qquad \frac{dL_1}{dy} > 0. \qquad (2.14)$$

Equation (2.14) is, in fact, quite similar to the quantity theory and, indeed, if dL_1/dy is assumed to be constant, then it is almost identical. However, the liquidity preference theory differs from the quantity theory by taking into account the speculative motive.

Let the demand for money to satisfy the speculative motive be known as 'the demand for idle balances', denoted by L_2. The demand for idle balances is considered to be a function of the rate of interest relative to the rate of interest expected to prevail in the future. This is so because the only other financial asset considered in the model is government interest-bearing debt in the form of annuities. Annuities are bonds which yield a fixed nominal amount, called the 'coupon', each year to their owner. If the coupon is £b, and if the interest rate r_0 is expected to prevail for the future, then it can be shown that the value of the bond is $£b/r_0$. A simple example illustrates: if the rate of interest is 10 per cent per annum, then interest on £100 is £10 per annum, so a bond yielding £10 per annum would be worth £100, i.e., £10/0.10 or $£b/r$. From the formula for the value of a bond, it is clear that as r rises the value of the bond falls, and as r falls the value of the bond rises. This means that capital gains or losses may be made on bond holdings. If people expect the interest rate to rise and bond values to fall they may wish to hold their wealth as money rather than bonds, while if they expect the interest rate to fall they may wish to buy bonds to try to reap capital gains. Obviously, the potential capital gains or losses may be important in people's decisions to hold bonds, as well as the size of the coupon payment. Keynes assumed that different people had different expectations about the future course of the interest rate, but that for some given state of expectations the lower the current interest rate, the more people expect the interest rate to rise and bonds to fall in price, and, hence, the greater the preference for liquidity or money. The demand for idle balances, therefore, may be assumed to vary inversely with the interest rate as follows:

$$L_2 = l_2(r) \qquad \frac{dL_2}{dr} < 0 \qquad (2.15)$$

The total demand for money, L, is the sum of L_1 plus L_2. For equilibrium in the money market, it is necessary that the total demand for money equal the total supply of money, M, as follows:

$$L = L_1 + L_2 = \bar{M}. \tag{2.16}$$

From equation (2.16) it is clear that, as income rises and L_1 rises, then, for equilibrium to hold with the money supply fixed at $\bar{M}$, it is necessary for L_2 to fall. L_2 will fall if r rises; therefore, for equilibrium in the money market, the higher the level of income, the higher must be the interest rate.

For a given money supply, the *LM* curve shows those combinations of income and interest rate consistent with equilibrium in the money market. It slopes upwards from left to right as in figure 2.4. The shape and position of the curve depend upon the parameters of the demand-for-money function, which is the sum of the demands for idle and active balances, and also upon the size of the money supply. Increasing the money supply moves the *LM* curve rightwards away from the origin, since for any level of the interest rate and given idle demand for money, the new larger money supply will be able to support a higher active demand for money, which will occur only if income is correspondingly increased. A reduction in the money supply moves the *LM* curve leftwards towards the origin for similar reasons. The reader may care to work out what happens if the L_1 or L_2 functions shift, and to interpret points off the *LM* curve.

Appendix 2.2 presents a diagrammatic derivation of the *LM* curve, and may help to clarify the above discussion.

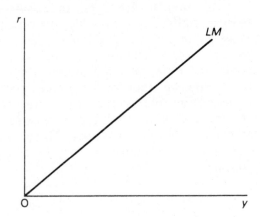

Figure 2.4   The *LM* curve

The IS–LM *Model of Goods and Money Market Interaction*   The *LM* curve provides a locus of combinations of y and r, any of which could equilibrate the money market, while the *IS* curve provides a locus of combinations of y and r, any of which could equilibrate the goods market. If the *IS* and *LM* curves intersect, then the y and r combination at the intersection is consistent with equilibrium in both the goods and the money markets. The equilibrium y and r combination for the economy as a whole is, therefore, that combination at the intersection of the *IS* and *LM* curves, as shown in figure 2.5.

The *IS–LM* model solves for the v .' ·· of y and r resulting from the simultaneous interaction of the goods and money markets. The level of output cannot be determined independently of the money market, as in the case of the Classical dichotomy. Nor can the equilibrium level of output be assumed to be necessarily consistent with full employment, and in figure 2.5 the equilibrium, y_e, is shown to be below the full-employment level of output y_{fe}. However, since the government may adjust the position of the *IS* and *LM* curves by its policy actions, it may take action to achieve the full-employment level of output. This policy conclusion harks back to that for the Classical model with money-wage rigidity, but Keynes's analysis provides a theoretical foundation for the use not only of monetary policy, but also of fiscal policy.

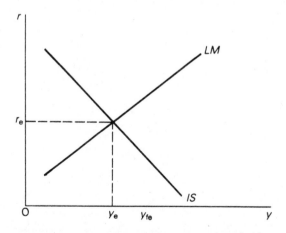

Figure 2.5   Simultaneous equilibrium in the goods and money markets: the *IS–LM* model

Fiscal and Monetary Policy in the IS–LM Model

The government enters the *IS–LM* model via its control of government spending, taxation and the money supply; these variables may thus be used by the government as instruments or tools for achieving its policy targets. Assume that the government's sole target is to achieve the full-employment level of output, y_{fe}, from a position of unemployment such as y_e in figure 2.6. The target of y_{fe} may be achieved by shifting one or both of the *IS* and *LM* curves rightwards such that their intersection shifts to a point vertically above y_{fe}. First of all, consider shifting the *IS* curve; this could be achieved by fiscal policy, by reducing taxation or by increasing government spending, since it has already been shown that these policy instruments determine the position of the *IS* curve. The result of a successful policy of this kind is illustrated in figure 2.6, which also shows quite clearly that, as well as causing output to rise from y_e to y_{fe}, the policy also causes the interest rate to rise from r_e to r_1.

It is worth examining the fiscal policy solution to unemployment in a little more detail. Considering the method of increasing government spending, it is, of course, reasonable to ask how this increase in spending is to be financed. If it is assumed that the government budget was in balance initially, that is, that the sum of government expenditures on real goods and services, G, plus any expenditures on transfer payments, such as unemployment benefits, or interest payments on government debt, was matched exactly by tax revenues, then it becomes easy to see that the government must

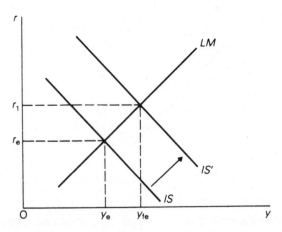

Figure 2.6 The fiscal policy solution to unemployment

finance the increase in government spending by either increasing taxation, borrowing more by selling government bonds, or 'printing money' and using the new money to pay for its extra spending.[10]

It may seem that increasing taxation to finance the increase in spending would offset any effects on the *IS* curve, but in this model this is not the case. The extra taxation only partly offsets the effects of the extra spending, and so it is possible to shift the *IS* curve by equal increases in spending and taxation. Increasing taxation by £1 will, in the first instance, reduce private sector disposable income by £1, which will reduce private sector consumption by less than £1, say by 80p; but if the government spends all of the £1 extra tax revenue, then aggregate demand rises by 20p, income will rise as a result, and the multiplier will come into play. Indeed, in the simple Keynesian multiplier model, the multiplier for a balanced budget increase in government spending – that is, one where the change in spending is matched by a similar change in lump-sum taxation – is unity, so that the change in *y* equals the change in *G*. For the *IS–LM* model, the balanced budget multiplier in normal circumstances is positive but less than unity, since as income rises the transactions demand for money rises, leaving less available for idle balances and putting pressure on the interest rate as individuals try to sell bonds to increase their money holdings. Aggregate money holdings do not rise, so the effect of the attempt to sell bonds is simply to lower their price and push up the interest rate. As the interest rate rises, private sector investment falls and this reduces the multiplier below that in the simple Keynesian multiplier model, since that model treats investment as exogenous. The reduction in investment as a result of increased government spending is known as 'crowding out'.

Financing the extra government spending by selling government bonds leads to a larger multiplier than in the balanced budget case, since the bond sales do not have the negative effects of taxation on private-sector consumption spending. Since the multiplier is larger in this case, then a given shift in the *IS* curve can be achieved for a smaller change in *G* than in the balanced budget case. Again, the multiplier in the *IS–LM* model is smaller than that in the simple Keynesian multiplier model as a result of the different treatments of investment. Notice that the *IS–LM* model does not need to examine conditions for bond market equilibrium separately from the conditions for goods and money market equilibrium, since if the goods market and money market are in equilibrium then nobody is trying to exchange bonds for goods or money so the bond market must be in equilibrium too.

It will be useful to leave analysis of a money-financed increase in government spending until after discussion of monetary policy effects on the *LM* curve, since money-financed increases in spending affect both the *IS* and *LM* curves simultaneously. Just as an increase in government spending from a balanced budget position requires an increase in taxation, or borrowing, or the printing of money so a reduction in taxation requires a commensurate reduction in government spending, or the sale of new bonds, or the printing of money to cover the gap left in government finances by the cut in taxation. The analysis in each case is very similar to the corresponding analysis for an increase in spending, and the reader should trace through the details as a useful exercise.

As an alternative to using fiscal policy to shift the *IS* curve to achieve the full-employment level of output, y_{fe}, the government could use monetary policy to shift the *LM* curve, as shown in figure 2.7. The *LM* curve moves rightwards as the money supply is increased; this causes the interest rate to fall, and investment, aggregate demand and income to rise. This shift of the *LM* curve results in y_{fe}, as did the *IS* curve shift in figure 2.6, but in the case of the *LM* shift the equilibrium rate of interest falls, while it rises in the case of the *IS* shift.

The increase in the money supply underlying the *LM* curve shift may be brought about by open-market operations, that is, by the purchase of bonds from the private sector in return for money in the form of currency or central bank deposits. Reductions in the money supply can also be brought about by open-market oper-

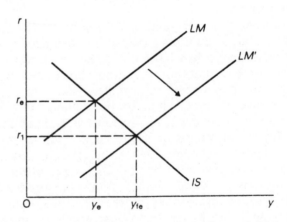

Figure 2.7   The monetary policy solution to unemployment

ations, in this case by selling bonds to the public and withdrawing the money so received from circulation.

Notice that with a bond-financed increase in government expenditure, the money supply remains constant. The money received from the sale of bonds is, in that case, returned to circulation by using it to pay for the extra government expenditure. It is useful to consider fiscal policy to be any policy which changes the levels of government spending or taxation while leaving the money stock unchanged, and monetary policy to be any policy which changes the money stock while leaving the levels of government spending or taxation unchanged. Such policies have been analysed above, but it is now useful to analyse combined fiscal and monetary policies.

Consider the case of a money-financed increase in government spending, as shown in figure 2.8. The initial equilibrium at $y_e r_e$ is assumed to be unsatisfactory to the government, which decides to increase its spending in order to shift the *IS* curve, and to finance this by printing money, which will increase the money supply and shift the *LM* curve. If the *IS* shift is brought about without shifting the *LM* curve, the solution in figure 2.8 will move from *A* to *B*, which will not achieve the government's target of y_{fe}, but will only cause income to rise to y_1 and the interest rate to rise to r_1. However, the increase in the money supply, and the shift in the *LM* curve, offsets the positive effect of the increased spending on the interest rate, thereby offsetting the crowding out of private investment and increasing the multiplier effects of the increased

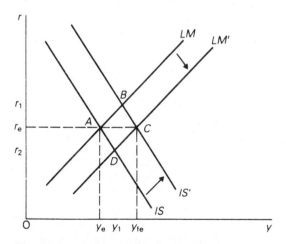

Figure 2.8   The joint use of fiscal and monetary policies

government spending. The solution in figure 2.8 moves, therefore, to *C*, where fiscal and monetary policy are combined and y_{fe} is achieved.

On the other hand, if only the *LM* curve shifted in figure 2.8, the solution would move from *A* to *D*, again failing to achieve y_{fe}, but this time reducing the interest rate to r_2 rather than increasing it to r_1. It is, therefore, clear that combined fiscal and monetary policies act together to create larger movements in income than if either policy were used alone, but act against each other with respect to the rate of interest; the net effect of combined policies on the rate of interest is, therefore, ambiguous. In the particular case of figure 2.8, it happens to be zero. This means that in order to achieve y_{fe} a government will need a smaller increase in spending if that increase is money-financed than if it is bond-financed (or tax-financed, which has a smaller multiplier even than the bond-financed case). It also means that by a judicious combination of policies the government can achieve not only a target level of income, but, simultaneously, a target rate of interest which it may desire to achieve in order to encourage private investment. For example, assume that the economy is initially at point *A* in figure 2.9 and that the government wishes to achieve y_{fe} and r_1 at point *C*. Point *C* may be reached by increasing government spending and money-financing this increase, which would take the economy to

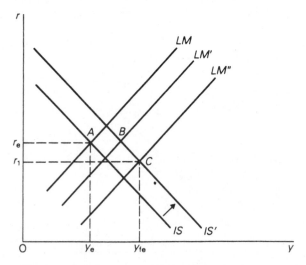

Figure 2.9 Fiscal and monetary policies for simultaneous income and interest rate targets

point *B* at the intersection of *IS'* and *LM'*, and then by further increasing the money supply by open-market operations to take the economy to point *C*, at the intersection of *IS'* and *LM"*.

The policy combination illustrated in figure 2.9 is an example of a more general result, due to Tinbergen (1952), that, in order to achieve a number of targets simultaneously, it is necessary to have at least as many independent instruments or tools as there are targets. Independent instruments are those which the government can adjust independently: that is to say, fiscal policy and monetary policy are independent if one can be adjusted without adjusting the other.

2.3 Keynes, Keynesians and Monetarists

The *IS–LM* model, even under the simplifying assumptions made so far, is quite a complicated tool of analysis, but it is extremely useful and a thorough grasp of it aids the understanding of the remaining developments to be examined in later chapters. Controlling the economy via sophisticated demand management techniques, or fine-tuning, as illustrated by the combined use of fiscal and monetary policies in the above example, is no easy task. Success would depend upon a knowledge of all the parameters underlying the *IS* and *LM* curves and accurate calculation of the right amounts by which to adjust fiscal and monetary policies. It is, therefore, possible to agree with Keynes that the economy does not always succeed in achieving full employment, and yet to argue against the use of fine-tuning demand management policies on the grounds that 'we are too ignorant of the structure of the economies we live in and of the manner in which that structure is changing to be able safely to implement activist stabilization policy in the present environment, or in the foreseeable future' (Laidler, 1981, p. 19).

The argument that 'we are too ignorant' has been one of the major planks of the monetarist case against Keynesian-style demand management since at least 1959 (see Friedman, 1959a). Monetarists tend to favour simple policies such as fixed rates of growth of the money stock, while Keynesians tend to favour more complicated fiscal and/or monetary policies which are adjusted in response to the state of the economy using cyclical fluctuations, in an attempt to maintain the economy as close to full employment as possible. It is possible to accept the Monetarist arguments about the infeasibility of stabilization policy while accepting Keynes's analysis of how the economy works. The labels 'Monetarist' and 'Keynesian' are, therefore, in some sense misnomers which might better be replaced by the alternatives, 'non-activists' and 'activists', activists being those who think the government knows enough, and is trustworthy enough, to adjust its policies in response to fluctuations in economic activity, and non-activists being those who lack such trust in the ability or intentions of the government. Indeed, it has been argued that Keynes himself did not favour activist fine-tuning, and did not accept the policies which came to be called Keynesian (see Hutchison, 1977; Meltzer, 1981).

To shed light on this issue it is instructive to see what policies Keynes favoured, and why. Clearly, he did not believe in the self-regulating ability of the market economy and favoured some sort of government intervention to rectify the inability of the market economy to maintain full employment. The following quotation illustrates this point:

> the outstanding features of our actual experience – namely, that we oscillate, avoiding the gravest extremes of fluctuation in employment and in prices in both directions, round an intermediate position appreciably below full employment. . . . The unimpeded rule of the above conditions is a fact of observation concerning the world as it is or has been, and not a necessary principle which cannot be changed. (Keynes, 1936, p. 254)

Keynes, therefore, wished to raise the 'intermediate position' towards full employment and also to minimize the fluctuations about this 'intermediate position'.

According to Keynes, the prime cause of economic fluctuations was the volatility of investment. We have previously assumed that investment is determined by the rate of interest under the explicit assumption of given expectations about the future net returns or profits. Keynes relaxed the assumption of given expectations and argued that 'The outstanding fact is the extreme precariousness of the basis of knowledge on which our estimates of prospective yield have to be made. Our knowledge of the factors which will govern the yield of an investment some years hence is usually very slight and often negligible' (1936, p. 149). Such precariously held expectations are highly volatile and are subject to 'the mass psychology of the market' (1936, p. 155) and 'the daily revaluations of the Stock Exchange', which 'exert a decisive influence on the rate of current investment. For there is no sense in building up a new enterprise at a cost greater than that at which a similar enterprise can be purchased; whilst there is an inducement to spend on a new project what may seem an extravagant sum, if it can be floated off on the Stock Exchange at an immediate profit' (1936, p. 151). None of this is improved by the existence of professional investors or speculators, since such agents are concerned not 'with what an investment is really worth to a man who buys it "for keeps", but with what the market will value it at . . . three months or a year hence. . . . The social object of skilled investment should be to defeat the dark forces of time and ignorance which envelop our future. The actual, private object of the most skilled investment today is "to beat the gun" . . .' (1936, pp. 154–5).

Thus, according to Keynes, expectations and, hence, investment are highly volatile. Aggregate demand will be volatile too, since there is no reason to believe that consumption will fluctuate in ways to offset investment fluctuations. Indeed, consumption by the stock-owning classes will tend to rise or fall as 'the value of their investments' (1936, p. 319) rises or falls.

To express these ideas in terms of the *IS–LM* analysis, Keynes argued that volatile expectations led to volatility of the *IS* curve and, hence, to fluctuations in output. These fluctuations could not be 'sufficiently offset by corresponding fluctuations in the rate of interest' (1936, p. 320), or in other words by activist monetary policy, to move the *LM* curve around to maintain the *IS–LM* intersection at the full-employment output level. Therefore, Keynes recommended a policy of social control of investment: as he put it, 'I conclude that the duty of ordering the current volume of investment cannot safely be left in private hands' (1936, p. 320). He later argued that, 'if the bulk of investment is under public or semi-public control and we go in for a stable long-term programme, serious fluctuations are enormously less likely to occur' (in a letter to Meade, 1943: see Moggridge, 1980, p. 326). This policy of a 'socially controlled rate of investment' (Keynes, 1936, p. 325) would help to eliminate fluctuations, but in order to increase the average level of activity Keynes also favoured policies to increase consumption. As he wrote in the *General Theory*, 'There is room . . . for both policies to operate together – to promote investment and, at the same time, to promote consumption . . .' (1936, p. 325).

According to the above interpretation of Keynes, which closely resembles that to be found in Meltzer (1981), Keynes did not wish to attempt to stabilize the economy by activist fine-tuning.[11] Rather, he wished to attack directly one of the major causes of fluctuations by recommending 'comprehensive socialisation of investment' (1936, p. 378). It should be noted that in this respect Keynes appeared to 'want it both ways', since he argued that:

[such state control of investment] need not exclude all manner of compromises and devices by which public authority will co-operate with private initiative. . . . It is not the ownership of the instruments of production which it is important for the State to assume. If the State is able to determine the aggregate amount of resources devoted to augmenting the instruments and the basic rate of reward to those who own them, it will have accomplished all that is necessary. . . . But there will still remain a wide field for the exercise of private initiative and responsibility. Within this field the traditional advantages of individualism will still hold good. (Keynes, 1936, pp. 378–80)[12]

Keynes elaborated upon his views on how to control the economy in a series of articles for *The Times* in January 1937. In these he reiterated his view that 'the production of investment goods tends to fluctuate widely; and it is these fluctuations which cause the fluctuations, first of profits, then of general business activity . . .' (*The Times*, 12 Jan. 1937, p. 13). His major proposal for stabilizing investment was to stabilize the long-term rate of interest, which 'must be kept *continuously* as near as possible to what we believe to be the long-term optimum. It is not possible to be used as a short-term weapon . . .' (*The Times*, 13 Jan. 1937, p. 13). This type of policy may be viewed as a non-activist policy, similar in type to the control of the money supply which, we shall soon see, was to be Friedman's major policy proposal. We shall compare these two proposals within the context of the *IS–LM* model in the final section of this chapter, where it will be shown that which of the two is preferable depends upon the sources and magnitudes of the shocks to the economy. For the moment, however, it is worth noting that Keynes's other arguments in the articles for *The Times* indicated a degree of belief in activist policies entirely in keeping with the fine-tuning proclivities of later Keynesians. Thus, although he recognized 'what a ticklish business it is to maintain stability' (*The Times*, 12 Jan. 1937, p. 14), he went on in the articles in the following two days to propose policies to switch from bond to tax finance of the government deficit to dampen aggregate demand as the economy neared a peak in the business cycle, to adjust government expenditure to maintain stable aggregate demand (this proposal to be facilitated by the appointment of 'a board of public investment to prepare sound schemes against the time that they are needed', *The Times*, 14 Jan. 1937, p. 13), and even for adjustments in tariffs on imports throughout the business cycle (this latter proposal may be better understood after the discussion of open economy issues in part VI of this book).

It can be seen, then, that although Keynes wished to develop institutional arrangements that increase long-term stability, he did not see these as substitutes for fine-tuning. He was quite prepared to propose a mixture of activist and non-activist policies at one and the same time. The Keynesians, therefore, in advocating fine-tuning policies were clearly taking their cue from their master.[13]

The Monetarist position clearly opposes the use of fine-tuning policies, and favours instead a policy of maintaining a steady rate of growth of the nominal money supply. This view is well represented by the following quotation from Milton Friedman:

> As I examine the past record of stability in the United States, I am impressed by the number of occasions on which major fluctuations have been a consequence of changing and at times erratic governmental policies with respect to money. This record offers much support for the view that, if the monetary framework were stable, our private enterprise economy is sufficiently adaptable to the other changes that occur to yield a high degree of economic stability in the short run as well as the long run.
>
> For this reason, the urgent need, I believe, is to keep monetary changes from being a destabilizing force. . . . In my view, this can best be done by assigning the monetary authorities the task of keeping the stock of money growing at a regular and steady state, month in and month out. . . .
>
> The elimination of monetary uncertainty would promote healthy economic growth by providing a stable environment for both individual planning and social action. (Friedman, 1959a, pp. 144–5)

Friedman based these views on two propositions. The first is that a close, regular and predictable relationship holds between the level of the money supply, output and the price level in the long run. The second is that this relationship is not predictable in the short run. Hence, he favoured a long-run steady rate of growth of the money supply, but did not favour attempting to use monetary policy as a means of offsetting short-run forces that generate fluctuations. The attempt at short-run control would, in his opinion, be 'likely merely to introduce additional instability into the economy, to make the economy less rather than more stable' (1959a, p. 144). Furthermore, he argued that 'this conclusion about short-run changes is valid not only for monetary policy but also for fiscal or other policies' (1959a, p. 144).

Thus, Friedman apparently believed, contrary to Keynes, that the *laissez-faire* economy is acceptably stable about full employment, and that fluctuations in activity are due primarily to ill-managed and erratic government intervention, specifically with regard to monetary policy. It is worth noting, however, that Friedman had earlier favoured controlling erratic government intervention by setting the rates of government spending and taxation according to long-run allocation and equity criteria, and not changing these instruments for short-run stabilization purposes (Friedman, 1948). Under this plan, the government budget deficit would rise or fall as tax receipts adjusted to income fluctuations, and Friedman at that time favoured allowing the money supply to adjust to finance these changing deficits.

Friedman has been consistent in wishing to minimize destabilizing government intervention, but has changed his mind as to the best way to do this. His reasons for changing his mind were that the new simpler rule would be easier for the public to understand and support, and that by separating the monetary from the fiscal aspects the rule would be easier to implement while producing similar results to his earlier, more complex, rule. Fixing the rate of growth of the money supply would remove the easy option of money finance for a government under pressure from various groups to raise spending or cut taxes; such fiscal policies would, instead, require debt finance and possibly unpopular increases in the interest rate, which would tend to prevent the government from following excessively expansionary fiscal policies. (See the reprint of Friedman, 1948, and the accompanying comment.) It should be noted that Friedman did not believe fluctuations could be removed entirely by adherence to either version of his rule, nor that reasonable levels of unemployment could be maintained without price and wage flexibility, but only that, given uncertainty and the ignorance of the government, stable and non-activist policies would be better than attempts to fine-tune the economy (see Friedman, 1948 and 1959a).

Before going on to the next section, it will be useful to summarize some of the above discussion, and to raise a few final points. First, in terms of the *IS–LM* model, Keynes may be viewed to have seen instability arising primarily out of shifts in the *IS* curve owing to the effects of volatile expectations on the demand for investment. He therefore favoured controlling investment. This assessment of Keynes is in contrast to the view, sometimes expressed, that he favoured fiscal policy rather than monetary policy because the *IS* curve was more stable than the *LM* curve. That view is wrong. He did not favour monetary policy, because he did not believe it could be manipulated well enough to offset *IS* shifts with policy-induced *LM* shifts. Rather, Keynes wished to stabilize directly the *IS* curve, shifts in which he viewed as the prime source of instability.

Friedman seems to have implied in several of his works that Keynes viewed the demand for money as the most unstable element in his system, which implies that the *LM* curve would be more volatile than the *IS* curve. Keynes certainly recognized that the demand for money depended, like investment, on expectations, and would be volatile. But the above interpretation of Keynes is that this was not given prominence over fluctuations in investment demand as the cause of economic instability. The empirical debate which arose concerning the relative stability of the demand for money and the demand for investment was, therefore, possibly misdirected. Nevertheless, within the context of the *IS–LM* model it would be useful to know the distributions of the shocks to both the *IS* and *LM* curves in order to try to design an optimal activist macroeconomic policy or to compare different non-activist rules, such as Friedman's rule for fixing the rate of growth of the money supply with Keynes's rule for fixing the rate of interest. The remaining section of this chapter offers a brief analysis of the choice between such non-activist rules.

The reader should note that the above discussion of the different schools of thought has not had to rely upon extreme assumptions about the slopes of the *IS* or *LM* functions, which can be used to generate certain special cases of the *IS–LM* model with associated special policy implications. Furthermore, the discussion of Keynes's ideas and policy recommendations did not rely upon money-wage and price rigidity except as simplifying assumptions. Nevertheless, special cases of the *IS–LM* model were the cause of much debate after the publication of the *General Theory* and Hicks's 1937 paper. It even became the orthodox view that Keynes's *General Theory* was a special case of the Classical model, dependent upon money-wage rigidity, and that his policy recommendations derived from a special case of the *IS–LM* model. It is with such issues that the next chapter of this book deals.

2.4 Interest Rate versus Money Stock Targets

We have seen, above, that Keynes proposed to use fiscal policy in a rather activist or fine-tuning manner, but that he also, like many later Keynesians, favoured controlling the rate of interest in order to stabilize investment. Friedman, on the other hand, eschewed fine-tuning and proposed a simple policy of controlling the rate of growth of the money supply in order to stabilize the economy. Friedman's dislike of fine-tuning stems, at least partly, from the view that knowledge of the economy is shrouded in uncertainty; the authorities do not really know where the economy is or where it is headed and, in such a situation, any attempt at fine-tuning is likely to destabilize the economy and move it in the wrong direction. Friedman's view was based not only on theoretical arguments, but also upon his interpretation of events, especially in the United States. However, even if Friedman is correct in arguing that fine-tuning should be avoided, it is not necessarily the case that aiming to fix the rate of growth of the money supply will stabilize the economy better than some other simple rule such as fixing the rate of interest. The choice between such alternative intermediate targets may be analysed by explicitly introducing uncertainty into the standard *IS–LM* model.[14] The terminology of intermediate or proximate targets is used since such targets are adopted only as a means to the end of stabilizing some other variable, such as output, which is the ultimate target of policy.

Assume that the government wishes to stabilize output at the level y_0, and that it is uncertain about the actual positions of the *IS* and *LM* curves representing the economy due to the variability of the demands for consumption, investment and money. The government cannot act quickly enough to stabilize output perfectly by changing its fiscal or monetary policies in response to the private sector induced movements in the *IS* and *LM* curves. It therefore decides to set fiscal policy according to criteria of equity and efficiency, and to use a non-activist monetary policy to stabilize output. The question is, then, whether it should aim to fix the interest rate or the money supply. The answer, within the context of a closed economy *IS–LM* model, will depend upon the relative variability of the shocks to, or unexpected movements of, the *IS* and *LM* curves.

For simplicity, assume initially that the demand for money and, hence, the position of the *LM* curve, is not subject to uncertainty, so that there is uncertainty only about the *IS* curve. This situation is illustrated in figure 2.10.

Figure 2.10 shows three *IS* curves, *IS*, *IS'*, and *IS''*, and two *LM* curves, $LM(M_0)$ and $LM(r_0)$. The curve *IS* represents the government's best guess as to the position of the *IS* curve, but the *IS* curve is subject to unpredictable shifts, for example to *IS'* or *IS''* if, say, investment or consumption demand changes suddenly.

If the government knew with certainty that the *IS* curve would be *IS*, then it could achieve its ultimate target of y_0 with certainty by setting an intermediate target for the money supply of M_0, thus producing the curve $LM(M_0)$ and *IS–LM* equilibrium at $y_0 r_0$. Alter-

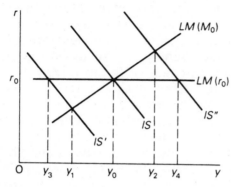

Figure 2.10 Intermediate targets and goods market uncertainty

natively, it could announce that it did not care what value the money supply achieved, but order the monetary authorities to buy or sell bonds until the interest rate r_0 was achieved. Setting r_0 as the intermediate target would result in the *LM* curve $LM(r_0)$, and would also result in *IS–LM* equilibrium at $y_0 r_0$ and with a money supply of M_0. Hence, under certainty the choice between money or interest rate targets is irrelevant, either will do the job with identical outcomes.

Now, however, consider the effects of uncertainty. If the *IS* curve deviates between *IS'* and *IS"* and the money supply is fixed at M_0, then the *IS–LM* equilibrium moves up and down the curve $LM(M_0)$, and income varies between y_1 and y_2. If, on the other hand, the interest rate is fixed at r_0, then the *IS–LM* equilibrium moves along the curve $LM (r_0)$, and income varies between y_3 and y_4. Clearly, the Monetarist prescription of fixing the money supply performs better than fixing the interest rate.

The reason behind this result is not difficult to understand. Consider, for example that starting from $y_0 r_0$ there is a sudden boost to investment demand which shifts the *IS* curve out to *IS"*. Under a fixed money supply target, the resulting increase in output causes an increase in the demand for active balances. People try to sell bonds to acquire more money, but in aggregate no more money is available so the effect is only to push down the price of bonds and push up the interest rate. The rising interest rate reduces the demand for idle balances and equilibrates the overall demand for money with the given supply of money. The rise in the interest rate partly offsets the initial boost to investment demand, thereby helping to stabilize output. Under an interest rate target, on the other hand, the increase in the demand for active balances would be met not by a rise in the interest rate, but by central bank purchases of bonds to maintain the interest rate at r_0 by, effectively, allowing the money supply to rise exactly in step with money demand at the interest rate r_0. In this case, then, the initial boost to investment is not offset at all as a result of the policy, and its effects on the economy are greater. These arguments are easily adjusted for the case of a decline in investment demand and the *IS* shift from *IS* to IS'. The point is, simply, that fixing the money supply involves letting the interest rate adjust to partly offset *IS* shifts (whether induced by changes in consumption or investment demands), whilst no such offset is possible under a fixed interest rate policy which entails letting the money supply rather than the interest rate adjust. The superiority of the Monetarist rule over an interest rate rule does not, however, carry over to the case where the *LM* curve rather than the *IS* curve is the subject of uncertainty, as figure 2.11 will be used to show.

Figure 2.11 shows one *IS* curve, known with certainty, and four *LM* curves, $LM(M_0)$, $LM'(M_0)$, $LM''(M_0)$ and $LM(r_0)$. If the demand for money and, hence, the position of the *LM* curve, could be determined with certainty then, again, the choice of a money supply or interest rate target would not matter. Either the money supply could be fixed at M_0, yielding $LM(M_0)$ and equilibrium of $y_0 r_0$, or the interest rate could be fixed at r_0, yielding $LM(r_0)$ and equilibrium of $y_0 r_0$. However, with uncertainty about the demand for money the choice of intermediate target does matter.

Consider first the fixed money supply target of M_0; as the demand for money rises above or falls below its average level, then the *LM* curve under the fixed money supply rule moves from $LM(M_0)$ to

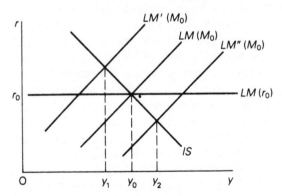

Figure 2.11   Intermediate targets and money market uncertainty

$LM'(M_0)$ or $LM''(M_0)$ respectively, causing the *IS–LM* intersection to move to income levels y_1 or y_2 respectively. The intuition is easy to grasp. A fall, say, in the demand for money for given r and y values causes the money market to move into disequilibrium with an excess supply of money, and the *LM* curve to shift rightwards indicating that either a rise in income or a fall in the interest rate, or some combination, is needed to clear the money market. Given a downward sloping (but not vertical) *IS* curve, what happens is that as members of the public try to reduce their money holdings by buying bonds, they cause the bond price to rise and the interest rate to fall, so inducing extra investment and causing income to rise. As interest rates fall and income rises, the demand for money increases until a new equilibrium is reached at a higher income level, say y_2, and a lower interest rate, but with the money demand back in equilibrium with the constant money supply M_0. The argument is easily adapted to the case of a rising demand for money, and the level of income can thus be seen to vary between y_1 and y_2 in figure 2.11 under a policy of fixing the money supply at M_0 (where y_1 and y_2 in figure 2.11 are not necessarily equal to y_1 and y_2 in figure 2.10).

On the other hand, if the interest rate were fixed at r_0, then as the demand for money falls, for example, and members of the public try to buy bonds, the monetary authority reacts by selling bonds to them. In this case, therefore, the bond price and interest rate are held constant and the money supply is reduced exactly in step with demand, since the money used to purchase bonds from the monetary authority is taken out of circulation. Crucially, since the interest rate is held at r_0, and the money supply allowed to vary up or down with demand, the money market variability has no implications for the goods market and output is stabilized perfectly about y_0. Clearly, if uncertainty arises in the money market, but not in the goods market, a policy of fixing the interest rate is preferable to fixing the money supply if the ultimate aim is to reduce the variability of output.

The above results generalize to the case where there is uncertainty about both the goods and money markets; then the choice between the interest rate and the money supply target will depend on the relative size of the variance of the random shocks experienced in each sector and on the model parameters. If the bigger shocks occur in the money market then an interest rate rule should be followed, whilst if the bigger shocks occur in the goods market a monetary rule should be followed. It is interesting to note that if Keynes's emphasis upon the volatility of investment demand may be taken to imply a view that the goods market was subject to greater shocks than the money market, then it would also probably imply support for a monetary rule rather than the interest rate rule favoured by Keynes. More importantly, however, is to note that which rule is to be preferred is partly an empirical issue and cannot be settled on purely theoretical grounds. Monetarists clearly feel that the evidence is in favour of unpredictable shocks to the goods market being the 'dominant driving forces of economic fluctuations' (Brunner, 1981, p. 24), especially since interest rates and output tend to move procyclically, which implies that output changes are brought about more by movements of the *IS* curve than of the *LM* curve.[15]

Finally, the reader should note that several proponents of intermediate targeting (of either the money supply, the interest rate or some other target) argue that targets should be set only over short periods, and that they should be adjusted frequently in the light of the changing behaviour of the economy. In this case the target rate of interest, say, may be higher when output is near its peak than when it is near its trough. Proponents of such policies presumably wish to avoid the dangers of fine-tuning in the short-run, but wish to allow the authorities the ability to respond to events in the medium term.

Appendix 2.1
A Diagrammatic Derivation of the *IS* Curve

Figure 2.12 derives the *IS* curve diagrammatically, under the assumption that government expenditure and tax receipts are independent of the level of income. The figure may be interpreted as follows. Quadrant (iv) shows the relationship between planned injections and the rate of interest under the assumptions that planned investment varies inversely with the rate of interest and that government spending is given exogenously. The broken line *I* shows that planned investment of I_0 will take place at the rate of interest r_0, while the $I + G$ line shows that total injections at r_0 will be $I_0 + G$. Similarly, at r_1, planned investment is I_1, while total injections are $I_1 + G$.

Quadrant (ii) shows the relationship between planned withdrawals and the level of income under the assumption that planned savings vary with the level of income and that taxation is given exogenously. The broken line *S* shows that planned savings of S_0 will take place when income is at y_0, while the $S + T$ line shows

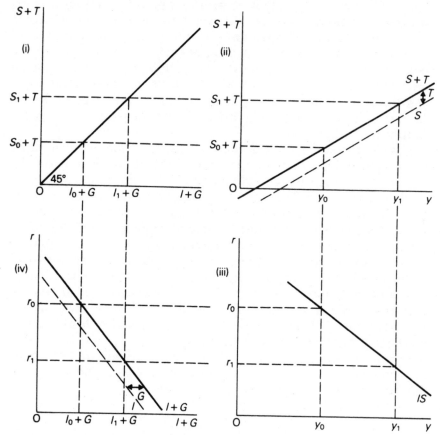

Figure 2.12   Derivation of the *IS* curve. (i) Equilibrium condition. (ii) Savings function. (iii) The *IS* curve. (iv) Investment function

that total withdrawals will be $S_0 + T$ at y_0. Similarly, at y_1, planned saving is at S_1 while total withdrawals are $S_1 + T$.

The *IS* curve in quadrant (iii) may now be derived as follows. Consider the rate of interest, r_0, which induces injections of $I_0 + G$ as shown in quadrant (iv). Follow the vertical dotted line about $I_0 + G$ upwards to quadrant (i). All points on the 45° line in quadrant (i) represent equality between planned injections and withdrawals; hence, when planned injections are $I_0 + G$ it is necessary for equilibrium that planned withdrawals be $S_0 + T$. Following the horizontal dotted line from $S_0 + T$ in quadrant (i) to quadrant (ii) shows that planned withdrawals of $S_0 + T$ will result if income is y_0. Planned withdrawals will, therefore, equal planned injections if the interest rate is r_0 and the level of income y_0. The intersection in quadrant (iii) of the dotted lines from r_0 in quadrant (iv) and from y_0 in quadrant (ii), therefore, provides a point on the *IS* curve. Similarly, it is possible to show that planned injections equal planned withdrawals when the interest rate is r_1. and the level of income is y_1. This provides another point on the *IS* curve. Repetition of this procedure would yield the *IS* curve shown in quadrant (iii).

It is clear from figure 2.12 and the accompanying discussion that the shape and position of the *IS* curve must depend upon the parameters of the savings and investment functions, and also upon the levels of G and T. Figure 2.13 shows how the *IS* curve moves as G changes from G_0 to $G_0 + \Delta G$, where the derivation of the *IS* curves follows from the same technique explained with regard to figure 2.12. The economic interpretation is that, with government spending of G_0 and an interest rate of r_0, planned injections and withdrawals will be equal if income is y_0, but when G is at $G_0 + \Delta G$, and the interest rate is r_0, planned injections will be higher than previously ($I_0 + G_0 + \Delta G$ compared with $I_0 + G_0$), and so, for equilibrium, planned withdrawals must be higher too, and will be the right amount higher when income is at y_1. As an exercise the reader should work through the effects of a change in exogenous or lump-sum taxes on the position of the *IS* curve, and also work out how to introduce income taxes into the analysis.

Appendix 2.2
A Diagrammatic Derivation of the *LM* Curve

Figure 2.14 derives the *LM* curve diagrammatically, and may be interpreted as follows. Quadrant (iv) shows the relationship between active balances and income, with L_1' active balances being demanded when income is y_0, L_1'' at y_1, and so on.

Quadrant (iii) shows the equilibrium condition in the money market. It is drawn for a fixed money supply equal to $\bar{M}$, all of which must be held in either active or idle balances. The points along the line indicate all of the possible ways in which the given money supply may be divided between L_1 and L_2. For example, when L_1' active balances are held, then idle balances of ($\bar{M} - L_1'$) or L_2' must be held for equilibrium in the money market, as shown by the distance between $\bar{M}$ and L_1' on the vertical axis, which may be translated using the properties of the 45° line to the horizontal axis.

Figure 2.13 The effects of an increase in government spending on the *IS* curve. (i) Equilibrium condition. (ii) Savings function. (iii) The *IS* curve. (iv) Investment function

Quadrant (ii) shows the relationship between idle balances and the rate of interest, with L_2' idle balances being demanded at r_0, L_2'' at r_1 and so on.

The *LM* curve in quadrant (i) is derived as follows. Consider the level of income y_0 in quadrant (iv) which causes active balances of L_1' to be demanded. Follow the dotted line from L_1' across to quadrant (iii), which shows that for equilibrium, with active balances of L_1' demanded, idle balances of L_2' must be demanded in order that the sum of idle plus active balances will equal the money supply, $\bar{M}$. Follow the dotted line from L_2' on the horizontal axis up to quadrant (ii), which shows that idle balances of L_2' will be

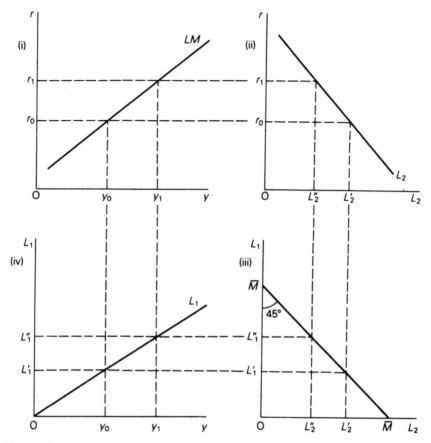

Figure 2.14 Derivation of the *LM* curve. (i) The *LM* curve. (ii) Idle balances. (iii) Equilibrium condition. (iv) Active balances

demanded when the interest rate is r_0. The money market will, therefore, be in equilibrium when the level of income is y_0 and the rate of interest r_0. Thus, $y_0 r_0$ provides a point on the *LM* curve, as is shown by the intersection in quadrant (i) of the dotted line from r_0 in quadrant (ii) with the dotted line from y_0 in quadrant (i). Similarly, $y_1 r_1$ is another point on the *LM* curve, and the reader may care to check its derivation as a useful exercise.

It is clear from figure 2.14 and the accompanying discussion that the shape and position of the *LM* curve must depend upon the parameters of the demand-for-money function, which is the sum of the demands for idle and active balances, and also upon the quantity of the money supply. Figure 2.15 shows how the *LM* curve moves as *M* changes from $\bar{M}$ to $\bar{M} + \Delta\bar{M}$, where the derivation of the *LM* curve follows from the same technique explained with regard to figure 2.14. Increasing the money supply moves the *LM* curve in parallel fashion rightwards away from the origin. The economic interpretation of this is quite simple. Consider, for example, initial equilibrium at $y_0 r_0$ with money supply $\bar{M}$, then let the money supply rise by $\Delta\bar{M}$. What level of income will be consistent with equilibrium in the money market for the new higher money supply if the interest rate remains at r_0? If the interest rate remains

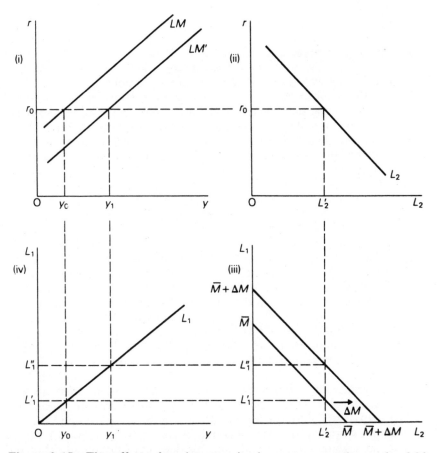

Figure 2.15 The effect of an increase in the money supply on the *LM* curve. (i) The *LM* curve. (ii) Idle balances. (iii) Equilibrium condition. (iv) Active balances

at r_0, then the demand for idle balances remains constant at L_2', so for equilibrium the extra money supply must all be demanded for extra active balances, which requires a higher level of income than y_0, in this case y_1, to cause the demand for idle balances to rise from L_1'' to L_1'''. Similarly, for any other interest rate, the level of income consistent with money market equilibrium rises when the money supply is increased. Put another way, for any level of income, the rate of interest consistent with money market equilibrium falls when the money supply is increased. With income unchanged, the extra money supply must be absorbed into extra idle balances, which will happen only as the rate of interest falls.

Notes

1   Similarly, concerted action by the trade union movement or central decree may be able to impose money-wage cuts on all workers simultaneously without affecting relative positions.
2   He also mentioned expectations and uncertainty as being crucial in determining employment and investment expenditure, and again questioned the ability of the market economy to ensure full employment. See chapter 12 of Keynes's *General Theory* for a readable and entertaining discussion of the role of expectations in determining investment.
3   See Keynes (1936, p. 27, and chapter 21, especially pp. 296–300).
4   The terminology is due to Kahn (1931). Kahn was a pupil and subsequently a colleague of Keynes at Cambridge.
5   It is interesting to note that in an article for *The Times* in January 1937 Keynes offered a verbal expression of this type of model.
6   Also, like the Classical model, the *IS–LM* model neglects the effects of positive net investment on the size of the capital stock.
7   This distinction is extremely useful. It was not, however, used by Keynes but originated in the writings of the Swedish economist Myrdahl and his colleagues of the 'Stockholm school' (see Ohlin, 1937). For a discussion of the relationship between the work of Keynes and the 'Stockholm school', see Patinkin (1982). See also Machlup (1939).
8   As an *aide-mémoire*, the *IS* curve stands for the planned I = planned S curve.
9   The reality of this assumption, or the lack of it, is often used to criticize the *IS–LM* model, and often also to criticize monetarist proposals to control the rate of growth of the money supply. It is the author's opinion that this assumption can easily be relaxed to allow for endogenous money and that this does not substantially alter the *IS–LM* model. The criticism of the monetarist proposal often goes along the lines that the money supply actually is, and has been,

endogenous, but this seems to miss the mark: the Monetarists are making a proposal about how the economy *should* be run, independently of how it has been, or is being, run. See section 2.4 for a discussion of the conditions under which it is better to fix the money supply or to fix the interest rate.

10   In the real world, the government need not actually print extra money; it can simply increase its deposits at the central bank. Also note that government budgets may include several elements neglected in the discussion in the text; for example, they may raise revenue by selling off assets, such as the British government's sale of shares in British Telecom in 1984.

11   Our interpretation does not exactly agree with that of Meltzer. Specifically, we view Keynes's unemployment equilibrium as a position of rest with the economy off the labour supply function. Meltzer views equilibrium as a point of intersection between the labour demand and supply functions. Our view on this point is nearer to that in Davidson's comment on Meltzer (Davidson, 1983).

12   In a similar manner, Keynes favoured a policy of maintaining a stable general level of money wages, while recognizing the advantages of 'some degree of flexibility . . . to expedite transfers from those [industries] which are relatively declining to those which are relatively expanding' (1936, p. 270). Just how to achieve these two desiderata simultaneously, he did not reveal.

13   Readers who remember the first edition of this book will recognize that this opinion represents a revision of my earlier views, which were closer to those of Hutchison and Meltzer.

14   The analysis to be presented is based upon that of Poole (1970).

15   The reader is referred to Brunner (1981) for a forceful statement of the case against monetary activism and in favour of monetary targeting. Gowland (1985, chapter 12) provides a recent review of the issues involved in the choice of target, and covers several ideas, such as the role of inflationary expectations, not discussed here. Chapter 8, section 1, below takes another look at the choice of target in a New Classical framework.

Part II

Was Keynes's *General Theory* Simply a Special Case of the Classical Model?

3

Special Cases of the *IS–LM* Model and the Neoclassical Synthesis

It has been suggested above that the fundamental issue between Keynes and the Classics concerned the dynamic stability of the economy, and the merits, or otherwise, of flexible wages and prices. This controversy can hardly be discussed within the confines of the comparative-static *IS–LM* model, but, nevertheless, that model does reasonably represent some of Keynes's ideas about the determination of output and the interest rate under the simplifying assumption of money-wage and price rigidity. It is not too surprising, therefore, that attention focused on the *IS–LM* model, and that the ideas of Keynes became associated with a special case of that model and with the assumption of money-wage and price rigidity.

It is unfortunate, however, that this focus on the tractable, and quite elegant, comparative-static *IS–LM* model diverted attention away from Keynes's dynamic arguments and led to an interpretation of the *General Theory* as simply a special case of the Classic model. This interpretation, now known as the Neoclassical Synthesis, since it synthesizes ideas from both Keynes and the Classics, clearly differs from the interpretation of Keynes that has been presented so far in this book. This chapter reviews the development of the Neoclassical Synthesis. The following chapter will examine the reaction against the Neoclassical Synthesis and the arguments of Clower and Leijonhufvud, who led an attempt to restore Keynes's status as an economic theorist.

The previous chapter presented the *IS–LM* model under the assumption that the *IS* curve sloped downwards from left to right and the *LM* curve sloped upwards from left to right. In these circumstances it was shown that both fiscal and monetary policies could be used to affect the equilibrium values of income and the interest rate. However, the potency of fiscal and monetary policies can be shown to depend upon the slopes of the *IS* and *LM* curves, and it can be shown that, in extreme cases, one or other of those policies loses all power in controlling the level of income. One of these extreme cases, known as the 'liquidity trap', has been especially important in the development of the Neoclassical Synthesis. The liquidity trap will, therefore, be reviewed below as a preliminary to the discussion of the Neoclassical Synthesis. A further preliminary dealt with below is the relaxation of the fixed-price assumption and the development of the *AS–AD* model.

The reader requiring a review of the factors determining the slopes of the *IS* and *LM* curves, and the relevance of those slopes for the potency of fiscal and monetary policy, is referred to the appendices to this chapter.[1]

3.1   The Liquidity Trap

The liquidity trap is the name which was given by Sir D. H. Robertson to the special case where, no matter how much the money supply is increased, the rate of interest refuses to fall to a level which induces a level of investment sufficient to generate full employment. Keynes recognized this case to be a theoretical possibility, but did not attach any practical significance to it (see Keynes, 1936, p. 207).

The liquidity trap may be represented in the *IS–LM* diagram as a horizontal segment of the *LM* curve at a certain minimum interest rate, r_{min}. At r_{min} the interest rate is so low that everybody expects it to rise in the future and so expects capital losses on bond holdings. Therefore, once the rate of interest reaches r_{min}, any increase in the money stock will be added to idle balances, and no one will use the money to buy bonds. In Keynes's words, 'liquidity-preference may become virtually absolute in the sense that almost everyone prefers cash to holding a debt which yields so low a rate of interest' (1936, p. 207). The price of bonds and the rate of interest do not, in these circumstances, change as the money supply is increased, and monetary policy becomes impotent as a means of increasing the level of income. All that happens as the money supply rises is that the demand for idle balances absorbs the increase in the money supply; the interest rate does not fall, more investment is not induced, and income remains unchanged.

Figure 3.1 illustrates the problem of the liquidity trap. The curves *LM* and *LM'* in quadrant (i) correspond to the money stocks $\bar{M}$

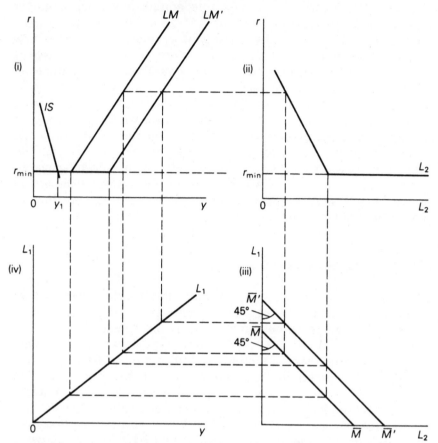

Figure 3.1 The liquidity trap and monetary policy. (i) *IS–LM*. (ii) Idle balances. (iii) Equilibrium condition. (iv) Active balances

and $\bar{M}'$ in quadrant (iii). The horizontal tail at r_{min} is common to both *LM* curves and is due to the horizontal section in quadrant (ii). The horizontal section in quadrant (ii) indicates that no one believes interest will fall below r_{min} and so no one will accept a bond at a rate below r_{min}. Technically, this implies that the elasticity of the demand for money with respect to the interest rate is infinite. The liquidity trap case is, therefore, associated with infinite interest elasticity of demand for money.

Given the *IS* curve in quadrant (i) and a money supply of $\bar{M}$, the equilibrium level of income is given by y_1 and the equilibrium interest rate is at r_{min}. Increasing the money stock to $\bar{M}'$ has no effect on the income or interest rate equilibrium since it moves only the upward-sloping part of the *LM* curve, but not the horizontal tail. *IS–LM* intersection remains at y_1 and r_{min} and monetary policy is ineffective. A fiscal policy which shifts the *IS* curve is necessary in such circumstances to bring about changes in the level of income or the interest rate.

Keynes, and especially his followers, advocated the use of fiscal policy, and the liquidity trap provided a case where, indeed, only fiscal policy could work. This seems to be the reason why the liquidity trap has come to be known as the 'extreme Keynesian' case. Paradoxically, Keynes attached little practical significance to the liquidity trap, but, as will be seen in the following discussion of the Neoclassical Synthesis, some writers have argued that his theory may have depended upon it.

3.2   The Aggregate Demand Curve

The final preliminary to the discussion of the Neoclassical Synthesis is the derivation of the aggregate demand curve in the *IS–LM* model. The aggregate demand curve in the Classical model has been presented in chapter 1. That curve was shown to be derived from the quantity theory of money and to be a relationship between the level of demand for real output, y, and the price level, P, determined by the equation, $y = MV/P$, where M is the nominal money stock and V its income velocity of circulation. The *IS–LM* model provides a more complex model of aggregate demand than does the quantity theory. In general, the *IS–LM* model allows a role for both fiscal and monetary policies in determining aggregate demand, although the special cases of the *IS–LM* model amount to special cases of the aggregate demand curve where, depending on the special case, either fiscal or monetary policy is irrelevant for the level of aggregate demand. The aggregate demand, or *AD*, curve to be derived from the *IS–LM* model indicates the relationship between the level of real aggregate demand and the price level and may be derived as follows.

It has already been shown that the *LM* curve shifts as a result of changes in the real money supply. Until now, these changes have been introduced by changing the nominal money supply, with the price level held at a fixed value. Changes in the price level, however, also change the real money supply and shift the *LM* curve even if the nominal money stock remains constant. As the price level rises, the real value of the money stock falls, and the *LM* curve shifts up to the left. Figure 3.2 illustrates the argument. The three *LM* curves shown in part (i) are all drawn for the same nominal money supply but for different price levels, P_0, P_1 and P_2. The position of the *IS* curve is independent of the price level, since the factors determining the *IS* relationship, as it has been developed so far, are all real variables which remain unaffected by price changes.

The position of the *LM* curves in part (i) clearly depends upon the price level. The higher the price level, the further to the left is the *LM* curve, and the higher the rate of interest and the lower the level of real income at the intersection with the common *IS* curve. When the price level is P_0, the *IS* and *LM* equilibrium is at r_0 and y_0. If the price level were lower, at P_1 say, the real money stock would be higher, inducing a lower rate of interest and a higher level of real income, at r_1 and y_1, respectively. Figure 3.2 (ii)

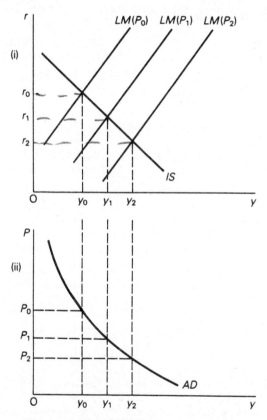

Figure 3.2 The aggregate demand curve. (i) *IS–LM.* (ii) *AD*

plots the price level against the corresponding real income level generated in part (i), the resulting points determining the AD schedule. The AD schedule shows that, for a given IS curve and a given nominal money stock, if the price level is a certain value, say P_0, then the level of aggregate demand generated by the $IS–LM$ model will take a certain value, say y_0.

The $IS–LM$ model is still necessary to determine the interest rate, r_0 in the case of P_0 and y_0 in figure 3.2. Notice that, whereas the Classical aggregate demand curve could be interpreted as saying, 'if the price level were P_0 the level of aggregate demand would be y_0' without mentioning aggregate supply, the $IS–LM$, or Keynesian, derivation of the aggregate demand curve must, strictly, be interpreted as saying, 'if the price level were P_0 and the level of aggregate supply were y_0, then the level of aggregate demand would be y_0 too'. This mention of aggregate supply is necessary since the Keynesian AD curve depends on the $IS–LM$ intersection and the IS curve represents goods market clearing. Of course, it is not possible to say whether, if the price level were P_0, the level of aggregate supply y_0 would be forthcoming without some knowledge of the aggregate supply curve too. Before completing the model in this way, the following section will show how fiscal and monetary policies affect the aggregate demand curve.

Fiscal and Monetary Policy and the AD Curve

The shape and position of the AD curve depend upon the factors determining the underlying IS and LM curves. Hence, any change in the elements which affect the IS and LM curves will affect the AD curve. For example, an increase in bond-financed real government spending which shifts the IS function to the right will move the AD curve to the right also.

Figure 3.3 shows two IS curves, IS and IS', where the level of bond-financed real government spending is higher in the case of IS'. Derivation of the AD curves shows that the AD curve, AD', corresponding to IS', lies everywhere to the right of the one corresponding to IS. The intuition is simple: the higher the level of bond-financed real government spending, the higher the level of real aggregate demand at any price level. Similarly, an increase in the nominal money stock, which shifts the LM curve rightwards for any price level, will also shift the AD curve rightwards.

Figure 3.4 shows two LM curves for the price level P_0, but where the nominal money stock is higher by the amount ΔM in the case of the LM' curve. It can be seen that, when the price level is P_0,

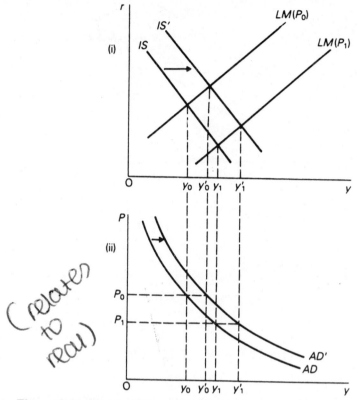

(relates to real)

Figure 3.3 Fiscal policy and the *AD* curve. (i) *IS–LM*. (ii) AD

the level of aggregate demand is y_0 given the *IS* curve and the nominal money stock M_0, but is higher at y_1 if the nominal money stock is higher at $M_0 + \Delta M$. Figure 3.4 (ii) shows that at P_0 the point on the *AD'* curve, given the higher nominal stock, lies to the right of the point at P_0 on the *AD* curve. Similarly, for any other price level the *AD'* curve lies to the right of the *AD* curve, as shown.

It is clear by now that the *IS–LM* model is really a model of real aggregate demand under the fixed-price assumption, and the *AD* curve extends the analysis to show how real aggregate demand varies as the price level changes.[2] To complete the model, it is necessary to introduce the aggregate supply curve.

Chapter 1 presented three versions of the aggregate supply, or *AS*, curve. The pure Classical aggregate supply curve derived from

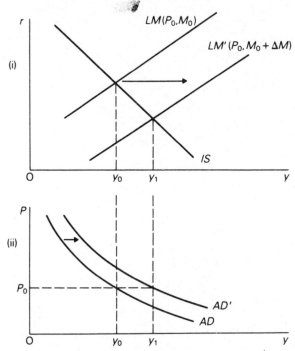

Figure 3.4   Monetary policy and the *AD* curve. (i) *IS–LM*. (ii) *AD*

the assumption of market clearing and real-wage adjustment, presented in figure 1.6, will be of use in the discussion of the Neoclassical Synthesis. So too will the *AS* curve derived under the assumption of money-wage rigidity presented in figure 1.8. Since much of the analysis of the *General Theory* assumed rigid money wages, and Keynes expressed the view that to induce an increase in real aggregate supply it would be necessary for the price level to rise, the *AS* curve of figure 1.8, which combines rigid money wages with flexible prices, has come to be called the Keynesian aggregate supply curve.[3] The reader whose memory of the derivation of the *AS* curves is not clear is advised to re-read the relevant sections of chapter 1 before proceeding with the development of the Neoclassical Synthesis below.

3.3   The Neoclassical Synthesis

Several important authors contributed, wittingly or otherwise, to the Neoclassical Synthesis. One of the most influential analyses was provided by Modigliani (1944), who concluded that the Keynesian explanation of the existence of involuntary unemployment depended upon either the liquidity trap or the assumption of rigid money wages. His argument was based upon an algebraic aggregate supply and demand model (which he later amended slightly; see Modigliani, 1963), but it is easily expressed using the diagrammatic approach developed above.

Consider first of all the assumption of money-wage rigidity and the resulting Keynesian *AS* curve shown in figure 3.5. The *AD* curve intersects the *AS* curve below the level of full-employment real output, as shown. The *AS* curve will not shift since money wages are assumed not to fall in the face of involuntary unemployment, which will, therefore, persist unless government demand management policies are used.

If the assumption of downward-rigid money wages is replaced by the assumption of perfectly flexible money wages and prices, so that the labour market clears, then the Keynesian *AS* curve must be replaced by the vertical Classical *AS* curve. *AS–AD* intersection with a Classical *AS* curve is, therefore, inconsistent with involuntary unemployment, but Modigliani, in effect, pointed out that involuntary unemployment could occur if the *AD* curve failed to intersect the *AS* curve. He argued that this could happen if the economy fell into a liquidity trap. Figure 3.6 illustrates that, as the price level falls from P_0 to P_1 in the diagram, the *IS–LM* intersection does not move, which implies a falling price level consistent with unchanging real aggregate demand. In other words, the *AD* curve becomes vertical and may fail to cross the *AS* curve, so that real aggregate demand may be insufficient to generate full employment even with wage and price flexibility.

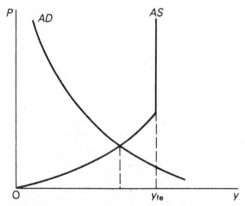

Figure 3.5 Rigid money wages and involuntary unemployment

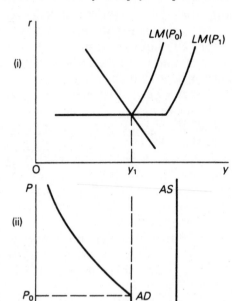

Figure 3.6   The liquidity trap and involuntary unemployment. (i) *IS–LM*.
(ii) *AD–AS*

Modigliani's conclusion, while influential, was modified with
respect to the role of the liquidity trap. The modification involves
departing from the simple *IS–LM* model, where real consumption
expenditures are determined by the level of income alone, and
adding wealth as a determinant of real consumption. This role for
wealth was pointed out by Pigou (1943) and was also emphasized
by Patinkin (1956): it is variously known as 'the Pigou effect',
'the wealth effect on consumption' or 'the real-balance effect on
consumption'. Strictly speaking, the Pigou effect denotes the effect
of falling prices on expenditures via the real balance effect, since
Pigou's arguments depend on falling prices and wealth effects.

In the presence of such wealth effects, a fall in the price level
will shift the *LM* curve rightwards as before by increasing the real
money supply, but now it will also shift the *IS* curve rightwards
too. The *IS* shift is caused by the falling price level increasing the
real value of the money (and bond) stock, thereby increasing wealth
and, thereby, increasing real consumption. Hence, even in the

liquidity trap, flexible money wages and prices can – in principle – shift the *IS-LM* intersection rightwards and increase real aggregate demand until full employment is achieved. Figure 3.7 shows the role of wealth effects in the liquidity trap by showing how the *IS* curve as well as the *LM* curve shifts in response to changes in the price level.

In the late 1950s and early 1960s, the orthodox view of the nature of the revolution wrought by Keynes was that 'the Pigou effect finally disposes of the Keynesian contention that under-employ-ment equilibrium does not depend on the assumption of wage rigidity' (Johnson, 1964, p. 239). In other words, the model which Keynes presented in the *General Theory* was said to be a special case of the Classical theory in the presence of money-wage rigidit-ies. This view minimized the importance of Keynes's theoretical

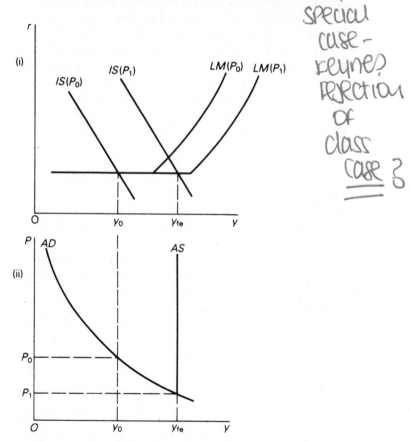

Figure 3.7 The liquidity trap and wealth effects. (i) *IS–LM*. (ii) *AD–AS*

contribution, but it was accepted that his contribution to the policy debate *was* important.[4] Even if monetary policy and wage and price flexibility could, via the Pigou effect, restore the economy to full employment, the process of adjustment by such means might be so slow that fiscal policy would be required to restore full employment more rapidly. Since such a view could be accepted by both Keynesians and those with Classical or neoclassical leanings, it came to be known as the Neoclassical Synthesis.

While the Neoclassical Synthesis owes much to the work of Patinkin, it should be noted that Patinkin did recognize that Keynes was attacking the Classical assumption of dynamic stability about full employment, and he endorsed Keynes's arguments about expectations and distribution effects of money-wage and price cuts preventing the economy from moving towards full employment. He even argued that the involuntary unemployment of the *General Theory* need not have its origin in wage rigidities as a result of such dynamic questions. However, Patinkin did appear to accept that money-wage and price cuts would eventually, via the real-balance effect, restore full employment. The unemployment Patinkin had in mind, then, was not the involuntary unemployment of the interpretation of the *General Theory* offered in this book. In both cases, involuntary unemployment clearly implies disequilibrium in the sense that the labour market is failing to clear and supply exceeds demand; but in Patinkin's case it also implies that the economy is in disequilibrium in the dynamic sense that forces will exist to move it away from the involuntary unemployment position, while the involuntary unemployment of the *General Theory* is an equilibrium phenomenon in the sense that is possible for the economy to achieve a position of rest with persistent involuntary unemployment.

The Neoclassical Synthesis was probably the dominant view of the *General Theory* in the late 1950s and early 1960s, but there was a reaction against it in the mid-1960s led by Clower (1965) and Leijonhufvud (1967, 1968), which re-interpreted the *General Theory* and attempted to restore Keynes's status as a theorist. The next chapter will review Clower and Leijonhufvud's re-interpretation of Keynes and, it is hoped, make clear that the interpretation offered in the first section of this book owes much to their arguments.

Appendix 3.1
The Slope of the *LM* Curve and Fiscal and Monetary Policy

It was shown in the previous chapter that the slope and position of the *LM* curve depend upon the quantity of money supplied, and upon the parameters of the demand-for-money function. The slope of both the demand for active balances with respect to income and the demand for idle balances with respect to the rate of interest determine the slope of the *LM* curve. There has been less controversy over the relationship between the demand for active balances and income, however, so it is useful to concentrate upon the relationship between the slope of the demand for idle balances and the slope of the *LM* curve. Figure 3.8 does this by showing how the slope of the *LM* curve differs according to the slope of the demand for idle balances, given the demand curve for active balances.

Figure 3.8 may be interpreted in the same way as figure 2.12 in the last chapter. The curve *LM* is derived using the curve marked L_2 in quadrant (ii), while the curve *LM'* is derived using the L'_2 curve. It can be seen that the less responsive is the demand for idle balances to changes in the interest rate or the steeper is the curve in quadrant (ii), the steeper is the *LM* curve in quadrant (i).

The relevance of the slope of the *LM* curve for policy is that the more steeply sloped is the *LM* curve, the less is the effect on income of any given change in fiscal policy, while the greater is the effect on income of any given change in monetary policy. Figures 3.9 and 3.10 illustrate this point with regard to fiscal and monetary policy, respectively.

Figure 3.9 shows two *LM* curves, *LM* and *LM'*, which both intersect with the original *IS* curve at point *A*. For a given fiscal policy stimulus which shifts the *IS* curve to *IS'*, the effect on income is larger, and that on the interest rate smaller, the flatter or less steeply sloped is the *LM* curve, as can be seen by comparing points *B* and *C*. This result may be interpreted as follows if the difference in slopes of the *LM* curves is due to differences in the relationship between the demand for idle balances and the interest rate. For the given change in fiscal policy shown in figure 3.9, as income rises the demand for active balances rises, and this demand can be met with a constant money supply only if the demand for idle balances falls. The demand for idle balances falls as the interest rate rises. When the demand for idle balances is not very responsive to changes in the interest rate, a larger rise in that rate is necessary to induce a given fall in idle balances than when the demand for

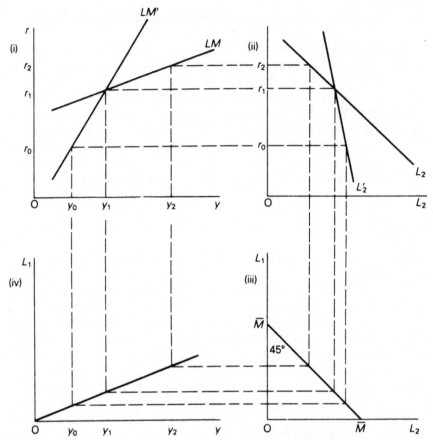

Figure 3.8 The slope of the *LM* curve and the demand for idle balances.
(i) The *LM* curve. (ii) Idle balances. (iii) Equilibrium condition. (iv)
Active balances

idle balances is more responsive to changes in the interest rate.
Hence, the less responsive the demand for idle balances to changes
in the interest rate, and the steeper the *LM* curve, the bigger will
be the change in the interest rate associated with any change in
income. This means that, as income rises in response to a fiscal
policy boost, the interest rate rises more sharply the more steeply
sloped is the *LM* curve, and, thus, more private sector investment
is crowded out and the lower is the multiplier effect on income.

Figure 3.10, on the other hand, shows that the more steeply
sloped is the *LM* curve, the bigger is the effect on both income

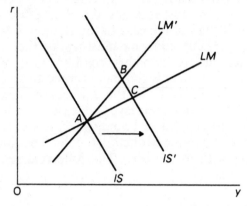

Figure 3.9 The slope of the *LM* curve and fiscal policy

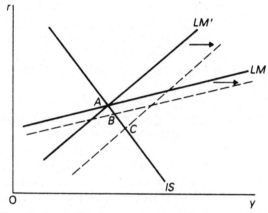

Figure 3.10 The slope of the *LM* curve and monetary policy

and interest rates of a given increase in the money supply. This is
shown by shifting the curves *LM* and *LM'* rightwards by equal
amounts, as shown by the arrows and broken lines.[5] The intersection with the steeper *LM* curve, *LM'*, moves further down the *IS*
curve, from *A* to *C*, than that of the less steep curve, from *A* to
B. The economic interpretation is similar to that given above with
regard to fiscal policy. We suppose again that the difference
between the slopes of the *LM* curves depends upon the interest
responsiveness of the demands for idle balances. In this case, the
increased money supply must be absorbed by increased demands

for active and idle balances. In the case of the steeper *LM* curve, a given fall in the interest rate has less of an effect on the demand for idle balances than in the case of the shallow *LM* curve. Hence, for the steeper *LM* curve income must rise further, and the interest rate fall further, before monetary equilibrium is restored.

Although the *LM* curve is generally agreed to be upward-sloping, there are two special cases of the *LM* curve which have, in the past, generated some controversy. One case has come to be known as the extreme Keynesian or liquidity trap case, and the other as the 'Classical' or 'extreme Monetarist' case. The liquidity trap case has been dealt with in the text. The following section deals with the Classical case.

The Classical or Extreme Monetarist Case

In this special case the *LM* curve is vertical. This is due to the demand for money being totally unresponsive to changes in the interest rate. The interest elasticity of the demand for money is said to be zero. If the demand for money is purely a function of the level of income, then the demand for money will equal the supply of money at some level of income regardless of the value of the interest rate.

The label 'the Classical case' is used since, with an interest-inelastic demand for money of this type, the income velocity of circulation of money is constant as in the Classical model. However, the key feature of the Classical model is the assumption of real-wage adjustment and market clearing in the labour market, rather than the constancy of the income velocity of circulation. The label 'Classical case' must, therefore, be carefully interpreted.

The relevance of the Classical case for policy is that it implies that fiscal policy cannot affect the level of income, but can affect only the rate of interest. Figure 3.11 illustrates the effects of a fiscal expansion which shifts the *IS* curve from *IS* to *IS'* by, say, a bond-financed increase in spending. The effect is only to push up the interest rate, leaving the level of income unchanged. The rising interest rate does nothing to release funds from idle to active balances, and causes total or complete crowding out, since the interest rate rises until private investment spending is cut by as much as government spending has been increased. As a result, the money market and goods market return to equilibrium at the same level of income as before the fiscal stimulus took place. In such circumstances only monetary policy has an effect on income. An increase in the money supply, shown in figure 3.12, will shift the

Figure 3.11 The Classical case and fiscal policy

Figure 3.12 The Classical case and monetary policy

LM curve outwards away from the origin by providing more funds for active balances; these will be voluntarily held only if the level of income rises, which occurs as a result of lower interest rates generating higher levels of private investment.

Since the Classical case emphasizes the relevance of monetary policy and rules out the usefulness of fiscal policy, it is sometimes given the alternative name of the 'extreme Monetarist' case. This name too must be very carefully interpreted. Neither Monetarists nor Classicists would argue that the level of real income could be permanently increased from y_1 to y_2 by an increase in the nominal money stock as in figure 3.12. Rather, as has been explained in the text, their case rests fundamentally on the assumed stability of the *laissez-faire* economy about full employment, and the inability of the government to intervene usefully in the economy. Consequently, Monetarists favour stable, predictable, non-activist policies.

The association of the vertical *LM* curve with the Monetarist case may stem from Friedman's empirical work (see Friedman, 1959b), which was consistent with such a result. Although Tobin (1972) has claimed that he thought the slope of the *LM* curve was the main issue between Keynesians and Monetarists, Friedman (1972) has explicitly denied this. Friedman's case would seem to depend not on a vertical *LM* curve, but upon the relative efficiency of the *laissez-faire* economy *vis-à-vis* the efficiency of the economy subject to activist government intervention (see Friedman, 1972, especially n. 7, p. 914).

Appendix 3.2
The Slope of the *IS* Curve and Fiscal and Monetary Policy

It was shown in the previous chapter that the slope and position of the *IS* curve depends upon the parameters of the savings and investment functions, and also upon the levels of *G* and *T*. The aspect of this which has generated most interest has been the interest elasticity of the investment function. Figure 3.13 shows that the more interest-responsive is the investment function, the less steeply sloped is the *IS* curve. The curve *IS* in quadrant (iii) of figure 3.13 is derived using the curve $(I + G)$ in quadrant (iv), while the curve *IS'* in quadrant (iii) is derived using the curve $(I + G)'$ in quadrant (iv). The curve $(I + G)'$ differs from the curve $(I + G)$ only by having a more interest-responsive investment function underlying it. The investment functions are not drawn separately in order to avoid cluttering the diagram any more than necessary.

There is a simple economic interpretation of the slopes of the curves *IS* and *IS'*. When the demand for investment is relatively more responsive to the interest rate, a fall (say) in the interest rate will induce a relatively large rise in investment demand, so requiring a relatively large rise in savings to maintain goods market equilibrium. A relatively large rise in savings requires a relatively large rise in income, and hence, produces a relatively flat *IS* curve

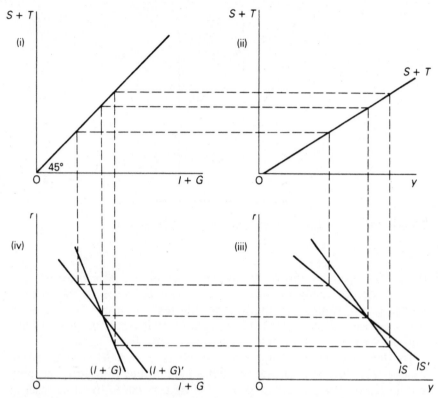

Figure 3.13 The slope of the *IS* curve and the investment function. (i) Equilibrium condition. (ii) Savings function. (iii) *IS* curve. (iv) Investment function

compared with the case of a less interest responsive investment demand function. The relevance for policy of the slope of the *IS* curve is that the more steeply sloped is the *IS* curve, the less is the effect on income of any given increase in the money supply, while the more effective on income is any given fiscal policy. Figures 3.14 and 3.15 illustrate this point with regard to fiscal and monetary policy, respectively.

Figure 3.14 shows two *IS* curves, *IS* and *IS′*, which both intersect with the *LM* curve at point *A*. A given fiscal stimulus shifts both curves outwards from the origin by equal horizontal amounts, as shown by the arrows.[6] In the case of the curve *IS*, the new equilibrium is achieved at point *B*, at higher levels of both the interest rate and income. Had the interest rate not risen then income would

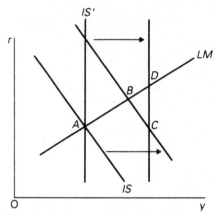

Figure 3.14   The slope of the *IS* curve and fiscal policy

have increased by more, as shown at point *C*. The interest rate rises since the rising income causes active balances to rise which, with a given money supply, means that less money is available for idle balances. The higher interest rate crowds out some investment and so weakens the effect on income of the fiscal stimulus.

In the case of the curve *IS'*, which is drawn for the extreme case of zero interest elasticity of the investment function, the new equilibrium is achieved at point *D*. In this case, the increase in income is greater and proceeds as far as it would have done as for point *C* with the curve *IS*, but the increase in the interest rate is also greater. The reason for this result is that, since investment does not respond to changes in the interest rate in this case, none of it is crowded out by rises in that rate as a result of the fiscal stimulus. Hence, the effect on income is greater, but this itself means that even more money is desired for extra active balances than in the previous case, which means that the rise in interest rate must be correspondingly higher in order to release more money from idle balances.

Figure 3.15, on the other hand, shows that the more steeply sloped is the *IS* curve, the less is the effect on income of any given increase in the money supply. Indeed, again using the extreme vertical case of the *IS* curve, it shows that this is akin to the liquidity trap in that increasing the money supply has no effect on the level of income. A vertical *IS* curve, therefore, is also sometimes said to represent an extreme Keynesian case. In figure 3.15 both *IS* and *IS'* intersect with the original *LM* curve at point *A*. An increase in

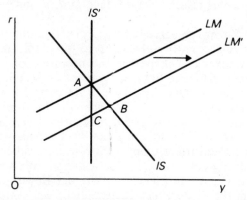

Figure 3.15 The slope of the *IS* curve and monetary policy

the money supply shifts the *LM* curve to *LM'*, which in the case of the curve *IS* causes equilibrium to move to point *B*. In the case of the curve *IS'*, the monetary stimulus serves only to lower the interest rate and the new equilibrium is achieved at point *C* without any effect on income. All that happens is that the extra money is absorbed into idle balances at the lower interest rate. There is no effect on income because the lower interest rate does not, in this case, stimulate private-sector investment.

Notes

1   The question of the slopes of the *IS* and *LM* curves is an empirical one. Most economists would probably now agree, on the basis of the evidence, that the extreme cases, which generated such controversy, are theoretically interesting but of little practical relevance. In so far as the *IS–LM* model is a useful representation of the economy, it is probably the standard version presented in the last chapter which is most useful rather than any of the special cases to be presented below. The most important proviso to this conclusion is that some Keynesian economists believe the money supply to be endogenously determined and not fixed by the government as in the standard *IS–LM* model. If, instead of fixing the money supply, the government allows the money supply to adjust to maintain a fixed interest rate, then the situation becomes akin to the interest targeting case of the previous chapter. (See Kaldor and Trevithick, 1981, for a discussion of the issues raised by endogeneity of the money supply.)

2   In Hicks's (1937) original article, it was assumed that money wages were given rather than the price level, which he did not mention.

However, it seems clearer to introduce *IS–LM* under the fixed-price assumption.

3 The extreme Keynesian aggregate supply curve in the textbooks shows supply to be perfectly price-elastic up to full employment. That is to say, it is of a reverse L-shape with no necessity for prices to rise to induce output to rise until full employment is reached, whereupon the *AS* curve becomes vertical. This type of *AS* curve has effectively been assumed in the *IS–LM* discussion under the fixed-price assumption. Its derivation is left as an exercise for the interested reader, who might note that it can be derived using the rigid money-wage analysis of figure 1.8 with the extra assumption of constant, rather than diminishing, marginal product of labour. See also appendix 4.1 below.

4 A question that is often asked is, 'Why did Keynes not foresee the significance of the Pigou effect?' Certainly he was aware of the significance of wealth in influencing spending patterns (1936, pp. 92–3), and ought to have recognized the effect of falling prices on the real value of wealth, even though it is only outside assets that matter in this respect. Outside assets are those, such as fiat money holdings, not matched by a debt of another person. Inside assets are those matched by a debt of another person, so that, as the real value of one person's asset rises, the real value of the debt of the debtor rises too, and in aggregate such effects would cancel out unless one allows for distributional effects.

There are at least three possible responses to the question posed in this note: (1) Keynes simply overlooked the significance of the Pigou effect; (2) like Pigou, Keynes recognized the minor empirical importance of the Pigou effect and so chose to neglect it; (3) Keynes ignored the Pigou effect because his fundamental criticism of the Classical model concerned the inability of the real economy to generate the market-clearing set of relative prices. Therefore, a reduction in all money wages and prices, generating a Pigou effect, would not resolve the problem of involuntary unemployment anyway. Whether Keynes's concern with relative prices made him overlook the Pigou effect altogether, or see it but choose to neglect it, is not clear, although he certainly recognized that the value of stocks and shares may exert an influence on the consumption behaviour of a '"stock-minded" public' (1936, p 319). The most important question, however, concerns not why Keynes neglected the Pigou effect, but the relevance of the Pigou effect to the interpretation of the *General Theory*. This issue is examined in the next chapter.

5 Since the *LM* and *LM'* curves differ only with respect to the underlying interest elasticity of demand for money, then, taking any given interest rate, each curve must shift by equal amounts in the horizontal direction for a given change in the money supply. This follows from noting that the horizontal shift depends only on the income elasticity of demand for money, which is assumed to be common to both curves so that both must move equal rightwards distances in response to a common

increase in the money supply. The reader may verify this argument by increasing the money supply in figure 3.8 and tracing through how the two different *LM* curves shift in response. In terms of figure 3.10, this means that the intersection of the dotted *LM* curves lies horizontally across from the intersection of the solid *LM* curves at point *A*.

6 Since the *IS* and *IS'* curves differ only with respect to the underlying interest elasticity of demand for investment, then, taking any given interest rate, each curve must shift by the same horizontal distance in response to a common fiscal stimulus. The associated common change in income for any interest rate restores the equality between planned injections and planned withdrawals in each case. The reader may verify this argument by tracing through the effects of an increase in *G* on the *IS* and *IS'* curves in figure 3.13. He may also show, using figure 3.13, that a change in the income tax rate (which affects the slope of the $S + T$ line in quadrant (ii)) affects the slope of the *IS* curve.

4

The Re-interpretation of Keynes

Although the Neoclassical Synthesis still has its adherents (see, e.g., Shapiro, 1982, ch. 9) it is certainly not universally accepted. The reaction against it was given impetus by the important work of Clower (1965), and its endorsement and development by Leijonhufvud (1967, 1968), which provided a defence of Keynes's *General Theory* to the criticism of it in the Neoclassical Synthesis. It will be useful to review Clower and Leijonhufvud's re-appraisal of Keynes, and then to relate it to some of the other interpretations of the *General Theory*, as well as to the perspective offered in Part I of this book.

4.1 Clower's Dual Decision Hypothesis

The dual decision hypothesis was put forward by Clower (1965) to provide choice-theoretic foundations for the central role accorded to aggregate demand and the multiplier by Keynes. As the name 'dual decision hypothesis' implies, the argument depends upon contrasting the decision-making underlying the Classical theory with that underlying Keynes's theory. The Classical (or Neoclassical) theory is essentially a theory of continuous competitive exchange equilibrium in which actual prices are always market-clearing prices. In this system individuals and firms take prices as given. On the basis of the set of market-clearing prices, individuals decide how much to buy and how much to sell of the factors and commodities in which they are interested, subject only to constraints imposed upon them by their endowments of factors and other assets. For example, a worker observes a price at which he can sell his labour and at which he can buy goods; given his initial endowment of wealth, he then decides how much labour to sell and goods to buy to maximize his utility, subject to his budget constraint.

In order to ensure that the set of prices always achieves market-clearing equilibrium, the Classical economists relied on the ideas of tâtonnement or re-contracting, that is, making offers to buy and sell but not carrying them out until a set of prices was found at which all markets cleared, or on the Walrasian auctioneer, who was imagined to call out prices until the market-clearing set was found, at which point only did trade take place. The Classical system, is, then, the general equilibrium system covered in the microeconomic textbooks, and the Classical macroeconomic model is just the macroeconomic analogue of that system.

According to Clower and Leijonhufvud, the innovation of Keynes was to work out (or to begin the task of working out) how the economy operates away from market-clearing equilibrium, when the price set will not clear all markets and no auctioneer can be relied upon to shout out the market-clearing price set. In this case agents in the economy face a slightly different optimization problem from that faced by agents in the Classical case. The worker from the above example now observes not only a price at which he can sell his labour and buy goods, but also an additional constraint on how much labour he can sell. This constraint is imposed by how much labour his employer is willing to hire. Thus faced with an extra constraint, he may be able to sell less labour than he would otherwise wish and, hence, may be able to buy fewer goods than he would otherwise wish.

The dual decision hypothesis contrasts decisions to supply and demand goods and services based on the assumption that all agents face infinitely elastic supply and demand schedules and are constrained in their decision-making only by prices and their initial endowments, with decisions to supply and demand goods and services subject to extra quantity constraints on the supply of, or demand for, certain goods or services. The former, or Classical, decision-making process gives rise to what Clower has called 'notional supply and demand curves', while the Keynesian, or quantity-constrained, decision-making process gives rise to what he has called 'effective supply and demand curves'.[1] What counts in the market is effective demand and supply, and only in full market-clearing equilibrium do the notional and effective magnitudes coincide.

The above concepts are illustrated by figure 4.1. The worker has an endowment of labour hours of $\bar{H}$ and of $\bar{M}$ wealth. He faces

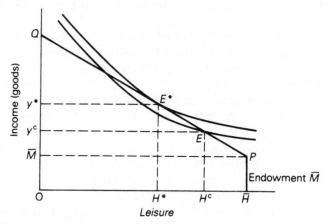

Figure 4.1 The dual decision hypothesis and the work–leisure choice

a fixed hourly real-wage rate which produces the budget constraint $\bar{H}PQ$. If the worker is free to choose his hours of work he may choose any point on $\bar{H}PQ$; if he chooses P he works for zero hours and consumes the goods equivalent of his wealth of $\bar{M}$ with $\bar{H}$ hours of leisure, if he chooses Q he works for $\bar{H}$ hours, consumes the goods equivalent of $\bar{M}$ plus $(Q - \bar{M})$, that is, his wealth plus earnings, and he takes no leisure. The utility-maximizing worker chooses to work for $(\bar{H} - H^*)$ hours and to consume the goods equivalent of y^* with H^* hours of leisure; that is, he chooses to operate at E^*, which puts him on his highest attainable indifference curve.

This decision is the type assumed in the Classical model; the worker is constrained only by a given set of relative prices and by his initial endowment. But what if he is also constrained by how much labour his employer is willing to hire? Specifically, if the employer will hire no more than $(\bar{H} - H^c)$ of the worker's time, then the worker must take this extra constraint into account in his decision-making process, and he will work $(\bar{H} - H^c)$ hours and consume more leisure (H^c) and fewer goods (y^c) than in the absence of the extra constraint. This decision is the type underlying Keynes's analysis.

The distinction between effective and notional demands may be seen as justifying Keynes's ideas about the consumption function. At market-clearing equilibrium the consumption function ought to depend on initial endowments and prices, just as the worker's demand for goods of y^* in figure 4.1 so depended; but away from market-clearing equilibrium, consumption will depend not only on endowments and prices, but also upon actual incomes, which may constrain effective demands to be below notional ones, just as the worker's demand for goods of y^c in figure 4.1 was below y^*.

Clower summed up his argument as follows: 'In a line, Keynesian economics brings current transactions into price theory whereas traditional analysis explicitly leaves them out' (1965, p. 295). Clearly, the dual decision hypothesis does provide some support for the argument that, if labour is ever forced to move 'off its supply curve', the economy may not produce the signals necessary to get labour back 'on to its supply curve' again; since unemployed workers may be unable to signal what their demands for output would be if firms would employ them. This insight brings into question the Classical assumption of stability about full employment.

Following Clower and Leijonhufvud, recent works on the micro-economic, choice-theoretic foundations of macroeconomics have focused attention on models where trade can take place at the non-market-clearing set of prices. In these models quantity constraints, as perceived by the economic agents, play a central role. Many such models are based upon an extreme, simple case where prices are fixed at the beginning of each period by sellers, in the light of their past experience and expectations of the future. Once quoted, prices are fixed until the beginning of the next period. At these prices the demands and supplies offered by all agents need not be compatible and markets may fail to clear. Then the economy moves to the next period and sellers can quote new prices. Equilibrium is reached when agents no longer wish to change prices from one period to the next, and this need not necessarily happen to be at full employment. This conclusion negates the statement by Johnson (1964), quoted in the last chapter, that 'the Pigou effect finally disposes of the Keynesian contention that under-employment equilibrium does not depend on the assumption of wage rigidity'. (For an introduction to non-market-clearing models see Benassy, 1982, and Weintraub, 1979.) Nevertheless, it remains the case that many of these models examine the implications of non-market-clearing, rather than provide an explanation of why markets fail to clear. Proponents of these models can, however, respond that assuming the presence of a Walrasian auctioneer allows models to examine the implications of market clearing but provides no explanation of why markets clear. Looked upon in this way the debate may appear to boil down to the empirical issue of which one of the two simplifying assumptions, market clearing or otherwise, leads to a better approximation of reality. However, the issue is not just empirical: a satisfactory resolution will require a theoretical explanation of why and how prices and quantities are adjusted in the real world. (See chapter 8 below for references to some recent work on this issue.)

4.2   Alternative Interpretations

Clower's work has not been without its critics. Grossman (1972), for example, has questioned Clower's interpretation of Keynes's analysis. Grossman argues that Keynes did not set out to attack the Classical theory of household choice, but simply specified the consumption function in an *ad hoc* manner, without appreciating the 'essential conceptual departure which the consumption function exemplifies' (1972, p. 28) Grossman argues that this must be the case, since the logical extension of the dual decision hypothesis to the behaviour of firms implies that they may be quantity-constrained too, and that they may be forced off the demand-for-labour curve. Keynes, however, was quite willing to accept the first Classical postulate and its implication that firms would be on their demand-for-labour curves.

The impact of quantity constraints on firms may be illustrated using figure 4.2, which shows the now-familiar labour supply and demand curves. Imagine that initially the economy is in full market-clearing equilibrium, with the real wage w_0 and employment level N_0. Then imagine that, for whatever reason, there is a reduction in aggregate demand, and that market forces fail to operate on either the price or money-wage level so that the real wage remains at w_0. Keynes's acceptance of the first Classical postulate would imply that with a real wage of w_0 firms would employ N_0 labourers and go on producing as much as before. The trouble with this is that, if aggregate demand has fallen, firms could no longer sell as much as before at the original price level. In the face of such a sales constraint, firms may be expected to reduce employment, and hence output, to match aggregate demand. Assume that firms reduce employment to N_1 to match output to aggregate demand; this puts firms at point B in figure 4.2. The labour demand curve D_N must, therefore, be interpreted as the unconstrained or notional labour demand curve, and it is in that sense that we have been using such curves earlier in this book.

The constrained labour demand curve must now be introduced. At B, firms are on the constrained labour demand curve, $\bar{D}_N$, given

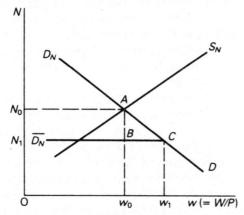

Figure 4.2 The case of sales-constrained firms

by the kinked line *DCB*, where the constraint is provided by the
level of aggregate demand. Notice that at point *B* there is involuntary unemployment even though the real wage is at its market
clearing level. Once the economy is allowed to operate off the
notional demand for labour curve, involuntary unemployment can
occur even if the market clearing set of relative prices is achieved.
This contrasts with Keynes's emphasis upon the failure of the price
system to produce the market clearing set of relative prices in his
explanation of involuntary unemployment and his acceptance of
the first Classical postulate (see chapter 2, section 2.1 above). Thus
at point *B* the real wage is below the marginal product of labour
and profit maximizing firms would, if they could, like to produce
and sell more output. If firms reduce prices in order to try to
increase sales then the real wage will rise for a given money wage
and the economy will move from point *B* towards point *C* in the
figure; for the economy to stay at point *B* implies that prices as
well as money wages do not fall, even though there is involuntary
unemployment and firms would like to sell more output. The
assumption of downward rigidity of prices as well as money wages
has interesting implications for the derivation of the aggregate
supply curve, as is shown in appendix 4.1.

Much modern Keynesian work attempts to explain how an economy could come to operate at a point like *B*. Such a possibility
was first recognized by Patinkin (1956, chapter 13) and, according
to Grossman, is consistent with Clower's treatment of constrained
consumer behaviour but inconsistent with Keynes's treatment of the

demand for labour. Therefore, Grossman argued, the Neoclassical Synthesis is nearer to a correct interpretation of the *General Theory* than Clower's attempted re-interpretation, even though the explicit introduction of quantity constraints may be a valid theoretical improvement upon both Keynes's own thinking and that behind the Neoclassical Synthesis.

Perhaps both Clower and Grossman go too far, albeit in opposite directions, and an intermediate position may be more appropriate. Certainly Keynes did not explicitly formulate anything like the dual decision hypothesis, and Clower never said he did; although Clower felt he must have had something similar 'at the back of his mind' (1965, p. 120). On the other hand, Keynes certainly attacked the stability assumption of the Classical model and attempted to put something else in its place. As Leijonhufvud put it,

> to make the transition from Walras' world to Keynes' world, it is . . . sufficient to dispense with the assumed *tâtonnement* mechanism. The removal of the auctioneer simply means that the generation of the information needed to co-ordinate economic activities in a large system where decision-making is decentralized will take time and will involve economic costs. No other 'classical' assumptions need to be relinquished. Apart from the absence of the auctioneer, the system remains as before: (a) individual traders still 'maximize utility' (or profit) – one need not assume that they are constrained from bargaining on their own, nor that they are 'money illusioned' or otherwise irrational; (b) price incentives are still effective – there is no inconsistency between Keynes' general 'elasticity optimism' and his theory of unemployment. (Leijonhufvud, 1967, p. 301)

Leijonhufvud's contention that Keynes removed the auctioneer is similar to our interpretation of his fundamental objection to the Classical model being concerned with its assumption of stability about full employment.[2]

Having dismissed the Classical model, Keynes offered something else in its place, and gave an important role to the consumption function in his own analysis. As Grossman points out, Keynes did not explicitly offer a choice-theoretic rationale for the importance of current income in the consumption function, but perhaps he thought it obvious that income constrains consumption and felt no need to offer a formal rationale, or to contrast this idea with the underlying assumption of the Classical model. This interpretation might not place a dual decision hypothesis at the back of Keynes's mind, but it does make him aware of income constraints on consumption. Trying to read Keynes's mind may not be a useful occupation, but certainly it is possible to read the following statement in the *General Theory*: 'The amount that the community spends on consumption obviously depends (i) partly on the amount of its income . . .' (1936, pp. 90–1).

As for Grossman's argument that, had Keynes recognized quantity constraints at all, he would have rejected the Classical aggregate demand-for-labour curve, there are two possible responses. One is simply that Keynes did not work out the logical extension of all his ideas, and that, had he done so, he would have been prepared to reject the Classical aggregate demand-for-labour curve. Some evidence for this response may be gleaned from the *General Theory*, where Keynes recognizes that employers might increase output as real wages fall only to find that 'the proceeds realized from the increased output will disappoint the entrepreneurs' (1936, p. 261) – in other words, firms will be sales-constrained. A second and possibly better, response would be to say that Keynes believed that excess supply in the goods market, unlike the labour market, would result in a fall in the price level, as predicted by the usual microeconomic arguments. In terms of figure 4.2, this implies that, as aggregate demand falls, firms at first supply more than is demanded and meet sales constraints. However, the result of this is not a move from A to B with constant real wages, but rather a fall in prices, with money wages fixed or falling more slowly, so that the real wage rises from w_0 to some level like w_1. As a result of the rise in real wages, firms reduce employment and output until employment has fallen to N_1, with firms, at point C, back on the Classical aggregate demand-for-labour curve – which in this case might be better called the 'notional aggregate demand-for-labour curve', since the point reached on it cannot be determined without knowledge of the sales constraint facing firms.[3, 4]

Even if this interpretation is accepted, it is not complete. Recognition of the role of quantity constraints deals only with the consequences of non-market-clearing. It tells us that there is no auctioneer in Keynes's system, but it does not tell us what forces actually determine the dynamics of the economic system and the fluctuations about equilibrium. The interpretation of Keynes offered in Part I of this book indicates that Keynes offered several suggestions. Clearly, uncertainty and expectations (in the labour, money, investment and consumption goods markets) are important for both the fluctuations in, and the general level of, activity. This view has been stressed by writers such as Shackle (1967) and Robinson (1971) and is sometimes said to indicate that Clower and Leijonhufvud neglected the most important elements of the *General Theory*. However, the two views would appear to be consistent with one another, the dark forces of time, ignorance and uncertainty being a cause of non-market-clearing and quantity constraints a result.[5]

Taken to their extreme, Keynes's views on uncertainty and the volatility and subjectivity of expectations lead to the iconoclastic conclusion that expectations are virtually incapable of being dealt with in the context of a formal economic model.[6] Instead, the economy must be treated as a historical process, with the typical policy recommendations of this school being against the fine-tuning of the majority of Keynesians and in favour of the replacement of market price signals by state control of important economic variables. These policy conclusions are in accord with our earlier interpretation of certain of the ideas of Keynes, although he seemed to wish to retain market forces and incentives, and to use the state only to ensure a sufficiently high and stable level of investment.

Along with uncertainty and expectations, Keynes also offered a role for distributional effects and relative wages. The former have featured prominently in the works of Kalecki and his followers (see, e.g., Sawyer, 1982), and the latter may well provide a sound reason as to why workers might accept a cut in real wages brought about by inflation, or general agreement on money-wage cuts, but not by piecemeal money-wage cuts.

As a final point, before offering a conclusion to this chapter, it should be noted that Clower and Leijonhufvud both criticized the *IS–LM* model as a distortion of Keynes's ideas. Since the *IS–LM* model played such an important role in the Neoclassical Synthesis, which they were attacking, their aversion to it is not surprising. Nevertheless, a more balanced view might be that the *IS–LM* model represented Keynes's views on the determination of aggregate demand under fixed money wages and prices quite well, but that this distracted attention from his more fundamental dynamic arguments.[7] Furthermore, by providing a formal rationale for income-constrained consumption behaviour, Clower's work itself provided a choice-theoretic rationale for the *IS–LM* and *AS–AD* models, which depend heavily on the consumption function embedded in them.[8]

It is possible to conclude, therefore, that the Neoclassical Synthesis offers an incorrect view of the *General Theory*. The *General Theory* did not simply propose a special case of the Classical model dependent upon rigid money wages. Rather, Keynes's was the more general model, since it did not assume stability about full employment, or instantaneous market clearing guaranteed by the presence of a Walrasian auctioneer. Instead, Keynes began to study the motion of the economy away from market clearing, without assuming that it would automatically move back to full-employment equilibrium. He offered several important insights concerning factors such as quantity constraints, expectations, concern about relative wages and so on. He also offered a more complicated comparative-static analysis of aggregate demand than that offered by the Quantity Theory. Thus, Keynes attacked the Classical model on several fronts, and it is not surprising, therefore, that different authors have stressed different aspects of Keynes's thought, and have offered apparently contradictory interpretations of the *General Theory*, nor that others (such as Blaug, 1978) have found it an untidy and badly written book.

The view offered here is that the alternative interpretations of the *General Theory* can partly be reconciled, and that it may be viewed as a reasonably consistent, if multi-faceted, attack on the Classical model. If the *General Theory* is untidy and confusing, or even confused, this appears to be more a result of the difficult problems Keynes chose to tackle, than of his deficiencies as a writer or theorist.

Lest this conclusion appear over-generous to Keynes, it should be pointed out that, even if it is accepted, it is not necessary to accept either Keynes's theory or his policy prescriptions. Specifically, it is worth pointing out again that, even if Keynes did discern correctly that the *laissez-faire* economy fails to deliver continuous full employment, this does not necessarily imply that the government has the knowledge, ability or desire to intervene in the economy for the public good, but only that the *laissez-faire* economy could be improved upon if the government has such knowledge, ability and desire.

The next chapter turns away from the rather fundamental issues concerning the correct interpretations of Keynes's *General Theory* covered in this and the previous chapter, and returns to the development of the *IS–LM* model. The developments examined, however, will be seen to have been inspired partly by aspects of the development of the Neoclassical Synthesis, and to have quite fundamental implications of their own.

Appendix 4.1
Derivation of the Aggregate Supply Curve under Downward Rigid Money Wages and Prices

The derivation of the aggregate supply curve under downward rigid money wages and prices is interesting since it gives some insight into the working of disequilibrium or non-market-clearing models and illustrates the role of quantity constraints in such models. The arguments may be illustrated using figure 4.3, which is drawn for the interesting case where the money wage and price level, although downward rigid, produce the market clearing real wage; but this is not, in the presence of quantity constraints and downward rigid money wages and prices, sufficient to produce market clearing.

The analysis may, perhaps, be best understood by contrasting it with the simpler Classical analysis. Start in part (iv) of the figure, where the line through the origin shows the relationship between money wages and prices necessary to produce the real wage $\bar{w}$. In the Classical analysis, firms employ labour up to the point where the real wage and the marginal product of labour are equated, in other words the demand for labour curve in the Classical analysis would be given by the line D_N–D in part (i) of the figure, and employment would be given by $\hat{N}$ at the intersection of the demand for and supply of labour curves. Reading across from part (i) to

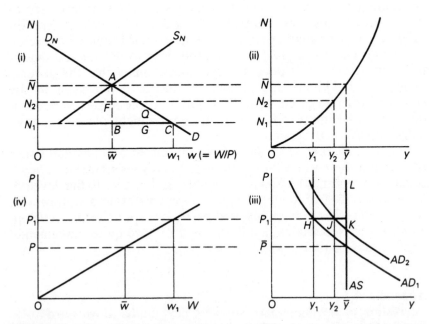

Figure 4.3 The aggregate supply curve with downward rigid money wages and prices. (i) The labour market. (ii) The production function. (iii) The AS–AD curves. (iv) Money wages and prices.

the production function in part (ii) of the figure would show that the output produced as a result of the employment level of $\bar{N}$ would be $\bar{y}$. The Classical aggregate supply curve may then be derived as the vertical line L–AS in part (iii), under the assumption that money wages and prices are perfectly flexible upwards or downwards to produce the market clearing real wage and output level, regardless of the position of the aggregate demand curve in part (iii). Thus if aggregate demand were given by the curve AD_1 the price level would be $\bar{P}$ as shown in part (iii), and the money wage would be $\bar{w}$ as shown by reading across from part (iii) to part (iv) for the price level $\bar{P}$.

Now, however, consider that the price level and money wage are downward rigid at the levels of P_1 and w_1 respectively. The resulting real wage is still at the market clearing level of $\bar{w}$ as shown in part (iv), but this no longer guarantees that the market clearing solution will result.

Consider that aggregate demand is still given by the curve AD_1 in part (iii), which implies that aggregate demand will be at the level y_1 as shown. Reading up to part (ii) shows that in order to produce y_1 firms need to hire only N_1 employees, which is exactly how many they will hire even though the real wage of w is below the marginal product of labour of w_1 when employment is N_1 as shown in part (i). Firms do not go on hiring workers until the marginal product is equated to the real wage since if they did so they would only produce output which they could not sell. Thus the economy locates at point B in part (i) (rather than at point A as in the Classical analysis) and at point H in part (iii) of the figure. There are a couple of points to notice here. First notice that away from market clearing it is assumed that quantities traded are set by the short side of the market, that is if supply differs from demand the smaller of the two yields the amount traded; thus in the labour market the short side is the demand side with N_1 being demanded and traded rather than the higher amount of $\bar{N}$ which would be voluntarily supplied at the real wage $\bar{w}$. Second notice that if firms were willing to reduce prices below P_1 then the economy would not locate at point B in part (i); for the given money wage of w_1, as the price level fell the real wage would rise and firms would move along the constrained labour demand curve DCB from B to C, at which point the real wage would equal the marginal product of labour, firms would have no more incentive to try to increase sales and the price level would stabilize. Thus the kinked line BCD represents the constrained demand for labour curve, given the constraint that at the price level P_1 the demand for output is y_1.

If aggregate demand were to shift for some reason to the new curve AD_2, demand at the price level P_1 would rise to y_2 as shown in part (iii) of the figure. Tracing through the figure shows that firms would now gladly hire N_2 employees at the going money and real wage rates and that the real wage would still be below the marginal product of labour, implying that firms would like to sell more output than the demand constraint allows them to sell. Thus firms would be willing to meet the demand for y_2 without requiring an increase in the price level above P_1. The economy therefore relocates to point F in part (i) of the figure (on a new constrained labour demand curve) and to point J in part (iii). If the aggregate demand curve were to continue shifting rightwards in part (iii) of the figure the forthcoming supply would continue shifting rightwards too, until the point K were reached, corresponding to the point A in part (i). If aggregate demand at the price level P_1 rose beyond $\bar{y}$ then it would exceed the voluntary supply of firms, since at point A in part (i) the real wage and marginal product of labour are equated, and there would be excess demand in the goods market. This would cause the price level to be bid up, so reducing the real wage and causing excess demand in the labour market too, which would cause the money wage to be bid up to restore the real wage to its market clearing level. Thus supply will not rise beyond $\bar{y}$ and the aggregate supply curve will become kinked at the point K in part (iii) of the figure. Thus the aggregate supply curve under the assumptions made here is the line $HJKL$, which is a reverse L-shape often associated with an extreme Keynesian view. Notice that the derivation of such a shaped aggregate supply curve here differs considerably from that outlined in note 3 of the previous chapter.

The reverse L-shape of the aggregate supply curve in figure 4.3 depends upon the real wage initially being at the market clearing level. The reader may show that if the analysis began at some point such as G in between B and C on the constrained labour demand curve in part (i) of the figure, the resulting aggregate supply curve would initially be horizontal; as aggregate demand rose, output would rise without any associated rise in price as the economy relocated along the vertical line GQ in part (i). Once the point Q was reached, however, firms would require a higher price level in order to induce them to increase output further; any further increase in aggregate demand would be met with an increase in both output and price, so that the aggregate supply curve would become upward sloping, as the rise in price, for the given money wage, reduced the real wage and increased labour demand exactly as was shown in chapter 1 for the case of a downward rigid money wage (see figure 1.8). Also just as in figure 1.8, and the accompanying analysis, the aggregate supply curve would again become vertical at full employment; indeed apart from the analysis of the horizontal section of the aggregate supply curve, the analysis would be identical to that accompanying figure 1.8. The analysis with a starting value for the real wage below the market clearing level is slightly more complicated and is left as an exercise for the interested reader, who may take as a clue that its shape is the same as for the aggregate supply curve just derived, but this time with the real wage rising as output and employment rise along the upward sloping part of the curve. The reader attempting this latter exercise should also remember that employment should be set according to the short side of the labour market.

Notes

1 Notice that Clower's definition of effective demand as the demand forthcoming given the operation of quantity constraints is similar to the definition offered by Keynes as 'the aggregate income (or proceeds) which the entrepreneurs expect to receive . . . from the amount of current employment which they decide to give' (1936, p. 55). Also notice the role given by Keynes to expectations.

2 It should be noted that it is quite possible to argue that Keynes moved much further away from the Classical model than is implied by Clower and Leijonhufvud. Keynes's removal of the auctioneer may well have been the result of relinquishing other Classical assumptions; in particular, Winslow convincingly argues that Keynes rejected the 'premise that economic behaviour is fully rational' and instead assumed that 'there are important elements of irrationality in motivation' (1989, p. 1).

3 This interpretation is in line with that of Davidson (e.g. 1983). Until this chapter we have been willing to call the line D_N in figure 4.2 the aggregate demand-for-labour curve, whereas Davidson thinks that so doing implies that the demand for labour is determined solely by the real wage, regardless of the level of aggregate demand. We certainly wish to make no such implication, however, and perhaps should have called the D_N curve the 'notional aggregate labour demand curve' throughout. We did not do so simply because it would have cluttered the argument when the D_N curve was first introduced in chapter 1. The notional aggregate labour demand curve may be interpreted as the relationship between the real wage and the amount of labour firms

would like to hire if they could sell all the ensuing output at the price level implied by the relationship between the money and real-wage levels. The notional aggregate labour demand curve might then be just a different label for Davidson's marginal product of labour curve, and the point on that curve at which employment and the real wage settle can be argued to be determined by the level of aggregate demand, as in Davidson.

4   It is open to question whether the constrained demand-for-labour curve should have a horizontal segment, or whether point *C* should show equal employment, and, therefore, output and aggregate demand, as point *B*. Perhaps, since the real wage is higher at point *C*, the level of aggregate demand might be different too, so that *B* and *C* could not both lie on the constrained labour demand curve.

5   This view contrasts with that of Leijonhufvud (1968, especially ch. 2) that the price mechanism fails because of the presence of money in the system. Rather, it views the existence of money as, at least partly, dependent upon its role as a useful device for facilitating transactions in the presence of uncertainty (or the absence of the Walrasian auctioneer) (see Goodhart, 1975, especially chs 2 and 3).

6   Keynes expressed this idea in a letter to G. F. Shove in 1936 when he wrote that, 'as soon as one is dealing with the influence of expectations and of transitory experience, one is, in the nature of things, outside the realm of the formally exact' (Moggridge, 1973, p. 2).

7   It might be noted here that, when confronted with evidence that it was real wages which were rigid rather than money wages, Keynes responded that rigid money wages were not essential for his theory, and that he could easily relax the rigid-money-wage assumption (see Meltzer, 1981, pp. 51–2 for discussion). This is direct support for the claim that the *General Theory* was more than a special case of the Classical model with rigid money wages.

8   Developments in modelling the consumption function have stressed the roles of future earnings and the credit market in determining current consumption. Such developments weaken the dependence of consumption on current income, but do not appear to affect the fundamental distinction between notional and effective demand introduced by Clower. For a discussion of modelling the consumption function, see a standard intermediate level textbook such as Greenaway and Shaw (1983).

Part III

Does Fiscal Policy Really Matter?
The Crowding-out Debate

5

Wealth Effects and the Government Budget Identity

We now return to the development of the *IS–LM* model. The special cases of the *IS–LM* model examined in chapter 3, and the wealth effects introduced in the Neoclassical Synthesis have contributed to an important debate on the issue of 'crowding out'.[1]

The crowding-out debate concerns the efficacy of fiscal policy in stimulating aggregate demand. In the usual *IS–LM* model, with finite interest elasticity in both the *IS* and *LM* curves, an increase in bond-financed government expenditure pushes up the interest rate; this releases some money from idle to active balances and allows the level of income to rise. Although the higher interest rate discourages, or 'crowds out', some private-sector investment, this is not enough to offset completely the increase in government expenditure, so the effect on income is positive and crowding out is said to be partial.

The special cases of the *IS–LM* model produce different extremes of crowding out. For example, under the assumption of an interest-inelastic demand for money function (see appendix 3.1), a bond-financed increase in government expenditure would result in complete crowding out. The reason for this is that the increase in government expenditure pushes up the interest rate without releasing any money from idle to active balances. The existing money stock cannot, therefore, support any increase in income, and the interest rate is pushed up until enough interest-elastic private-sector investment expenditure is discouraged to offset exactly the effect on aggregate demand of the increased government expenditure. Crowding out is thus complete, and the bond-financed increase in government expenditure fails to stimulate aggregate demand. On the other hand, in the liquidity trap there is no crowding out associated with a bond-financed increase in government expenditure. The interest rate does not rise until the economy is out of the trap, and no private sector investment expenditure is crowded out. Also, in the interest-inelastic investment case (see appendix 3.2), there is no crowding out associated with such a policy, since any rise in interest rates has no effect on investment demand.

It is now generally accepted that the relevant interest elasticities of the *IS–LM* model do not take their extreme values, although the empirical magnitude of such elasticities is still important in determining the degree of crowding out. Important roles are also played in the debate by the issues of wealth effects and the government budget identity. These latter issues are dealt with below.

5.1 Wealth Effects

It was shown in chapter 3 that wealth effects in the consumption function have played an important role in macroeconomic debate since the work of Pigou and Patinkin drew attention to them. It is useful, therefore, to incorporate such effects fully into the *IS–LM* and *AS–AD* models. In order to do this, it is necessary first of all to define wealth; second, to see how policies may change wealth, either directly or indirectly; third, to introduce wealth effects into the behavioural assumptions underlying the models; and, finally, to examine the impact of recognizing wealth effects upon the policy implications derived from the models.

Defining Wealth

Wealth may be defined as the sum of the assets minus the sum of the liabilities of the private sector. Assume, for simplicity, that the private sector has no liabilities and that assets consist of holdings of money and government bonds. This assumption neglects the role of stocks of real private assets and the value of human capital, but will allow analysis of the role of wealth none the less.[2]

Since wealth is a stock variable, it must be measured at a point in time. In discrete-time models it is often useful to measure wealth at the beginning and end of each period, and in order to do this it is useful to adopt the following notation:

$$a_t = a_{t-1} + \Delta a_t \qquad (5.1)$$

where

a_t = the real value of the private-sector wealth stock as measured at the end of period t, or the beginning of period $t + 1$.

a_{t-1} = the real value of the private-sector wealth stock as measured at the end of period $t - 1$, or the beginning of period t.

Δa_t = the change in the real value of the private-sector wealth stock from the beginning to the end of the period t.

The value of a_t, given that wealth consists of money and bond holdings, is given by

$$a_t = \frac{1}{P_t}\left(M_t + \frac{B_t}{r_t}\right) \qquad (5.2)$$

where

P_t = the price level in period t
M_t = the nominal money stock at the end of period t
r_t = the nominal interest rate in period t
B_t = the nominal value of the interest payable on the government debt, all of which, for simplicity, is assumed to consist of fixed coupon annuities

Equation (5.2) simply shows the real value of wealth to be the nominal value divided by the price level.

Changes in the Real Value of the Wealth Stock

Using equations (5.1) and (5.2), it is possible to see that the real value of the wealth stock may change in two ways: directly or indirectly. Direct changes in the real value of wealth are brought about by changes in the nominal value of the money stock, or by changes in the nominal value of coupon payments on the government debt. For example, if, *ceteris paribus*, the government increased the nominal money stock to finance an increase in government spending, this would directly change the real value of wealth. Indirect changes in the real value of wealth are brought about by changes in the real value of existing assets, as a result of a change in either the price level or the nominal interest rate.

Wealth Effects in the IS–LM *and* AS–AD *models*

The Neoclassical Synthesis introduced wealth effects in the context of a falling price level, raising the real value of the money stock and inducing higher real consumption at any real level of income. The analysis, therefore, concerned a price-induced indirect wealth effect from the real value of the money supply on real consumption. Given equation (5.2), it is possible to argue that the wealth effect on consumption as prices fall would have come about as a result of not only a rising real-money stock, but also a rising real-bond stock, so long as interest rate changes did not negate the indirect price effects on the real value of the bond stock. It also seems sensible (see Silber, 1970) to argue that real wealth would be an important determinant not only of consumption spending, but also of the demand for money, the argument being that the wealthier a person is, the more he or she will spend and, also, the more money he or she will wish to hold. Recognizing that wealth effects occur in the demand-for-money function has important policy implications, as is shown below.

Wealth Effects and the Crowding-out Debate

We have already seen, in appendix 3.1, that interest inelasticity of the demand for money was, perhaps wrongly, thought to be one of the supporting arguments for the Monetarist case against active fiscal stabilization policy. It has also been argued (e.g. by Blinder and Solow, 1973; Burrows, 1979; and Cohen, 1982) that the Monetarist case relies upon an extreme case of wealth effects in an *IS–LM* framework. This argument may be examined after comparing the effects of a bond-financed increase in real government spending with a money-financed increase in real government spending in the *IS–LM* and *AS–AD* models.

Consider, firstly, the money-financed increase in government spending, in which case the results of the analysis are alike in either the presence or the absence of wealth effects. Section (i) of figure 5.1 shows initial *IS–LM* intersection at A for price level P_0, and for given values of the underlying parameters and policy variables. Section (ii) shows the corresponding aggregate demand curve, AD_0, and, for comparison, the Classical and extreme Keynesian AS curves, AS_1 and AS_2, respectively. If the government money-finances an increase in government spending, the analysis, in the absence of wealth effects in either the consumption or the demand-

Figure 5.1 Wealth effects and a money-financed increase in real government spending. (i) *IS–LM*. (ii) *AD–AS*

for-money function, would show the *IS–LM* curves shifting to *IS*₁ and *LM*₁, respectively, for price level P_0, and the *AD* curve shifting to AD_1. The final result would be an increase in either prices to P_1 or income to y_1, depending on which version of the *AS* curve is considered. For the Classical *AS* curve case there would be further shifts in the *LM* curve as the price level rose towards P_1; for the extreme Keynesian *AS* curve case, the intersection of IS_1 and LM_1 at *B* would remain relevant.

Introducing wealth effects somewhat complicates the standard result. (For simplicity, interest-induced wealth effects are ignored in what follows; should they be introduced, they would affect the slopes of the *IS* and *LM* curves with wealth effects compared with those without, but would not, otherwise, affect the analysis. The interested reader may calculate how the slopes of the IS and LM curves would be affected.) With wealth effects on consumption, the IS curve would move beyond IS_1 to IS_2, since the money financing of the extra government spending would increase wealth and so increase consumption for any income and price level. Furthermore, since the value of the wealth stock depends on the price levels, the position of the IS curves will depend on the price level too.

Thus, wealth effects on consumption would tend to increase the IS curve shift, and thereby would increase the AD shift too. However, wealth effects on the demand for money mean that the shift of the LM curve would be smaller than in their absence, say to LM_2 rather than LM_1. This is so because the increased wealth causes increased demand for money at any level of (real) income and interest rates, which means that points on LM_1 (which neglects wealth effects) would represent points of excess demand for money in the presence of wealth effects in the demand-for-money function.[3] The shift to LM_2 rather than LM_1 tends to reduce the effect of policy and reduce the shift of the AD schedule in the lower part of the diagram.

Recognizing wealth effects, therefore, leads to recognizing two offsetting effects as far as the policy goes. The wealth effects on the IS curve tend to increase the demand-stimulating aspects of the policy, while those on the LM curve tend to reduce them. For the price level P_0, therefore, the IS–LM intersection at point C could lie to the right or left of B; or, in other words, the AD schedule, AD_2, with wealth effects, could lie to the right or left of AD_1. With or without recognizing wealth effects, however, one conclusion is unambiguous: the policy will stimulate aggregate demand, since both IS and LM curves move rightwards, as does the AD curve. Just what effects the policy has on the price level and real income depend on the AS curve as well as the AD curve, as is illustrated in section (ii) of figure 5.1. Notice that, for the aggregate demand curve AD_2 and the aggregate supply curve AS_1, the eventual effect on income is zero, and the price level rises from P_0 to P_2 in section (ii) of the figure. In terms of the IS–LM analysis, the IS and LM curves in section (i) would need redrawing as the price level changed; this is not done as it would clutter up the figure. Readers may wish to draw in the IS and LM curves for price level P_2; if so, they should note that, in order to be consistent with AD_2, the curves must intersect above the real-income level y_0.

In a discrete-time model, it might be argued that the measure of wealth which is relevant for behaviour in any period is the real value of wealth at the beginning of the period. If this is so, then the analysis becomes dynamic to some extent, since the wealth effects of the money financing would not take place until the period after the policy was enacted. In figure 5.1 the *IS* and *LM* curves would shift from IS_0 and LM_0 to IS_1 and LM_1 for the price level P_0 in the period in which the policy was carried out, as a result of the standard effects of the policy, and to IS_2 and LM_2 for the price level P_0 in the subsequent period, as a result of the wealth effects. The *AD* curve would similarly move to AD_1 in the period in which the policy was carried out, and then to AD_2 subsequently. The total effects of the policy, therefore, take two periods to manifest themselves, but this does not radically affect any policy conclusions.

It should be noted that the analysis assumes that in subsequent periods the level of government spending is maintained at its new high level, and that no further subsequent increases in the money supply occur. This latter assumption will be relaxed, with significant effects, in section 5.2 below. For now, however, it is sufficient to notice that recognizing wealth effects does not significantly affect the conclusions regarding a money-financed increase in real government spending. The same cannot be said for the case of a bond-financed increase in real government spending, as figure 5.2 makes clear.

Figure 5.2 (i) shows initial *IS–LM* intersection at *A* for price level P_0, and for given values of the underlying parameters and policy variables. Part (ii) shows the corresponding aggregate demand curve, AD_0, and, as for figure 5.1, plots the Classical and extreme Keynesian *AS* curves, AS_1 and AS_2, respectively.

Now consider the effects of a bond-financed increase in real government spending, and this time explicitly allow for the argument that wealth effects manifest themselves in the period after the policy is carried out. The analysis for the period in which the policy is carried out is, thus, the standard analysis in the absence of wealth effects. The *IS* curve moves to IS_1 and the *LM* curve remains at LM_0 for the price level P_0, in part (i) of the figure. Correspondingly, the *AD* curve moves to AD_1 in part (ii), and the effects on price and income levels depend on the nature of the *AS* curve. The first-round effects of the policy are, therefore, to stimulate aggregate demand, but to a lesser extent than for the money-financed case since the *LM* curve does not move this time. However, wealth effects now significantly affect the analysis in subsequent periods. Counting the increase in the bond stock as a direct increase in wealth (and still ignoring any interest-induced wealth effects), the subsequent wealth effects on consumption, in the

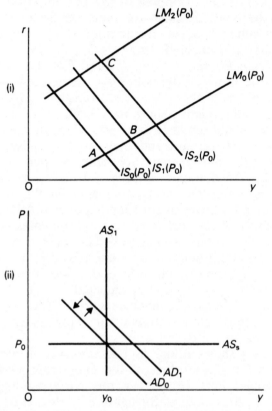

Figure 5.2 Wealth effects and a bond-financed increase in real government spending. (i) *IS–LM*. (ii) *AD–AS*

period after the policy is carried out, will cause the *IS* curve to shift out further to *IS₂*, in just the same way as for the money-financed policy. But now the wealth effects on the demand for money cause the *LM* curve to move upwards to *LM₂*. Again, the wealth-induced *LM* shift tends to offset the expansionary effect of the wealth-induced *IS* shift, but this time, since the final *LM* curve lies above the initial *LM* curve, it may even offset the expansionary effect of the policy altogether. Indeed, as shown in figure 5.2, for the price level P_0 the final *IS–LM* intersection is above the initial *IS–LM* intersection at the output level y_0, and the final *AD* shift is back from AD_1 to AD_0 again. Figure 5.2, therefore, shows complete crowding out, since ultimately the bond-financed increase in real government spending has no effect on aggregate demand.

Again, it is necessary to assume that the new higher level of government spending is maintained, and that no further increases in the bond stock take place, for this conclusion to hold in future periods.

It is possible, then, that wealth effects will cause complete crowding out of the effects of bond-financed real government expenditure. There is no need to rely upon a vertical *LM* curve to generate the complete crowding-out result. Blinder and Solow, therefore, argued that 'Friedman has indicated that he now believes that these wealth effects, rather than the oft-cited slope of the *LM* curve, constitute the main issue separating Monetarists from Keynesians' (1973, pp. 322–3). However, a careful reading of the article by Friedman (1972) to which Blinder and Solow refer shows that Friedman was not talking about wealth effects at all: he was talking about the money financing of an increase in the government budget deficit, as for example, brought about by an increase in real government spending. Friedman argued that this policy

> shifts the *LM* curve to the right (so long as prices are assumed constant). But this is not a once-for-all shift. So long as the deficit continues, and continues to be financed by creating money, the nominal money stock continues to grow and the *LM* curve (at initial prices) continues to move to the right. Is there any doubt that this effect must swamp the effect of the once-for-all shift of the *IS* curve? Of course, if prices react, we get into a new set of issues. The rightward movement of the *LM* curve is then offset. . . . (Friedman, 1972, p. 916)

As this quotation shows, Friedman was clearly not talking about wealth effects, otherwise the *IS* shift would not have been once-for-all. Instead, he was pointing out that an increased government budget deficit in one period would be likely to lead to deficits in subsequent periods too, so that, for money financing, the nominal money stock would go on rising with subsequent effects in the *IS–LM* model.

In terms of figure 5.1, Friedman was arguing that neither point *B*, for the case without wealth effects, nor point *C*, for the case with wealth effects, need necessarily represent the ultimate *IS–LM* intersection (at the initial price level), since it is likely that further increases in the nominal money supply will be necessary to finance and maintain the new higher level of real government spending. A similar logic could, of course, be applied to the bond-financed case. In order to trace the implications of Friedman's insight more fully, it is necessary explicitly to incorporate the government budget identity into the analysis. Somewhat ironically, this task was carried out not by Friedman, but by Blinder and Solow (although earlier authors had included the government budget identity in their work – e.g. Christ, 1968; Brunner and Meltzer, 1972).[4] The next section, therefore, turns to an analysis of the government budget identity.

5.2   The Government Budget Identity

The government budget identity may be viewed as little more than an accounting relationship which states that government expenditure on goods and services, plus interest payments on outstanding government bonds, plus non-interest transfer payments, must be financed either out of tax revenues or from new money creation or from the receipts of bond sales. The government budget identity is also commonly called the government budget constraint, although it does not imply any constraint upon the level of the government's spending, since the government can, in principle, raise more taxes, print more money or sell more bonds if it wishes to finance more spending. Any constraint upon the level of government spending comes not from the government budget constraint, but from the physical and political limitations the economy places upon the government. The government budget constraint, therefore, operates rather differently than its counterpart of the individual budget constraint in elementary microeconomic analysis, where a constraint on the level of spending often is implied, which is why the alternative term of 'government budget identity' is used here. Another term for the government budget identity would be the 'government financing requirement', which gives the correct implication that government spending, like that of individuals, must be financed in one way or another. This is hardly a controversial point; for example, it neither conflicts with nor supports the Keynesian argument that a government can and should increase spending in a recession as a countercyclical policy. Nevertheless, the implications of recognizing the government budget identity, and of tracing the effects of financing government policies, are very important and interesting.

Consider the following algebraic version of the government budget identity:

$$G_t + B_{t-1} \equiv T_t + \Delta M_t + \frac{\Delta B_t}{r_t} \tag{5.3}$$

where

G_t = government spending on goods and services plus transfers in period t

B_{t-1} = interest payable in period t on the outstanding government debt at the beginning of period t

T_t = tax receipts in period t

ΔM_t = increase in the (high-powered) money supply in period t

$\dfrac{\Delta B_t}{r_t}$ = value of bond sales in period t.

Assume, for simplicity, that prices are constant (with $P = 1$) so that the variables in (5.3) may be regarded as either real or nominal. Further, assume that there are no banks, so that ΔM_t represents the total change in the domestic money stock which consists entirely of high-powered money. Also, assume that all bonds take the form of consols and that interest is first paid in the period following the period of issue. It would, of course, be possible to complicate (5.3) by allowing for different types of bonds, profits from nationalized industries and so on, but the simple form of (5.3) still allows a number of points to be clarified.

One value of recognizing (5.3) is that it makes it clear that government policies are not completely independent of one another, in the sense that at least one policy variable must be set to accommodate the values of the other policy variables and satisfy the government budget identity (5.3). In other words, of the four policy variables, G, T, ΔM and $\Delta B/r$ in (5.3), the government may choose values for three but must let the fourth one adjust to satisfy the budget identity. For example, the government could choose to set values for G, T and ΔM, but then it would have to let $\Delta B/r$ adjust to satisfy (5.3). In practice, the government is likely to be under pressure simultaneously to increase spending, reduce taxes, control the change in the money supply and control bond sales so as to prevent government borrowing pushing up interest rates. The government must balance these pressures and adjust the variables under its control while still satisfying the government budget identity.[5]

Another benefit of recognizing the government budget identity is that it introduces some intrinsically dynamic elements into the otherwise comparative-static *IS–LM* model. For example, consider a money-financed once-and-for-all increase in government spending. In the standard *IS–LM* model, such a policy causes the *IS* and *LM* curves to shift once (as for example from *IS* to IS_1 and *LM* to LM_1 in figure 5.1); but now it becomes obvious that, unless the budget is balanced, that is unless $G_t + B_t = T_t$, at the level of income given by the new *IS–LM* intersection, further changes must take place which will continue to move either the *IS* or the *LM* curve or both. A simple case is where the new *IS–LM* intersection leads not to a balanced budget, but to a deficit on the budget which is money-financed; in this case the *LM* curve will continue to move outwards as long as the deficit persists and continues to be money-financed. In the absence of wealth effects on the *IS* curve, it will move only once, when the money-financed increase in spending occurs, but clearly the *LM* curve may continue to shift for several periods.

It was precisely this case that Friedman was talking about when he said, 'is there any doubt that this [latter] effect must swamp the once-for-all shift of the *IS* function' (1972, p. 916), although later writers have (wrongly!) inferred this to be a statement about wealth effects. The government budget identity is conceptually different from the wealth effects arguments presented in the last section, but since it helps to define changes in the stock of wealth (money plus bonds), it does have implications for those arguments.

By introducing dynamic elements into the *IS–LM* model, the government budget identity might provide a link between Keynesian and Monetarist approaches by pointing out the linkages between time periods. After all, Friedman has said that 'One way to characterize the Keynesian approach is that it gives almost exclusive importance to the first-round effect . . . Similarly, one way to characterize the quantity theory approach is to say that it gives almost no importance to first-round effects' (1972, p. 922). The government budget identity links first-round effects to subsequent-round effects and helps to provide a more complete model. It also links the flow variables, such as G_t, with stock variables, such as M_t, via the changes in stock variables, such as ΔM_t, included within it. This, too, may well link Keynesian and Monetarist analyses, since the former is often said to be too preoccupied with flows to the neglect of stocks, which are the focus of attention of the Monetarists' approach. However, recognition of the government budget identity need not bring any closer together the Keynesian and Monetarist views about the truly fundamental issues of the relative efficacy of *laissez-faire* versus government intervention.

Consideration of how flows affect stocks, and of how the variables in the model change over time and drive the economy from one position to another, also forces consideration of the question of model stability. Once a movement is set in train, will the economy ever converge on equilibrium again? It is quite clear that the

IS–LM equilibria examined so far may represent only temporary equilibria, that is, points at which demands and supplies for both flows (e.g., in the goods market) and stocks (e.g., in the money market) are equated, but at which forces are in train to change the values of the variables in the economy and move it to a new position. For example, consider the continuing increase in the money stock and consequent *LM* shifts in the discussion of a money-financed increase in government spending above. A condition for full, or stock-flow, equilibrium (in a non-inflationary no-growth framework) is that neither stocks nor flows be changing; this condition requires a balanced budget to prevent changes in the money or bond stocks, and also requires that the government undertake no open-market operations such as bond sales, which would, from a balanced government budget position, cause the money stock to fall and the bond stock to rise (since the private sector in this case would use money to buy bonds and, therefore, would increase its bond holdings but diminish its money holdings as the government takes the money receipts and keeps them out of circulation). The balanced budget requirement may be written as

$$G_t + B_{t-1} = T_t \tag{5.5}$$

It is now possible to see how the government budget identity may be introduced into the *IS–LM* model, and to see how it affects policy analysis within that model. Three cases will be considered: (1) a once-and-for-all increase in government spending where tax rates are held fixed and any subsequent budget deficits (or surpluses) are financed by issuing money; (2) a once-and-for-all increase in government spending under constant tax rates where any subsequent budget deficits (or surpluses) are financed by bond sales; (3) an open-market purchase of bonds where any subsequent budget deficits (or surpluses) are financed by issuing money. An examination of these three cases will make clear the importance of the role played by the government budget identity.

The Money-financed Expenditure Case

This case is illustrated in figure 5.3. Part (i) of the figure shows the *IS–LM* curves, and part (ii) shows the government budget identity. For simplicity, maintain the assumption of fixed prices (with $P = 1$); this assumption will be relaxed later. Further, assume that wealth effects play a role in determining the position of the *IS* and

Figure 5.3   Money-financed spending, wealth effects and the government budget identity. (i) *IS–LM*. (ii) Government budget

LM curves as described in the previous section. Consider that, initially, the *IS–LM* intersection was at point *A* on IS_1 and LM_1, with a level of income y_1 and interest rate r_1, as shown in figure 5.3 (i). Part (ii) of the figure shows government expenditure, *G*, plus interest payments, *B*, on the vertical axis and income along the horizontal axis. (Time subscripts are neglected.)

Tax revenues are also measured on the vertical axis. The line $T = ty$ indicates that tax revenues are some proportion t $(0 < t < 1)$ of income. This assumption could easily be relaxed and the tax function made more realistic – for example, to include taxes on interest payments. The horizontal line $G + B$ embodies the assumption that government spending plus interest payments are independent of the level of income. The intersection of $G + B$ and T above y_1 indicates that, initially, the government budget is in balance at y_1. The *IS–LM* equilibrium at the intersection of IS_1

and LM_1 could represent a full equilibrium, in the sense that there are no pressures in the economy tending to cause either stocks or flows to change.

Now, however, assume that the government intervenes to increase the level of government spending by the amount ΔG, and decides to finance this spending and any subsequent deficits by issuing money. The standard *IS–LM* analysis of this policy would show the *IS* and *LM* curves moving to IS_2 and LM_2 respectively, but in the presence of wealth effects the *IS* curve will move further, to IS_3 and the *LM* curve will not move so far, to LM_3. Thus, recognizing wealth effects modifies the *IS–LM* analysis, but only slightly.

Recognizing the government budget identity forces a more significant modification upon the analysis. The intersection of IS_3 and LM_3 at C leads to a level of income of y_3, but inspection of figure 5.3 (ii) shows that this intersection can represent only a temporary equilibrium. The increase in government spending by ΔG has shifted the $G + B$ line upwards by the amount ΔG to $G + \Delta G + B$, while the tax revenue line has not moved. Clearly, at income level y_3, tax revenues are less than total government outgoings $(G + \Delta G + B)$. The government must money-finance the deficit, further increasing the money stock and causing further shifts in the *IS* and *LM* curves. Full equilibrium cannot be reached until the *IS–LM* curves intersect above y_m, the level of income now needed to bring about a balanced government budget. Such a position will be achieved if the money financing of deficits eventually shifts the *LM* curve to LM_m and the *IS* curve to IS_m (via wealth effects), in which case the *IS–LM* intersection at D will represent a full equilibrium.

To check whether the new full equilibrium would, in fact, ever be reached would require detailed algebraic treatment and knowledge of the parameters of the system of equations, but since the money financing of deficits tends to move both the *IS* and *LM* curves out from the origin, it clearly tends to move the economy towards the new equilibrium. It is likely, therefore, that the money-financed increase in spending will eventually move the economy to the new equilibrium at y_m, which is determined by the intersection of the $G + \Delta G + B$ line and the tax function in figure 5.3 (ii).[6] The *IS–LM* curves, however, determine the path the economy takes on its way to that new equilibrium, and also determine the path and new equilibrium level for the interest rate. The government budget identity, therefore, complements, but does not replace, the *IS–LM* analysis.

The Bond-financed Expenditure Case

This case is illustrated in figure 5.4, of which part (i) shows the *IS–LM* curves and part (ii) the government budget identity. Again, assume that an initial full-equilibrium position occurs at the intersection of IS_1 and LM_1, at point A in part (i), at an income level of y_1 which coincides with a balanced budget in part (ii). Now, however, assume that the government intervenes to increase the level of government spending by the amount ΔG and decides to finance this spending and any subsequent deficits by selling bonds. The standard *IS–LM* analysis of this policy would show the *IS* curve moving to IS_2 and the *LM* curve remaining unmoved; but, after recognizing wealth effects, the analysis shows *IS* moving further, to IS_3, and the *LM* curve moving upwards to LM_2. Wealth effects thus introduce ambiguities into the analysis of this policy, since the *LM* shift may offset the expansionary effect of the *IS* shift.

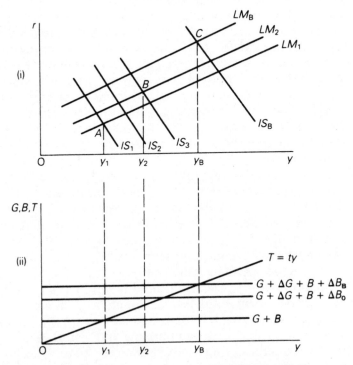

Figure 5.4 Bond-financed spending, wealth effects and the government budget identity. (i) *IS–LM*. (ii) Government budget

Whether wealth effects are recognized or not, the *IS–LM* analysis is at least clear on one point: the bond-financed case is less expansionary than the money-financed case for a similar increase in government spending. The implication of the government budget identity is that this comparison may no longer hold. The intersection at B of the IS_3 and LM_2 curves in part (i) of figure 5.4 leads to a level of income of y_2, which will indeed be less than would be achieved under money financing, but at this level the government budget will be in deficit. The deficit can be seen in part (ii) by noting that the $G + B$ line moves upwards to $G + \Delta G + B + \Delta B_0$ on the initial bond-financed increase in spending, and that at y_2 taxes do not match total government outgoings. More bonds will be sold in order to finance the deficit, and this will induce further shifts in the IS and LM curves owing to wealth effects.[7] If the system is stable it will eventually converge on a new equilibrium, such as that shown where the IS_B and LM_B curves intersect at C with an income level of y_B, which balances the government budget at an outgoings level of $G + \Delta G + B + \Delta B_B$ in part (ii).

There are two things to compare with the money-financed case. First, since the IS and LM shifts tend to offset one another in the bond-financed case, it is more likely that those shifts may not move the economy to a new full equilibrium. It could be that the extra bond sales push up interest payments more than their wealth effects on the $IS–LM$ curves push up income and taxes, so that the deficit simply grows and grows as ever more bonds are sold each period to finance it. The $IS–LM$ intersection may either move income away from the level necessary for full equilibrium, or move it so slowly in the right direction that ever-increasing interest payments keep moving the level necessary for full equilibrium away from that level generated by the $IS–LM$ intersection. In either case, instability results.

Second, if the system does converge on a new equilibrium, it is likely that this will be at a higher level of income than in the money-financed case. The reason for this is that, as long as the government goes on selling bonds, the $G + \Delta G + B + \Delta B$ line goes on shifting upwards, owing to the extra interest payments, and this moves the eventual balanced budget position up to ever higher income le/els, and beyond the full equilibrium for the money-financed case for which ΔB is, by definition, zero. The basic intuition is that, the more interest payments the government commits itself to, the higher must income be to generate the taxes to finance those payments.

However, it is not always the case that the bond-financed full-equilibrium level of income is greater than for the money-financed case. In some models the initial expansion when government spending increases may be so great as to move the government into a budget surplus, in which case, instead of selling bonds, it would use the surplus to buy back bonds, and thereby hold the money stock constant but reduce interest payments and pull the $G + \Delta G + B + \Delta B$ line downwards by making ΔB negative. Whether the bond-financed case is more expansionary in full equilibrium than the money-financed case, therefore, depends upon whether the eventual ΔB is positive or negative; if it is positive, bond financing is more expansionary. (For a discussion of such issues see Blinder and Solow, 1973; Hiller, 1977, 1980; and Shieh, 1980.)

The Open Market Purchase Case

This case is illustrated in figure 5.5. Again, initially assume full equilibrium at the intersection of IS_1 and LM_1 at A, with an income level of y_1 at which the government budget is balanced. Now consider that the government issues money to finance a purchase of bonds on the open market. In the immediate term there are no wealth effects, since the private sector simply exchanges bond holdings for money holdings and both bonds and money are considered to be part of wealth. The standard analysis of a shift of the LM curve to LM_2 with the IS curve unmoved is, therefore, applicable. The immediate effect of this policy, therefore, would move the IS–LM intersection to B and would be expansionary, with income rising to y_2.

Recognition of the government budget identity again indicates that this position represents only a temporary equilibrium. At y_2, figure 5.5 (ii) shows the government to be running a surplus on its budget, since taxes have risen with income and interest payments have fallen as bonds have been bought back. If the government uses this surplus to buy back more bonds, thereby reducing the bond stock further while holding the money supply fixed at its new higher levels, the full-equilibrium result will be to cause income to fall if the economy is to converge on a new equilibrium. The fall in income occurs because as bonds are bought back wealth declines, and the IS curve shifts towards the origin causing income to fall, although this effect is somewhat offset by the fall in wealth, reducing the demand for money and shifting the LM curve downwards too. Since all the bond purchases reduce interest payments, any new equilibrium which requires a balanced government budget

Figure 5.5 An open-market purchase, wealth effects and the government budget identity. (i) *IS–LM*. (ii) Government budget

must be at a level of income below the initial level, y_1. A new equilibrium is shown at y_p in the diagram, at the intersection of IS_p and LM_p at C in part (i) and with interest payments down by ΔB_p in part (ii). Thus, in this case the government budget identity implies that the full-equilibrium effect on policy on income is in the opposite direction to the effect implied by analysis which does not recognize the role of that constraint. Of course, it is possible that the policy could be destabilizing and no new equilibrium ever attained.

The three policy examples discussed above illustrate the importance of the government budget identity in introducing dynamic elements into the analysis and improving the comparison of full-equilibrium and intermediate policy effects. The reader may care to use it in analysing other policies, such as a tax-financed increase in spending, or for more complicated policies, such as an open-market purchase followed by a rise in spending to eliminate the surplus instead of using the surplus to withdraw bonds.

Notice, however, that, useful as the government budget identity may be for policy analysis, it does not solve the really important questions. Will the changes in aggregate demand analysed in the above examples cause changes in the level of real income, or will they instead cause changes in the price level, or in both the price level and real income? And how should policy be set to stabilize undesirable fluctuations in output and prices? The answers to these questions depend upon a view of the aggregate supply side of the economy, of the sources of shocks to the economy, and of the ability of the government to intervene usefully.

It should also be noted that the standard *IS–LM* model is a comparative-static framework which implies that all the dynamic relationships in the economy are assumed to work themselves out in a time space so short that capital stock changes and financial asset stock changes can be neglected. This is a rather strong assumption, which is relaxed upon introduction of the government budget identity into the model. The government budget identity introduces some dynamics, but when this is done and changes in the capital stock are still neglected it implies that, in the time necessary for the dynamic relationships to work themselves out, it is necessary to take into account changes in financial asset stocks, but still possible to neglect changes in the real capital stock. The implication that changes in financial asset stocks are more important than changes in the real capital stock is rather unsatisfactory, but to introduce changes in the real capital stock would be beyond the scope of this book.

So far in this section, the assumption has been made of fixed prices; that is, a horizontal aggregate supply curve has been assumed. It is useful now to contrast this with the extreme Classical vertical aggregate supply curve.[8] It is possible to interpret figure 5.5 as showing that, in full equilibrium, aggregate demand is lower at any price level as a result of an open-market purchase which increases the money supply. If the aggregate supply schedule is vertical, as in the Classical model, this implies that an increase in the money supply as a result of an open-market purchase will initially raise the price level but eventually reduce it. It would also, with our simplifying assumptions, destabilize the model; the government surplus would go on getting ever larger as the bond stock and interest payments declined without real income falling to reduce real tax receipts. Of course, in the real world, governments would offset such pressures by reducing tax rates or increasing real expenditure, or by some combination of such vote-winning policies.

Similarly, with a Classical aggregate supply curve it is possible to interpret the other examples as showing that in full equilibrium bond financing has a bigger impact on the price level than money financing for a similar increase in expenditure. These policies too would destabilize the model, since the increase in real government expenditure would never be matched by an increase in tax receipts under the assumptions of fixed tax rates and fixed real income levels. Again, in the real world governments could take actions to restore stability by cutting expenditure or increasing tax rates, and also in the real world, real tax receipts often rise with inflation (owing to imperfect adjustment of nominal tax allowances, etc.).

These results may seem very un-Monetarist at first glance, but there are leading Monetarists, such as Brunner, who would prob- ably accept them. However, Brunner would argue that, although bond financing would eventually lead to a higher price level than money financing, this would take much longer to come about than the increase in the price level for the money-financed case. Since inflation is the speed at which prices change, and not the eventual change in their level, then, in practice, it is money financing of ever larger government expenditure which has generated the high levels of inflation in recent times, not bond financing of such expenditure (see Brunner, 1976). In terms of our analysis, this is due to the *IS* and *LM* shifts both being expansionary under money financing but the *LM* shifts being contractionary under the bond-financing case and so reducing the speed at which the aggregate demand curve moves rightward. This is the same factor which makes bond financing more likely to destabilize the economy in the above discussion under the fixed-price assumption. Even with variable prices, bond financing remains more likely to be unstable than money financing.

Notice that, while the increase in the money supply is crucial for Brunner's argument, it is also important that it is usually increased in order to finance extra government expenditure, and that Brunner looks at the mix of fiscal and monetary policies, not just the rate of growth of the money supply. Examining the mix of policies in this way is an obvious corollary of recognizing the government budget identity and the relationships it implies between policy variables. Further, notice that Friedman's (1959a) proposal to fix the rate of growth of the money supply while also fixing the levels of government spending and taxation according to allocation and equity criteria, implies allowing the bond stock to adjust to finance the imbalances on the government budget arising from the inevitable fluctuations in economic activity. In the light of the indications that bond financing tends to induce instability, perhaps Friedman would have been wiser to stick to his original proposal (Friedman, 1948), which fixed the bond stock and allowed the money supply to adjust. (For a similar comment see McCallum, 1984.) On the other hand, Keynesians who wish to fine-tune the economy must be aware of the implications of the government budget constraint, if the full-equilibrium effects of their policies are to be taken into account to ensure that immediate success does not lead to later failure.

Finally, notice that since the impact of monetary policy depends upon the fiscal policy with which it is combined, and that short-run effects on variables such as output and the price level may well be reversed in the long-run, it is unlikely that simple and straightforward empirical relationships between income or prices and monetary or fiscal policy will be easy to find. The analysis indicates, for example, that whether, and if so by how much, the price level changes in response to a given monetary stimulus would vary over time and according to the fiscal policy being carried out alongside, and after, the monetary stimulus.

Having touched upon some aspects of the inflation debate in this chapter, the ground has been prepared for a discussion of the inflation–unemployment trade-off to which attention turns in the next chapter.

Notes

1   This chapter deals only with indirect crowding out, that is, with private expenditure crowded out by the interest rate effects of public expenditure. There may also be some direct crowding out where public expenditure directly replaces private expenditure (e.g., public provision of free health care may directly replace some private expenditure on health care). Direct crowding out is neglected here for simplicity's sake. For a taxonomic discussion see Buiter, 1977.
2   It also sidesteps the considerable debate about whether bonds constitute part of the wealth stock or not. See, e.g., Barro (1974), Feldstein (1982), and the discussion in chapter 8 below.
3   The interested reader is left to work out the extreme circumstances under which the *LM* curve would not move at all from LM_0 after an increase in nominal money supply for the price level P_0.
4   Clearly the 'main issue separating Monetarists from Keynesians' is not the role of wealth effects, nor the slope of the *LM* curve, nor the government budget identity, rather it is, as argued in chapter 2 above,

the issue of how the government may best pursue macroeconomic policy. Keynesians believe that the government should actively intervene in an attempt to fine-tune the economy by frequently adjusting its macroeconomic policies. Monetarists believe that such policy adjustments are likely to lead to more rather than less instability; therefore they favour simple and infrequently adjusted macroeconomic policies.

5 Another way of looking at this is to re-write (5.3) to yield

$$G_t + B_{t-1} - T_t \equiv \Delta M_t + \frac{\Delta B_t}{r_t} \equiv PSBR \tag{5.4}$$

Equation (5.4) shows that the public sector borrowing requirement (PSBR) is just the difference between public sector outgoings $(G_t + B_{t-1})$ and incomings (T_t), and may be financed by either issuing money or selling bonds. This version makes clear why governments say things like 'It is necessary to control government spending to control the size of the PSBR and limit the growth of the money supply.'

6 Notice that at the new equilibrium level of y_m, the increase in taxes, ΔT, compared with the initial position of y_1, equals the increase in government expenditure, ΔG. Since ΔT equals $t\Delta y$, then $t\Delta y$ equals ΔG, and the long-run multiplier, $\Delta y/\Delta G$, equals $1/t$. Thus, for a money-financed increase in expenditure, the long-run multiplier is simply the reciprocal of the marginal tax rate, with no behavioural parameters such as the marginal propensity to consume having any role to play! Such parameters do, however, determine the path taken to the new equilibrium, and, indeed, determine whether the system converges on the new equilibrium or not (see Hillier, 1977).

7 Notice that it is also possible to argue that the higher interest payments received by the private sector will induce higher consumption expenditure for any level of earned income, y, and interest rate, r, and so will shift the IS curve to the right even without the presence of wealth effects. It is, however, possible to show that the standard IS-LM model, complemented with a government budget identity and recognizing such interest payment effects to the neglect of wealth effects, produces instability of the system under bond financing (see Alpine, 1985). Furthermore, it would seem that, if interest payments enter into the consumption function, they should also enter the demand-for-money function and induce LM shifts.

8 Formally, this requires rewriting the government budget identity to include the price level as a variable. This could be done as follows:

$$G_t + \frac{B_{t-1}}{P_t} \equiv T_t + \frac{\Delta M_t}{P_t} + \frac{\Delta B_t}{r_t P_t} \tag{5.6}$$

where G_t and T_t are maintained as real values but it is necessary to deflate the nominal variables B_{t-1}, ΔM_t and ΔB_t by the price level,

P_t, to express all the variables in the government budget identity as real variables. This implies that the real value of interest payments on the existing government debt declines as the price level rises. The reader may care to work out the consequences of this for the diagrammatic analysis in the text. See also chapter 12 below for an open economy model with endogenous prices and explicit treatment of the government budget identity.

Part IV

Inflation and Unemployment: Is There a Trade-Off?

6

Inflation and Unemployment

Some of the most heated debates in macroeconomics in recent years have been concerned with the causes and consequences of inflation, the relationship between inflation and unemployment, and the appropriate policy responses. The topic of inflation was touched upon in the previous chapter, and it is now time to turn to an analysis of the issues involved in this important area.

The relevant ideas will be presented in their approximate chronological order. Accordingly, after discussing the definition of inflation, section 6.1 makes use of the *AS–AD* model, before the final two sections trace the development of the Phillips curve upon the debate, and introduce expectations as an endogenous variable into the analysis. This approach will enable the reader to gain some perspective upon how debates and controversies have contributed to the development of economic models, and will, fairly naturally, lead into the topics of rational expectations and New Classical Macroeconomics to be covered in the following chapters.[1]

6.1 Inflation and Unemployment in the *AS–AD* Model

Before going any further with the theoretical modelling of inflation-related issues, it is best to pause to offer a concise definition of inflation. Inflation may be defined, for our purposes, as the proportionate increase in the price level per period of time. Another way of looking at inflation would be to point out that as the price level rises the real value of a given nominal amount of money falls, so that is to say that as the price level rises £1 will buy fewer and fewer goods. Thus, inflation might, alternatively, be defined as the proportionate decline in the purchasing power of a given nominal amount of money. In this sense, inflation is a monetary phenomenon. Therefore, Laidler and Parkin argue that its importance 'stems from the pervasive role played by money in a modern economy' (1975, p. 741). Friedman goes further than this and argues that inflation 'is always and everywhere a monetary phenomenon . . . and can be produced only by a more rapid increase in the quantity of money than in output' (1970, p. 24). He clearly has views not only on what inflation is, but also on what causes it.

By no means all economists agree with Friedman on the causes of inflation, and it is such issues which are the focus of much of this chapter. There is also much disagreement about the consequences of inflation. Most would agree that a short bout of inflation, or a persistent but well-predicted one, would not be as harmful as a persistent and unpredictable bout of inflation. Even for the latter case there are those who argue that the consequences are not that serious, while others argue that unpredictable inflation distorts the mechanism of the price system and creates various inefficiencies and inequities, and even unemployment.

By imagining shifts in the *AS* or *AD* curves taking place over time, it is possible to use the essentially comparative-static *AS–AD* model as an introduction to the problems of inflation and unemployment. This interpretation of the model accords with the analyses of inflation offered after the Second World War and in the 1950s and early 1960s, when it was popular to contrast two alternative views of the causes of inflation, the demand-pull and the cost-push theories.

Demand-pull Inflation

Demand-pull inflation is said to occur as a result of an increase in real aggregate demand at any price level. This is illustrated in figure 6.1 by the outward shift of the *AD* curve from AD_0 to AD_1. If the relevant *AS* curve is the Classical type AS_0, the price level rises from P_0 to P_2 while output remains fixed at y_0, but if the relevant *AS* curve is the Keynesian type AS_1, the price level rises only to P_1 with output also rising to y_1, with a simultaneous increase in employment and reduction in unemployment. Remember that, in either case, the inflation is the proportionate rate of change of prices over time, and depends upon the speed with which the *AD* curve moves from AD_0 to AD_1, not just upon the difference between the eventual and original price level.

The theory of demand-pull inflation was consistent with Keynes's emphasis in the *General Theory* on the importance of aggregate demand, and, especially, with his analysis in a series of articles he

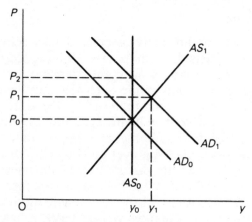

Figure 6.1 Demand-pull inflation

wrote at the onset of the Second World War, collectively published as *How to Pay for the War* (Keynes, 1940). Keynesians have, therefore, been willing to consider demand-pull theories, while such theories have also been put forward by those of a more Monetarist persuasion. The difference between the two sets of views, however, is that, while Keynesians might believe that shifts in aggregate demand are caused by changes in private sector consumption or investment behaviour, or fiscal policy, for Monetarists the dominant cause of the increase in aggregate demand would be thought to be an increase in the money supply, usually viewed as being brought about by governments attempting to reduce interest rates to encourage investment and growth.[2] Friedman clearly expressed the Monetarist view when he wrote:

> Many countries in the post-war period, including the United States, pursued cheap-money policies, partly under the influence of the ideas derived from Keynes . . . Every such country experienced either open inflation or a network of partly effective, partly ineffective, controls designed to suppress the inflationary pressure. In every case, the stock of money rose as a result of the cheap-money policies and so did prices . . . (Friedman, 1959a, p. 138)

Many Keynesians are willing to accept the close correlation between growth of the money supply and inflation, but do not accept the growth of the money supply as the causal factor. Just how they can hold to this view will be made clear by considering cost-push theories of inflation.

Cost-push Inflation

Cost-push theories are normally associated with Keynesians and eschewed by Monetarists. In such theories, it is argued that inflation is caused not by an increase in aggregate demand, but rather by a shift in the aggregate supply curve such that any level of output will require a higher price level than before the shift. The shift in the aggregate supply curve may be brought about by one of several factors, such as a push for higher money wages by unionized labour, an increase in the price mark-up over costs by employers, or, more generally, a struggle over the distribution of incomes, or possibly by a rise in raw material prices. Such views are not inconsistent with the *General Theory* and Keynes's emphasis there on the relationship between costs, prices and the money-wage level. It has been shown earlier that the position of the AS curve depends on the money-wage level and the production function (although the earlier analysis assumed firms to be perfectly competitive and not to fix prices according to some cost mark-up theory). While Monetarists might accept the importance of changes in raw material prices for inflation, they would probably by unhappy with other cost-push arguments. For instance, Johnson argued that inflation was due to expansionary monetary policies, and the attempts to bring other factors into the argument represented a distressing 'resort to amateur sociology and politics' (1972a, p. 310).

The cost-push analysis is illustrated in figure 6.2. Assume aggregate demand to be initially represented by the curve AD_0. The cost-push factor causes the aggregate supply curve to shift from AS_0 to AS_1, and prices to rise to P_1 from P_0, with output falling from y_0 to y_1. Of course, as output falls to y_1, employment falls too and unemployment rises. The government may, then, decide to act to offset the increase in unemployment by increasing aggregate demand, causing the AD curve to shift to AD_1. This latter shift reinforces the price rise, which now pushes prices up to P_2, but offsets the fall in employment, since output returns to y_0.

If the government chooses to increase aggregate demand by increasing the money supply, it is said to follow an 'accommodating monetary policy', since the change in money supply accommodates the cost-push shift of the AS curve. Empirically, such a policy would lead to a close correlation between inflation and changes in the money supply. Such a correlation would not, therefore, necessarily support the Monetarist contention that increases in the money supply cause inflation. The Monetarists might argue, at this point,

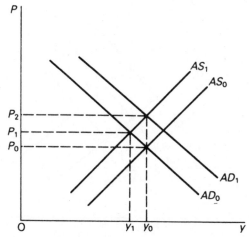

Figure 6.2 Cost-push inflation and accommodating monetary policy

that they see no reason why cost-push forces should continuously push the *AS* curve upwards, even if they could do so in rare instances, unless the monetary authorities continue to try to offset the adverse effects of such cost-push forces on output and unemployment by following accommodating monetary policy, which perpetuates a cost-price inflationary spiral as the *AS* and *AD* curves chase each other upwards. Thus, the Monetarists would argue that persistent inflation is not possible if the monetary authorities control the rate of growth of the money supply within certain limits.

A cost-push inflationary spiral is illustrated in figure 6.3. Let the initial equilibrium in the economy be at point *A*, on the intersection of AS_0 with AD_0, at an output level y_0 and price level P_0. Now consider a cost-push factor to shift the *AS* curve to AS_1. The economy moves towards point *B*, with a reduction in output and an increase in prices and unemployment (since employment falls with output). If the government's monetary policy accommodates the cost-push, the money supply will rise and pull the aggregate demand curve out to AD_1, causing prices to rise further and output to return to its original level as the economy moves towards point *C*. Imagine that the cost-push factor was an increase in money wages as a result of union pressures, and it is easy to see that the rise in prices to P_2 will have reduced real wages again, causing the unions to push for a further rise in money wages. This latter push

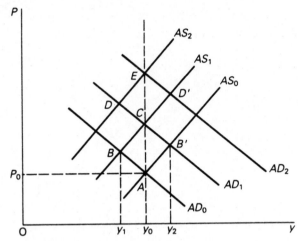

Figure 6.3   Cost-price inflationary spiral

moves the *AS* curve further up to AS_2, and the cycle is underway again.

Alternatively, starting from *A* once more, now consider the initial impetus to be caused by a shift in the aggregate demand curve, possibly engineered by government policy in an attempt to increase output above y_0. The economy will move towards point *B'*, with rising prices, rising output and falling unemployment. The economy is unlikely to remain at *B'*, however, since the higher price level will probably result in higher money wages being bargained for in the labour market, which will cause the *AS* curve to shift upwards to AS_1, moving the economy towards *C*, with a further rise in prices but a reduction in output back to y_0 and an increase in unemployment. If the government reacts to the reduction in output back to y_0 by a further stimulus to aggregate demand, to pull the *AD* curve to AD_2, then the cycle begins again.

Notice that, if the economy were at *A* for a long period and then the cost-price spiral began it would be possible to ascertain the initial impulse by seeing whether output rose or fell at the onset of the cycle. If output rose and the economy moved towards *B'*, then the initial impulse could be seen to be demand-pull; whereas if output initially fell, then the initial impulse could be seen to be cost-push. However, in either case, once the cycle is underway, it consists of rising prices with output alternately rising and falling, and it may be difficult to tell whether the initial impetus was cost-push or demand-pull. Notice too that, although the Monetarists would generally have faith in the ability of the labour market to clear, that does not imply a belief in a vertical aggregate supply curve in anything other than the long run. Thus, they might well accept the analysis in figure 6.3, but the upward-sloping AS curves drawn there would be said to hold only in the short run for given money wages. In the long run, as prices rise, so do money wages and the short-run AS curves drift upwards from AS_0 to AS_1 and so on as described above. In the long run, the Monetarists would argue that the labour market would clear at, or at least close to, full employment as money wages and prices adjusted to produce the market-clearing real wage and level of employment and output. Continuing inflation will not, therefore, be a result of cost-push pressures. Let the full-employment level be y_0 in figure 6.3, in which case the long-run aggregate supply curve would be the broken line vertically above y_0 through the points ACE.

Monetarists would recognize the existence of frictional unemployment arising from people entering the labour force, changing jobs and so on, and would not associate full employment with the absence of unemployment. Keynesians would probably accept the Monetarist ideas of full employment, but would not accept the view that the market economy, if left to itself, will operate close enough to full employment without direct intervention from the government. Such differences in opinion have been described in earlier chapters and will be examined again later, but for now it will be useful to leave such issues until we have discussed an empirical and theoretical attempt to improve the debate about inflation and unemployment, initiated by the publication in 1958 of an article by A. W. Phillips which gave rise to the concept now known as the 'Phillips curve'.

6.2 The Phillips Curve

The arguments above have been concerned with relationships between levels of output and prices expressed in the AS and AD curves. The discussion of dynamic questions such as inflation, which is the rate of change of prices over time, has had to be conducted in terms of movements of the AS and AD curves over time. The Phillips curve, on the other hand, led to a great amount of literature concerned directly with the relationship between variables expressed as time rates of change and other variables. The seminal article was published by Phillips in 1958, and showed an estimated relationship between the proportionate rate of change of money-wage rates and the unemployment rate for the period 1861–1957 in the United Kingdom.[3]

The relationship Phillips found looked like that shown in figure 6.4 and appeared to indicate a close relationship between the growth rate of money wages per period, denoted by $\dot{W}$, and the rate of unemployment (expressed as a percentage of the total labour force, i.e., the proportion of unemployed to employed plus unemployed people), such that the higher the rate of unemployment, the lower the growth rate of money wages. The theoretical basis for the curve was expressed by Phillips as follows:

> When the demand for labour is high and there are very few unemployed we should expect employers to bid wage rates up quite rapidly, each firm and each industry being continually tempted to offer a little above the prevailing rates to attract the most suitable labour from other firms and industries. On the other hand it appears that workers are reluctant to offer their services at less than the prevailing rates when the demand for labour is low and unemployment is high, so that wage rates fall only very slowly. The relation between unemployment and the rate of change of wage rates is therefore likely to be highly non-linear. (Phillips, 1958, p. 283)

The next development was to relate prices to money wages as a major cost component, and so to use the Phillips curve to explain wage inflation, with wage inflation then helping to determine price inflation in another equation. Samuelson and Solow (1960) took this process to its logical conclusion and estimated directly a relationship

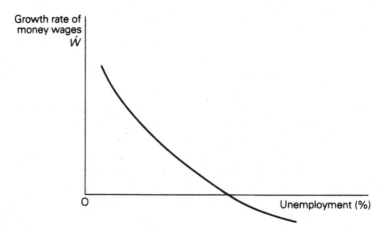

Figure 6.4   The Phillips curve

between the rate of unemployment and the rate of price inflation. The resulting relationship is usually called a Phillips curve in the literature, and although this is, strictly, a misnomer, we shall do likewise. Figure 6.5 illustrates, with price inflation, denoted by $\dot{P}$, on the vertical axis instead of $\dot{W}$, as in the original Phillips curve.

Phillips curves became part of the conventional wisdom in macroeconomics in the early 1960s. They were accepted by proponents of both demand-pull and cost-push theories, since the excess demand for labour signalled by low unemployment and associated with high levels of wage inflation in the Phillips curve could be ascribed to either high levels of demand for goods (and, hence, labour) by the demand-pull theorists, or to unions restricting labour supply by the cost-push theorists (though profits-push would probably have to show up in the pricing equation rather than in the Phillips curve itself).

The Phillips curve was adopted too by politicians and the popular press, to explain the concept of a trade-off between inflation and unemployment. Given the position of the Phillips curve, lower inflation could be achieved only at the expense of higher unemployment (for example, as in moving from A to B in figure 6.5) and vice versa, thus providing a reason for the failure of governments to achieve desirable levels of inflation and unemployment simultaneously.[4] There were even attempts at analysing government reaction functions to see how governments ranked various combinations of inflation and unemployment to determine where, on the

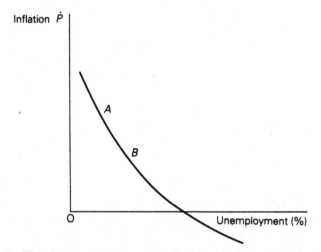

Figure 6.5 The Phillips curve with inflation on the vertical axis

Phillips curve, the government would decide to place the economy (see for example Reuber, 1964). A natural development of this line of thought was an analysis of how to shift the Phillips curve by prices and incomes policies in order to improve the trade-off facing policy-makers (see for example Lipsey and Parkin, 1970).

Another, and more cynical, reason for the widespread adoption of the Phillips curve may be that it provided a vehicle for economists to display their prowess in the use of statistical techniques to estimate the parameters of the Phillips curve. As Rowley and Wilton put it

> one cannot help but be astounded by the ingenious and pragmatic approaches of the Phillips curve analysts. There appears to be an unending list of explanatory variables which have been found signifi-cant in various 'augmented' Phillips curves. Perhaps even more disturbing is the inter-temporal instability of the estimated coef-ficients, particularly the coefficient on the unemployment variable. In short, studies which appear to have excellent statistical credentials (in inferential terms) have produced the following consensus on the Phillips curve:
>
> (1) it clearly exists
> (2) it is definitely not invariant to time nor author
>
> Paradoxically, then, the greatest attack on the Phillips curve may implicitly rest in the diversity of the empirical evidence purported to prove its very existence! (Rowley and Wilton, 1973, p. 90)

While agreeing with Rowley and Wilton that the empirical basis for the Phillips curve was tenuous, and noting that by the late 1960s this was gradually being recognized, it seems that the greatest attack on the Phillips curve was not empirical but theoretical. This theoretical attack is based largely upon the work of Friedman (1968) and Phelps (1967), though their ideas differ in certain import-ant respects. The contribution of Friedman provides the basis for the discussion in section 6.3.

6.3   The Role of Expectations and the Natural Rate Hypothesis

Friedman (1968) argued that there is no long-run, stable trade-off between inflation and unemployment such as the trade-off illus-trated in figure 6.5. His reasoning was that it is the real wage, and not the money wage, which matters in the labour market. There is, therefore, no long-run relationship between the rate of change of money wages or prices and unemployment, and no true theoretical basis for the Phillips curve. Instead, the real wage adjusts over time to clear the labour market about the natural rate of unemployment, which is roughly equal to the full-employment rate of unemployment, that is, that rate consistent with the unemployment being due to the natural frictions in the labour market and not due to any lack of aggregate demand. Friedman himself defined the natural rate of unemployment as being

> ground out by the Walrasian system of general equilibrium equations, provided there is embedded in them the actual structural characteristics of the labor and commodity markets, including market imperfections, stochastic variability in demand and supplies, the cost of gathering information about job vacancies and labor availabilities, the costs of mobility, and so on. (Friedman, 1968, p. 8)

Acceptance of the natural rate hypothesis implies the view that any inflation-unemployment trade-off must be temporary or depend upon continually accelerating inflation to maintain unemployment below the natural rate. The reasoning behind this result, and the importance of expectations of inflation, may be illustrated using figure 6.6. Imagine the economy represented by the figure to be initially at the point A on the short-run Phillips curve 1, (SRPC 1), which holds when expectations of inflation are that it will continue at the rate $\dot{P}_1$, as indicated by the notation $E(\dot{P}) = \dot{P}_1$. At

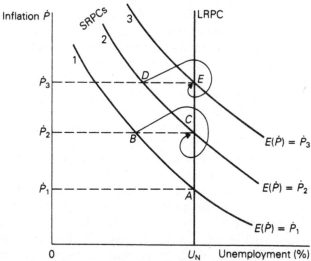

Figure 6.6 Expectations-adjusted Phillips curves

point A, expectations are being fulfilled and the labour market is generating the natural rate of unemployment, U_N. Now let the government decide to reduce the unemployment rate below U_N, and to accept the trade-off of a higher rate of inflation by increasing aggregate demand and moving the economy to point B on the short-run Phillips curve 1. According to Friedman, any such trade-off will be temporary. The short-run Phillips curve will prove to be an unstable basis for policy since it was formed when expectations were of inflation at the rate $\dot{P}_1$, but once point B is achieved, the inflation rate is $\dot{P}_2$ not $\dot{P}_1$. Workers and firms thus adjust their expectations of inflation towards $\dot{P}_2$, until eventually money-wage contracts adjust fully to reflect the rate of inflation and real wages return to their market-clearing level and the economy moves to point C on the new short-run Phillips curve 2. The route from A to B to C may well be like the loop drawn in figure 6.6, depending on the process of adjustment of inflation expectations from $\dot{P}_1$ to $\dot{P}_2$. As long as inflation expectations lag behind the actual rate of inflation, workers perceive increases in money wages (which firms are tempted to offer as aggregate demand and prices rise) to be worth more in terms of goods than they really are, and hence, they accept more employment than they otherwise would and the unemployment rate falls below U_N. When inflation expectations exceed the actual rate, workers refuse employment they would otherwise take and the unemployment rate is above U_N in those parts of the adjustment process.

Thus, expectations of inflation play a crucial role in determining both actual inflation and unemployment by affecting behaviour in the labour market. In Friedman's version of the story, firms know the inflation rate but workers react to money-wage offers according to their expectations of inflation, and so it is workers who can be said to be fooled by unanticipatedly high inflation into accepting jobs at money wages which they would not find acceptable if they knew the actual inflation rate. (On the other hand, when the expected rate of inflation exceeds the actual rate, workers reject jobs at money-wage offers which would be acceptable if only they knew the actual inflation rate.) Friedman's version of the story, therefore, depends on workers being unemployed because they refuse money-wage offers which seem unacceptable to them; the unemployed thus consist of a pool of workers who have either quit their jobs or refused jobs in order to hold out for, or search for, a job at an acceptable money wage, given their expectations of inflation, this acceptable wage being known as the 'reservation wage'.

Such a search theory of unemployment, as it is called, would appear to conflict with the empirical evidence that many of the unemployed did not quit their last job, but were fired. However, Phelps's (1967) version of the story depends on firms rather than workers reacting to inflation expections and hiring or firing employees accordingly. It is possible that there is some truth in both versions of the story, and that unemployment and inflation will depend, to some extent, upon the inflation expectations of both firms and workers.

If, as is now widely agreed, expectations of price inflation have a role to play in determining the position of the Phillips curve, then it is natural to wonder why Phillips' original work achieved such good statistical results. Part of the answer might be that although prices did vary for the period examined by Phillips, they rose in some years and fell in others; the average expectation of inflation was low and fairly steady so that, in effect, the short-run Phillips curves did not move very much and allowed reasonable statistical results to be produced. These results were not, however, robust to the changed inflationary atmosphere of the 1960s and 1970s.

It should also be pointed out that the Phillips curve is the outcome of some underlying economic behaviour which may be expected to change as circumstances change. Morley, therefore, argues that:

> In retrospect, the century of stability of the Phillips curve for Britain, and the decade of stability shown by the curves for other countries during the 1950s and early 1960s, can be attributed to the fixed exchange rates which prevailed during most of the peacetime years which provide the data for the curves . . . The exceptions to the stability of the Phillips curve were those years when import prices rose noticeably. Phillips had warned in his article that nominal wage increases were higher than predicted by the curve in such years . . ..
> (Morley, 1988, pp. 42–3)

The period of empirical breakdown of the Phillips curve coincided with the breakdown of the Bretton Woods system of fixed exchange rates and the ushering in of a new era of floating exchange rates. It would not be surprising if such a significant macroeconomic change induced changes in previously reliable macroeconomic relationships. See part VI of this book for a discussion of open-economy macroeconomics and of the different exchange rate systems.

Returning to the analysis of figure 6.6, when the economy reaches point C, the unemployment rate is back to the natural rate; and inflation, and expectations of inflation, at $\dot{P}_2$, are higher than at A. Any trade-off has been temporary and has involved inducing periods of unemployment rates higher than the natural rate for part of the cycle. Any attempt by the government to reduce the unemployment rate by further stimulating aggregate demand will simply cause the economy to move into another inflation-unemployment spiral such as the one shown from C to D to E. The points ACE lie on the long-run Phillips curve, which is vertical above U_N, showing that when inflation expectations are being fulfilled the labour market will adjust and achieve the natural rate of unemployment. The rate of unemployment could be maintained below the natural rate only if the government could go on accelerating aggregate demand and inflation at such a rate that private sector expectations of inflation always lagged behind the actual inflation rate. Such a policy would hardly be popular, and, furthermore, would only work to maintain unemployment below the natural rate if private sector inflation expectations failed ever to catch up with the actual rate of inflation. If the private sector ever began to predict inflation rates accurately, and to adjust money wage rates accordingly, there would be no trade-off between inflation and unemployment.

Friedman's and Phelps's emphasis upon the role of expectations in determining the relationship between unemployment and inflation led to attempts to formulate expectations as an endogenous variable within economic models.[5] It will be useful to examine, briefly, two of these attempts: adaptive and rational expectations.[6]

Adaptive Expectations versus Rational Expectations

Adaptive expectations were actually first modelled before the Phillips curve literature, by Cagan (1956), within the context of a model of hyperinflation. The adaptive expectations hypothesis is that economic agents adapt their expectations in the light of past experience and, in particular, that they learn from mistakes.

Formally, adaptive expectations may be represented as follows:

$$_tE(\dot{P}_{t+1}) = {}_{t-1}E(\dot{P}_t) + \alpha[\dot{P}_t - {}_{t-1}E(\dot{P}_t)] \quad (0 < \alpha \leqslant 1). \quad (6.1)$$

Equation 6.1 shows that the expectation of inflation for the next period, $t + 1$, held as of the end of period t, $_tE(\dot{P}_{t+1})$, depends on the expectation of inflation held for the present period, $_{t-1}E(\dot{P}_t)$, as of the end of period $t-1$, plus some correction factor based on a proportion α of the gap between the expectation of inflation for the present period and the actual rate experienced, $\dot{P}_t$. Since this period's expectation $_{t-1}\dot{E}(P_t)$ depended on the actual experience and expectation of inflation in the previous period (i.e., $_{t-1}E(\dot{P}_t) =$

$_{t-2}E(\dot{P}_{t-1}) + \alpha[\dot{P}_{t-1} - {}_{t-2}E(\dot{P}_{t-1})]$]) and so on, then expectations depend upon all past experience and past expectations, with the property that, as long as α is less then one, the distant past has less influence on present expectations than the near past.

The adaptive expectations hypothesis, therefore, allows some learning from previous experience and past mistakes, and seems a sensible, simple way of modelling expectations. However, agents forming adaptive expectations learn only from the past; they do not, in formulating their expectations, take into account any announcements of future policies made by governments, but react only to what has already happened. Some economists find this feature of adaptive expectations to be highly unsatisfactory. Such economists argue that, in formulating their expectations of inflation for the next period, agents do take into account readily available information such as government announcements of policies for that period, and make predictions about the effects of those policies; if those predictions are based on the correct model of the economy, then they are said to be rational expectations.

The rational expectations hypothesis is highly controversial, and is one of the major building blocks of the New Classical macro-economic model which is examined in the next part of this book. For the moment, however, it will suffice to compare the implications of adaptive expectations versus rational expectations in the expect-ations-augmented Phillips curve treatment of inflation and unem-ployment.

Under adaptive expectations, government manipulation of aggre-gate demand leads to unanticipated changes in inflation and changes in unemployment, at least in the short-run. Let the Phillips curve be written as:

$$\dot{P}_t = a(U_t - U_N) + b_{t-1}E(\dot{P}_t) \qquad (6.2)$$

where U_N is the natural rate of unemployment. If b is positive but less than one, it can be seen that the long-run Phillips curve (when inflation expectations are correct) is downward sloping and not vertical, implying that the short-run trade-off is eroded but not eliminated even in the long-run. If, however, b is equal to one, the trade-off disappears completely in the long-run since the long-run Phillips curve is vertical in this case, although even then the short-run trade-off still exists and offers potential for government fine-tuning intervention.

The adaptive expectations hypothesis also implies that mainten-ance of unemployment at any level below the natural rate would require accelerating inflation. The acceleration is needed to offset the effects of the adaptive expectations correction factor moving expectations closer and closer to a non-accelerating rate of inflation and eroding the stimulus to employment, which, as was shown above, depends upon expectations falling below the actual level of inflation. On the other hand, the adaptive expectations hypothesis implies that any reduction in aggregate demand in order to combat inflation should be carried out gradually; otherwise the reduction will cause a large increase in unemployment, since it will not be predicted by the private sector, which takes time to adjust to new government policies and will not predict the reduction in inflation. A slight reduction in aggregate demand will have small effects on inflation and unemployment, but *continued* gradual reductions in aggregate demand will slowly eliminate inflation without causing a dramatic increase in unemployment.

This is illustrated in figure 6.7, which shows a vertical long-run Phillips curve (LRPC) and three short-run Phillips curves. Consider the economy to be in equilibrium at point A at the intersection of the long-run Phillips curve and the short-run Phillips curve corresponding to ongoing inflation at the rate $\dot{P}_1$. Now let the government wish to reduce inflation to the rate $\dot{P}_3$. If the government tries to achieve this immediately, it will require a large reduction in aggregate demand and a shift down the short-run Phillips curve from A to B with heavy costs in terms of unemployment. The case for gradualism is that a smaller reduction in aggregate demand would move the economy from A to C rather than

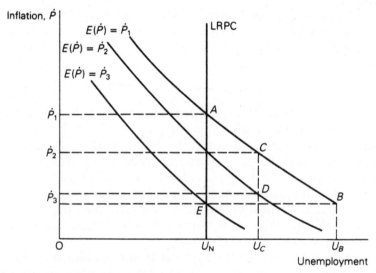

Figure 6.7 The case for gradualism

B, with a smaller reduction in inflation but at a lower cost in unemployment. As the economy adjusts to a new lower rate of inflation and moves on to the lower short-run Phillips curve $E(\dot{P}) = \dot{P}_2$, a further reduction in aggregate demand could move the economy to point D and thereby further reduce the inflation rate. Such gradual reductions in aggregate demand could be continued until the low inflation target $\dot{P}_3$ is achieved, without ever imposing serious unemployment costs.

The case for gradualism is not universally accepted. For one thing, it is not obvious to everyone that a sustained moderate increase in unemployment is preferable to a bigger increase which lasts for a shorter period of time. Also, some economists argue that a gradual policy would not work because private agents would not have confidence in its being continued and would not react to slight reductions in aggregate demand, whereas they would react to a 'stronger' policy. This argument may be valid, but it is clearly taking us into the realm of psychology and politics, although this may be inevitable when trying to model expectations.

The rational expectations hypothesis, when allied to the assumption of continuous market clearing in the labour market based on real-wage bargaining, leads to conclusions which differ starkly from those reached under the adaptive expectations hypothesis. For example, in figure 6.7 a pre-announced reduction in aggregate demand would lead to a movement not from A to B, but rather from A to E, the new lower inflation rate being taken into account by wage-bargainers on the basis of their predictions of the effects of the announced policy. In other words, with rational expectations and real-wage bargaining clearing the labour market, the economy immediately moves from one short-run Phillips curve to another in response to predictable policy consequences, and, apart from responses to unexpected shocks, is never pulled away from the vertical long-run Phillips curve. This implies not only that there is no need for gradualism, but also that there is no short-run trade-off between inflation and unemployment, while even accelerating inflation cannot reduce unemployment below the natural rate, as long as government policies are pre-announced or otherwise predictable. Only unpredictable events shock the economy away from the natural rate of unemployment. This obviously leaves little scope for activist fine-tuning policies, since if they can be predicted they will have no effect on unemployment, even in the short run.

The irrelevance hypothesis, as this latter conclusion has come to be known, provides an argument against activist fine-tuning that is different from the more traditional Monetarist case. In the traditional case, it is argued that governments do not know enough to successfully fine-tune the economy; the irrelevance hypothesis is that predictable activist policies would not work anyway. The irrelevance hypothesis belongs to the New Classical macro-economics rather than Monetarism, but the mutual dislike of both schools for activist policies has led some writers to lump them both together.

The extreme case of the irrelevance hypothesis depends upon the market-clearing assumption as well as the rational expectations hypothesis, and it is possible to include rational expectations in a model without coming to the extreme conclusions reached above. Such issues form the basis of much of the next chapter. For the present, however, it will be useful to conclude with some discussion of suitable policies to combat unemployment if the natural rate hypothesis holds, and to look at a later statement by Friedman (1977) on the relationship between inflation and unemployment.

If the natural rate hypothesis holds, then, even with adaptive expectations, a given reduction in unemployment below the natural rate requires accelerating inflation, and cannot be achieved at all under rational expectations and the market-clearing assumption. The Monetarist and New Classical macroeconomists, therefore, conclude that aggregate demand management is an inappropriate tool for attempting to reduce unemployment. In its place they recommend using fiscal policy to influence resource allocation and income distribution targets rather than to fine-tune the economy, and they recommend micro-policies to reduce unemployment by reducing the natural rate of unemployment itself. (See Laidler, 1978, p. 40 for a concise statement to this effect.) That is to say, they recommend such policies as improved dissemination of information about vacancies, retraining schemes, mobility allowances and so on to try to remove or offset the frictions producing unemployment.

Of course, any such policy needs to be carefully considered, taking into account its various effects on incentives facing private sector agents, and also recognizing any financial costs or revenues the policy involves for the government. For example, hiring civil servants to work in job centres might be just as costly as a more conventional public works programme, with similar consequences for the government budget and implications for tax rates, money creation or bond sales. Another way of putting this is that macro-policy is just the sum of all micro-policies, so that concern about fiscal expenditure by the government implies constraints on the resources available for micro-policies. To some extent the micro–

macro policy split is misleading, and the Monetarist contention that micro-policies be used to reduce unemployment is just a reiteration of Friedman's earlier claims that government expenditure and tax rates should be set according to equity and efficiency criteria and should not be adjusted for fine-tuning purposes, while fixing the rate growth of the money supply and allowing the bond stock to adjust to finance any government budget imbalances.

Finally, it is worth looking at Friedman's later views on inflation and unemployment expressed in his Nobel Lecture (Friedman, 1977). There he noted that the debate on inflation and unemployment had proceeded through stages from the original Phillips curve, to the expectations-augmented Phillips curve with a vertical long-run Phillips curve at the natural rate of unemployment, to a third stage, 'occasioned by the empirical phenomenon of an apparent positive relation between inflation and unemployment' (1977, p. 451). Friedman went on to argue that this apparent relationship would hold only during a transitional period, 'to be measured by quinquennia or decades, not years' (1977, p. 470), while economies adjusted to the new monetary environment of high and volatile inflation.

The positive association between inflation and unemployment during this period may be explained by two factors. First, increased volatility of the inflation rate (which, Friedman observed, tends to be associated with high levels of inflation) shortens the optimum length of unindexed contracts and makes indexation more advantageous. Until indexation is carried out, rigidities reduce the effectiveness of markets, and even indexation is inferior to stability and predictability of the inflation rate because of the lags involved in producing and applying indices. Thus, market efficiency is reduced by volatile inflation experience and may well involve higher unemployment, But, as Friedman noted, it is not necessarily the case that higher unemployment would result; for instance, firms may decide to hoard labour to avoid hiring and firing costs, and may increase average employment rates in such circumstances, or they may shorten contracts and find it easier to fire people and increase average employment rates. Empirical evidence would be needed to find the answers.

Second, Friedman argued that increased volatility of inflation renders market prices a less efficient system for disseminating useful information and co-ordinating economic activity. The higher the volatility of inflation, the harder it is to extract information about relative price changes, future prices and so on, and the harder it is to make efficient decisions. In other words, volatile inflation strengthens the dark forces of time and ignorance and so hinders the workings of the market economy, possibly causing a higher level of unemployment.

This is rather reminiscent of Keynes's views on the role of uncertainty in investment decisions, and so Keynesians might well agree that volatile inflation increases uncertainty, reduces investment demand and increases unemployment. The Keynesian policy conclusions would, however, differ from those reached by Friedman. Friedman argued that

> [the effects of] volatile inflation rates will lead governments to try to repress inflation in still other areas by explicit price and wage control, or by pressuring private business or unions 'voluntarily' to exercise 'restraint' . . . [leading to] reduction in the capacity of the price system to guide economic activity . . . the introduction of greater friction, as it were, in all markets; and, very likely, a higher recorded rate of unemployment. (Friedman, 1977, pp. 467–8)

That is to say, for Friedman, more intervention would probably occur and make matters worse, while Keynesians might well propose more intervention to make matters better.

Once the economy had adjusted to high and volatile inflation, Friedman believed it would return to the natural rate of unemployment (which he seemed to believe would not itself have been influenced by the inflation experience). He did not, however, believe that a positive association between inflation and unemployment implies an easy choice for government in reducing inflation and unemployment simultaneously. The positive relationship is due to an unanticipated increase in the level and volatility of inflation, not to the level or volatility *per se*. Once an economy had become used to high and variable inflation, a reduction in the level and variability of inflation would be unanticipated and would generate new frictions, giving rise to the return of a negative relationship between inflation and unemployment.

Friedman's views on the third stage of the relationship between inflation and unemployment are, therefore, consistent with his earlier work, with his emphasis upon the importance of anticipations and market adjustments to changes, and the rigidities in the way of such adjustments. The New Classical Macroeconomics similarly places great emphasis on anticipations, and, like Monetarism, tends to dislike activist government policies. It is to such issues that attention turns in the next part of this book.

Notes

1 The reader may care to note that the major developments introduced in this chapter closely parallel in time the development discussed in the previous three chapters, as will be evident from the dates of the major references.
2 Some Monetarists would emphasize the importance of the government budget identity and argue that monetary growth may be explained as a counterpart of government spending (see for example Brunner and Meltzer, 1972).
3 The idea can be traced back earlier to Brown (1955) and Fisher (1926).
4 Notice that movements along the Phillips curve would be brought about by aggregate demand management. The Phillips curve on its own represented only a part of a theory of inflation and unemployment; an aggregate demand story was needed to explain how the economy moved up or down the Phillips curve.
5 While Friedman and Phelps are generally accredited with recognizing the importance of expectations in this context, Hicks (1967) seems to have spotted it too. According to Hicks,

> Inflation does give a stimulus, but the stimulus is greatest when the inflation starts – when it starts from a condition that has been non-inflationary. If the inflation continues, people get adjusted to it. But when people are adjusted to it, when they expect rising prices, the mere occurrence of what has been expected is no longer stimulating. Nor can the fade-out be prevented by accelerating the inflation; for acceleration of inflation can be expected too. It is perfectly possible to have an 'inflationary equilibrium' in which prices go on rising, even for years, more or less as they are expected to rise; but then there is no stimulus. (Hicks, 1967, p. 260)

6 These attempts stand in contrast to Keynes's treatment of expectations as important but exogenous. Begg (1982a) has suggested that Keynes's conclusion, that expectations are almost impossible to model formally, may have confused the possibility of modelling expectations with the impossibility of predicting unanticipated events. Perhaps it is possible to model expectations, Keynes's 'short-run expectation', but not to model future shocks, Keynes's 'long-run expectation'. In which case, the *General Theory* could be restated to include endogenous, even rational, expectations without seriously upsetting Keynes's ideas, so long as it is remembered that Keynes had no faith in the ability of the price system to generate market clearing.

Part V

Does Macroeconomic Policy Really Matter? The New Classical Macroeconomics and the Activist–Non-activist Debate

7

The New Classical Macroeconomics: An Introduction

The New Classical macroeconomics may be viewed as a development of the introduction of endogenous expectations into the Phillips curve by Friedman and Phelps, discussed in the previous chapter. As Grossman put it,

> The natural rate hypothesis associates variations in economic aggregates relative to their natural levels with expectational errors involving differences between actual and expected rates of inflation. The idea of rational expectations takes this line of thought one fundamental step further by proposing a general theoretical approach to the study of expectations. The resulting analysis suggests that monetary and fiscal policies may not be able to produce systematic expectational errors, and this implies that the ability of the government to improve the aggregate performance of the economy is even more limited than we inferred either from the natural rate hypothesis or from a realistic view of the political process. Specifically, the idea of rational expectations suggests that it may not be feasible to design monetary and fiscal policies that can actively stabilize aggregate output and employment relative to their natural levels. More generally, the idea of rational expectations suggests a new set of questions about the causes of business cycles and their relation to government behaviour. (Grossman, 1980, p. 9)

In other words, any predictable, systematic effects of government policies (or of the decline of oil reserves or some other such factor likely to affect the economy) will be taken into account by agents in the economy when forming rational expectations. If deviations of output and employment from their natural levels are due only to expectational errors, and if expectations are rational, then only unexpected shocks to the economy will cause actuality to differ from those expectations and output and employment to differ from their natural levels. Unexpected policy actions could come only from sudden policy changes or from a deliberately random policy. Introducing such random shocks to the economy would hardly seem likely to improve stability, and predictable policy has no effects, so there is no stabilization role for government under this scenario. Furthermore, if deviations of variables from their natural levels are due only to unexpected shocks, then how is the cyclical nature of deviations to be explained? Why are deviations not just random about the natural levels?

The combination of the natural rate hypothesis and rational expectations forms the basis of the New Classical model. The name is appropriate since the two underlying assumptions imply continuous market clearing in the absence of expectational errors, and the New Classical model is virtually the Classical model with the addition of random shocks or disturbances to explain economic fluctuations, while both models provide similar policy conclusions.

The New Classical policy conclusions are similar to those of the Monetarists, too, but conceptually the two camps are quite different. Indeed, the Monetarists may be viewed as lying somewhere along a spectrum between Keynes and the New Classicals. According to this view, Keynes saw the economy failing to achieve full employment because of factors in the way of instantaneous market clearing in the real world, and he saw business cycles being generated by volatile and inefficient investment behaviour on the part of the private sector. Thus, he favoured policies to encourage consumption so as to maintain aggregate demand at a level near to full employment, and state control of investment so as to smooth away fluctuations. The Monetarists may be viewed as accepting that there are factors preventing continuous market clearing, but blaming fluctuations predominantly on unstable government behaviour and not sharing Keynes's belief in the ability of the government to control investment better than the private sector. The Monetarists also doubt the ability of the government to intervene successfully in the economy by finely tuning its macroeconomic policies in response to the state of the economy, although such policies may have some real short-run effects. The New Classicals go further than the Monetarists by virtually assuming away any factors preventing continuous market clearing apart from inevitable random elements producing expectational errors. For the New Classicals, the private sector is optimizing as efficiently as it can and there is no need or role for government intervention in the economy. Even a perfectly wise and benevolent government could not improve upon the outcome of private sector behaviour; at best, government can do no good, and at worst, it could generate more expectational errors with a complicated or random policy.

In this chapter and the next, we will outline a simple version of the New Classical model which exemplifies the similarity with the Classical model, and will show clearly how the irrelevance hypothesis results and how it can be modified. We will also examine some New Classical ideas about the generation of business cycles, as well as some criticisms of the New Classical model, and some alternative models which accept the rational expectations assumption but reject the natural rate hypothesis. Finally, an evaluation of the New Classical and New Keynesian models will be offered, along with some general conclusions on the activist–non-activist debate and a brief review of more recent developments.

7.1 New Classical Macroeconomics: A Diagrammatic Treatment

The New Classical model differs from the Classical model by introducing expectations and random errors, so that, effectively, the Classical model becomes a special case of the New Classical model when random errors are zero and expectations are correct. In order to show the close relationship between the two models, it will be useful to present a diagrammatic version of the New Classical model which can be compared with the diagrammatic version of the Classical model presented in chapter 1.[1]

In the Classical model, the labour market is assumed to clear by real-wage adjustment which equates the supply of and demand for labour. This is shown in figure 7.1 (i). Part (ii) of the figure shows the labour supply and demand curves with money wages rather than real wages on the horizontal axis. Since, according to both Classical and New Classical models, the supply of labour by workers and the demand for labour by employers both depend upon real rather than money wages, the supply and demand curves in part (ii) must be drawn dependent upon the price level, hence the inclusion of P_0 or P_1 in brackets besides the curves in part (ii). Consider the curve $S_N(P_0)$, which shows that workers will be willing to supply N^* units of labour at money wage W_0. The curve $S_N(P_1)$, however, for the higher price level P_1, shows that workers will supply only N_1 units of labour at money wage W_0, since the real wage represented by W_0 is lower for the price level P_1 than for P_0 and it is the real wage which determines labour supply.

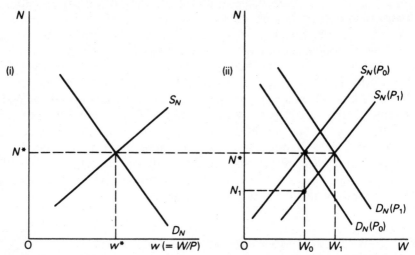

Figure 7.1   The labour market. (i) Real-wage adjustment. (ii) Money-wage adjustment

Similarly, the demand curves $D_N(P_0)$ and $D_N(P_1)$ show that the demand for labour rises as money wage falls only because they are drawn for given price levels, P_0 and P_1 respectively, so that, as the money wage falls, so does the real wage. Thus, in both parts of the figure the market-clearing level of employment is N^*. In part (i) the real wage w^* clears the labour market at N^*, while in part (ii) the real wage w^* is achieved by the money wage adjusting according to the price level (to W_0 for P_0 and W_1 for P_1, respectively).

Now assume that, while firms know the price level in the current period, t, and act accordingly, their employees act according to their expectation of the current price level formed at the end of the previous period, $_{t-1}E(P_t)$. Let $_{t-1}E(P_t) = P_0$. Now the money wage and real wage no longer necessarily adjust to clear the labour market at the long-run equilibrium, or natural, level of employment, N^*. Instead, if the actual price level diverges from P_0, then workers will misinterpret the real-wage value of any money-wage offer and will be led to offer their employment for levels other than N^*. Only if the actual price level is P_0 will workers correctly interpret money-wage offers, and will employment and the real wage settle at N^* and w^*, respectively. These ideas are illustrated in figure 7.2, which shows the expectations-augmented labour supply

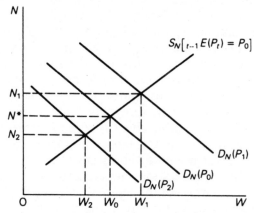

Figure 7.2 The labour market and the expectations-augmented labour supply curve

curve $S_N[_{t-1}E(P_t) = P_0]$ and labour demand curves $D_N(P_0)$, $D_N(P_1)$ and $D_N(P_2)$, where P_1 is greater than P_0 but P_2 is less than P_0. If the price level actually is P_0 the money wage will be set at W_0 and the real wage w^* and employment N^* will be achieved in the absence of any expectational errors on the part of workers or firms. However, if the price level is P_1, then firms will be induced to bid up the money wage, while workers, still expecting the price level to be P_0 not P_1, believe the real wage rises with the rising money wage and so are induced to accept more employment. Given workers' expectations of P_0 and an actual price of P_1 known to firms, employment is set at N_1 and the money wage at W_1. Employment at N_1 is in excess of N^* and W_1 exceeds W_0, but the real wage W_1/P_1 will, in fact, be below w^* (otherwise firms would not wish to hire more than N^* employees, as can be seen from part (i) of figure 7.1). Alternatively, if the price level is P_2, firms will be induced to lower the money wage; workers will, incorrectly, interpret this as a reduction in the real wage and will reduce their willing supply of labour accordingly. Given workers' expectations, the labour market will clear at money wage W_2 and employment level N_2. Readers ought to work out whether the real wage is above or below w^*.

Notice that the analysis underlying figure 7.2 implies market clearing and flexible money wages, but with fluctuations in employment about the natural level N^* occurring as a result of expectational errors; that is, the analysis is that of the natural rate hypothesis with flexible money wages clearing the labour market given workers' price expectations. Figure 7.2 takes the analysis a step away from that of the Classical model by explicitly introducing expectations, but it is necessary to go further by defining how expectations are formed and introducing random shocks to complete the New Classical model. Before carrying out these tasks, however, it will be useful to derive the expectations-augmented supply curve, or *EAS*, which shows the output that the economy will supply at any price level given a certain expected price level and an expectations-augmented labour supply curve.

The expectations-augmented supply curve is derived in figure 7.3 for the underlying expectations-augmented labour supply curve $S_N[_{t-1}E(P_t) = P_0]$. Part (i) of the figure illustrates the labour market and shows the levels of employment and money wages that will be determined for values of the price level P_0, P_1, P_2. Consider the

Figure 7.3   The expectations-augmented aggregate supply curve. (i) Labour market. (ii) Production function. (iii) Aggregate supply

price level P_0, at which workers' expectations are correct and employment is at its natural level of N^*. Part (ii), which represents the production function, shows that employment of N^* will result in output of y^*, the natural level of output. Part (iii), therefore, plots the point $P_0 y^*$ as a point on the expectations-augmented aggregate supply curve, $EAS\,[_{t-1}E(P_t) = P_0]$. Only at the price level P_0 are workers' expectations being fulfilled, with output and employment at their natural levels. For other price levels, workers are making expectational errors and accepting employment at levels away from N^*, as shown in part (i), with corresponding changes in output. Tracing through from part (i) to part (iii) of figure 7.3 for the price levels P_1 and P_2 shows that output and employment rise as the price level rises above P_0, and fall as the price level falls below P_0. It is not desirable that output or employment rise or fall from their natural levels, for in each case the cause is expectational error. For the higher price level P_1, workers are accepting employment N_1 for a money wage W_1, which they wrongly believe is giving them a real wage W_1/P_0, instead of its real value of W_1/P_1. On the other hand, for the lower price level P_2 they are underestimating the real value of the money wage W_2, and correspondingly accept less employment, N_2, than they would if they knew its true value.

It is possible to draw a different expectations-augmented supply curve for each price level expectation held by workers. In each case, the EAS would show output at its natural level, y^*, for the price level equal to the price expectation. Figure 7.4 shows a family of such curves and an aggregate demand curve, AD.

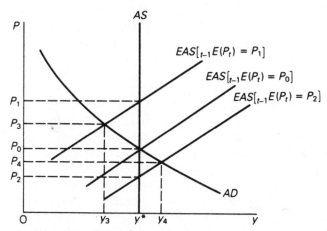

Figure 7.4 The determination of output and price levels, given price expectations

For any given *EAS* in figure 7.4, the actual output and price level are determined at the intersection of the *EAS* and *AD* curves; for *EAS* $[_{t-1}E(P_t) = P_0)]$ the price level is P_0, expectations are fulfilled, and output is at its natural level, y^*; for the other *EAS* curves output would be at y^* only if expectations were being fulfilled, at P_1 and P_2 respectively. The *AS* curve shows the locus of price and output combinations at which expectations are being fulfilled and is a vertical line above y^*. However, given the *AD* curve, price expectations of P_1 or P_2 would not be fulfilled, but would result in price levels of P_3 or P_4 respectively, with corresponding output levels of y_3 or y_4.

Notice again that, as the price level exceeds the expected price level (P_4 exceeds P_2), output exceeds its natural level (y_4 exceeds y^*), and as the price level falls below the expected price level (P_3 is less than P_1), output falls below the natural level (y^* exceeds y_3).

In order to close the model to derive the output and price levels, it is obviously necessary to determine price expectations. The New Classical way of doing this is to assume that workers form *rational expectations*, that is, expectations based upon an accurate knowledge of the parameters of the model describing the economy and all available information. In other words, rational expectations are formed given knowledge of the positions of the *EAS* and *AD* curves in figure 7.4, subject only to possible expectational errors arising from unknown random shocks to the economy. In such circumstances, for the economy represented in figure 7.4, workers will obviously predict the price level to be P_0 and will produce the relevant *EAS* $[_{t-1}E(P_t) = P_0]$ curve. Any other prediction or expectation about the price level would prove to be wrong even in the absence of shocks to the economy, and will, therefore, not be made by workers since they would foresee that it would be so proven.

The New Classical model may now be completed by explicitly adding random shocks and discussing the effects of anticipated-versus-unanticipated government policies. Figure 7.5 illustrates the complete model. Consider that workers estimate the aggregate demand curve to be given by *AD*; they will then produce the price expectation P_0 and the *EAS* $[_{t-1}E(P_t) = (P_0]$ curve. If workers' expectations are rational and no unexpected shocks occur, the outcome will indeed be the price level P_0 and output y^*. However, if there is a sudden unanticipated increase in aggregate demand, resulting in the curve *AD'*, firms will respond by increasing the price of output, and also by paying higher money wages to attract more labour. Given the curve *EAS* $[_{t-1}E(P_t) = P_0]$, output will

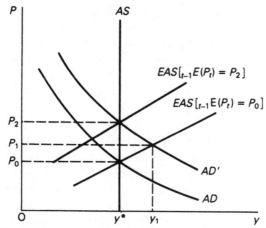

Figure 7.5 The effects of anticipated and unanticipated shocks to aggregate demand

rise to y_1 and the price level to P_1 in this case. This result is not, however, to be desired. It involves expectational errors and entails workers accepting employment at a money wage for which they overestimate the real value; if they did know the value of the real wage, they would not accept so much employment.

This model implies that the government may not engineer increases in output and employment by deliberate increases in aggregate demand according to any policy which is well-known to the private sector. For example, assume the government deliberately brings about AD' to try to increase output to y_1. If the private sector is aware of the government's policy plans then it will frustrate them, since it would be possible to calculate that, with AD' and $EAS\ [_{t-1}E(P_t) = P_0]$, the expected price level would be P_1 not P_0. Workers would, therefore, revise their price expectations to P_2 and would produce the $EAS\ [_{t-1}E(P_t) = P_2]$ curve, which with AD' would, indeed, produce the price level P_2 and the natural level of output y^*.

Thus, predictable government policy cannot affect real output and employment, but only nominal values; this is the irrelevance hypothesis. Only unpredictable elements in policy can affect real variables, but if the government introduces randomness into its policies the presumption is that it will only increase the variance of output and employment about their natural levels rather than successfully stabilize the economy. There is no usable Phillips-curve-type trade-off between output and the price level, nor any real role for government aggregate demand management. All the government can do is accept the fluctuations in output and employment about their natural levels caused by the inevitable shocks to the aggregate demand and supply curves, and avoid adding to these shocks by its own policy actions.[2]

This policy conclusion is very reminiscent of that of the Classical model. New Classical economists, like their Classical predecessors, point to unemployment as being due to rigidities preventing the price mechanism from working properly, but they also point to expectational errors (arising from unexpected shocks) causing voluntary employment and unemployment to fluctuate about their natural levels. The root cause of the voluntary unemployment of the New Classical model is associated with the inability of workers to bargain for real wages, which is, rather ironically, reminiscent of Keynes's discussion of the cause of involuntary unemployment.

Notice that, in the New Classical model, shocks to aggregate demand cause prices and output to move together, an unexpected increase in aggregate demand causing the price level to be above its expected level and output to be above its natural level, and conversely for an unexpected reduction in aggregate demand. Unexpected shocks to aggregate supply, however, cause prices and output to move in opposite directions. Hence it is possible to observe prices and output rising and falling together, or to observe prices moving one way and output the other. The model would, therefore, seem capable of offering a description of the relationship between price and output changes in the real world, dependent upon the sources of the shocks hitting the economy. If the shocks are truly independent random disturbances with no obvious time pattern, this raises the question of why, in the real world, output does not fluctuate randomly about a discernible natural or average value instead of tending to fluctuate cyclically, with a high level of output in one year followed by a high level in the next year and only gradually converging back to its normal value in a roughly systematic manner. The New Classical answer to this question is presented in the following section.

7.2   Business Cycles and the New Classical Model

The New Classical model presented above explains fluctuations in output and employment about their natural levels as being due to expectational errors – workers accepting more employment than the natural level when they believe the real wage is above its natural level, and less employment when it is below. The model does not really allow for the possibility of involuntary unemployment but models only voluntary employment decisions, with workers choosing to take more leisure when they perceive, rightly or wrongly, a low real wage relative to the natural level. Such a view of the business cycle has aroused the anger of Keynesian economists, who see redundancies and unemployment as evidence of market failure rather than market adjustment (see for example Solow, 1980). Furthermore, the New Classical model would not seem to explain the cylical nature of output and employment fluctuations, although, with only a few extra complications, it can be made to do so.

Lucas has explained the cyclical nature of output and employment fluctuations in the New Classical model in the following way:

> imagine that some event occurs which would, if correctly perceived by all, induce an increase in prices generally. Sooner or later, then, this adjustment will occur. Initially, however, more traders than not perceive a relative price movement, possibly permanent, in their favor. As a result, employment and investment both increase. Through time, as price information diffuses through the economy, these traders will see they have been mistaken. In the meantime, however, the added capacity *retards* price increases generally, postponing the recognition of the initial shock. In this way, unsystematic or short-term shocks to prices can lead to much longer swings in prices. (Lucas, 1977, p. 22; italics in original)

A similar story applies to factors causing a reduction in output and employment. In either case, the effects of the shock on the capital stock cause gradual adjustment and introduce cyclical swings in output, employment and prices. Notice that Lucas's story does not depend on workers making expectational errors while employers are always correct. Rather, for Lucas, both workers and employers are prone to make errors and to confuse general price changes with changes in the relative price of the goods or factors which they supply, and to adjust their behaviour according to their perceptions.

Similarly, it is possible to argue that firms do not adjust their employment levels instantaneously in response to shocks hitting the economy; rather, in order to economize on hiring and firing costs (such as interviewing applicants, training new workers, redundancy payments and so on), they adjust their employment levels gradually, and so impart gradual adjustment to output and employment.

Alternatively, inventory adjustment can be made to generate cyclical behaviour in models which generally fit within the New Classical school (e.g. Brunner, Cukierman and Meltzer, 1983). On the other hand, models with rational expectations but some money-wage rigidities, arising from long and overlapping contracts in the labour market, exhibit prolonged effects of random shocks, since contracts may not be renegotiated after a shock has occurred and, hence, the effect of the shock continues until the contract expires. The latter type of model is known as 'New Keynesian', that is models which accept the rational expectations idea but reject that of instantaneous market clearing found in the New Classical model. New Keynesian models may provide a rationale for government intervention if the government can respond to shocks more quickly than the private sector, which is locked into insufficiently flexible contracts. This argument will be examined in more detail in the next chapter, which deals with some criticisms and modifications of the, rather extreme, New Classical model presented so far. The final section of the present chapter presents an algebraic version of the New Classical model.

7.3   New Classical Macroeconomics: An Algebraic Treatment

It may be useful to conclude this chapter with an algebraic version of the New Classical model to reinforce the diagrammatic treatment offerred above.[3] It will suffice to work with a version of the *IS–LM* model supplemented with an expectations-augmented supply schedule as follows:

$$y_t = y^* + a_1[P_t - _{t-1}E(P_t)] + u_{1t} \quad a_1 > 0 \tag{7.1}$$

$$y_t = b_1 + b_2 r_t + b_3 G_t + b_4 \frac{r_t B_t}{P_t} + u_{2t} \tag{7.2}$$
$$b_1, b_3, b_4 > 0, b_2 < 0$$

$$M_t = c_1 P_t + c_2 y_t + c_3 r_t + u_{3t} \quad c_1, c_2 > 0, c_3 < 0. \tag{7.3}$$

Equation (7.1) represents the expectations-augmented supply schedule. It defines real aggregate supply, y_t, as a function of the natural level of output, y^*, and the difference between the expected and actual price level for period t. Since a_1 is positive, output exceeds its natural level if the actual price level exceeds the expected price level. The difference between actual and expected price levels is often said to represent a surprise to economic agents, and the expectations-augmented supply schedule is often known as the surprise supply schedule. The final term in equation (7.1), u_{1t}, represents a random disturbance to the supply schedule, and may be the source of a surprise since it cannot be predicted in advance by economic agents.

Equation (7.2) is an *IS* schedule where, for simplicity, r_t is the nominal interest rate, G_t is the level of real government spending on goods and services, and $r_t B_t / P_t$ is the level of real interest payments made by the government. B_t is the number of variable interest rate bonds of fixed nominal value of unity.[4,5] Equation (7.3) is an *LM* schedule where M_t is the nominal money stock and u_{2t} and u_{3t} are random disturbances which shift the *IS* and *LM* schedules. All the disturbance terms have zero means, constant and finite variances, and are independent of one another and of their own past values.

Manipulating equations (7.1)–(7.3) by linearizing and taking expectations, it is possible to derive the following result:

$$P_t - {}_{t-1}E(P_t) = f_1[G_t - {}_{t-1}E(G_t)] + f_2[B_t - {}_{t-1}E(B_t)]$$
$$+ f_3[M_t - {}_{t-1}E(M_t)] + f_4 u_{1t} + f_5 u_{2t} + f_6 u_{3t} \qquad (7.7)$$

where the f parameters depend upon the underlying parameters in (7.1)–(7.3).[6] Equation (7.7) may be interpreted as saying that the forecast, or expectational, errors on the price level $P_t - {}_{t-1}E(P_t)$ depend upon any errors made in forecasting government policy variables G_t, B_t and M_t and upon the inevitable shocks to the economy u_{1t}, u_{2t} and u_{3t}. If expectations are formed rationally, then in the absence of any shocks, u_{1t}, u_{2t} or u_{3t}, and in the absence of unpredictable policy components $G_t - {}_{t-1}E(G_t)$, $B_t - {}_{t-1}E(B_t)$, or $M_t - {}_{t-1}E(M_t)$, there will be no expectational errors and, from (7.1), output and employment will be at their natural levels. Furthermore, it is only the unforecastable elements of policy variables which cause forecast errors and affect the distribution of output about its natural level.

Thus, we have derived the irrelevance hypothesis from our algebraic model, and predictable government policy will have no real effects. This result lies at the heart of the New Classical macroeconomics and stems from the nature of the surprise supply schedule. Output deviates from its natural level only in response to exogenous shocks and unanticipated price movements.

Notes

1 The diagrammatic treatment of the New Classical model presented here is based upon that of Parkin and Bade (1982).
2 An argument which is closely related to the irrelevance hypothesis is the 'Lucas critique of econometric policy evaluation'. Lucas (1976) argued that the practice of estimating macroeconometric models and then using the estimated results to simulate behaviour of the economy in response to a number of different government policies, or to choose an optimum government policy, was invalid. He argued that econometric relationships will not remain stable in the face of policy changes, since economic behaviour would adjust to those changes. Therefore, estimates based on evidence drawn from data collected under past policies need be of no use in predicting behaviour under new and different policies. In principle, Lucas's critique has shattering implications for econometric analysis of policy. It could be taken to imply that policy evaluation should only be carried out using models that allowed estimation of the 'underlying' parameters of tastes and technology, which might be considered to be invariant with respect to government policy changes; this would rule out most of the macroeconometric models currently in use. However, it is possible to argue that, in practice, if models can produce paths for their endogenous variables which closely fit those that they have followed in the past, and that if the policies under consideration are similar to those which have been tried in the past, then the econometric evidence may well be useful: the model may be a reasonable approximation to reality even if government policies are changed. Of course, if government policies change dramatically and are very different to any previously experienced, then it would not be possible to have much confidence in the results of the econometric exercise. For a further discussion of the Lucas critique see chapter 3 of Cuthbertson and Taylor (1987).
3 The algebraic version presented here is based upon that of Sargent and Wallace (1975).
4 Notice that earlier in the book we have assumed bonds to have a fixed coupon or interest payment and to be of variable value. The bonds in the present model are of fixed value and offer variable interest payments. In the real world there are various different types of bond in existence.
5 Equation (7.2) may be derived from the following underlying investment and consumption schedules:

$$I_t = dr_t \qquad\qquad d < 0 \qquad\qquad (7.4)$$

$$C_t = e_1 + e_2 \left(y_t + \frac{r_t B_t}{P_t} - \frac{T_t}{P_t} \right) \quad e_1 > 0, 1 > e_2 > 0 \qquad (7.5)$$

where I_t, C_t represent real investment and consumption expenditure, respectively, and T_t represents nominal tax payments as defined in (7.6):

$$T_t = v(P_t y_t + r_t B_t). \tag{7.6}$$

The coefficients in (7.2) depend upon those in (7.4)–(7.6) as follows:

$$b_1 = e_1/[1 - e_2(1 - v)]$$
$$b_1 = d_2/[1 - e_2(1 - v)]$$
$$b_3 = 1/[1 - e_2(1 - v)]$$
$$b_4 = e_2(1 - v)/[1 - e_2(1 - v)].$$

Notice that the real value of interest payments enters into the consumption function as part of current disposable income in a simple extension of the absolute income hypothesis, yet this makes the *IS* schedule dependent on the price level even though wealth effects, as traditionally defined, are absent from the model. It would, of course, be possible to enter wealth effects into the consumption and demand-for-money functions but, for simplicity, this is not done here.

6 The reader need not worry about the details of this manipulation.

8

The New Classical Macroeconomics: Some Responses

The preceding chapter has outlined the basic New Classical model and derived the irrelevance hypothesis. It is now appropriate to critically evaluate that model and its policy implications. This chapter, therefore, proceeds by first of all showing that, even in the basic New Classical model, the incorporation of the government budget identity has important implications for policy. The New Classical model and its policy implications are then further modified by recognizing that the natural values of variables are not invariant to policy. Next, criticisms of the New Classical model are examined, and it is shown that neither of its basic assumptions of continuous market clearing and rational expectations is universally accepted. Finally, the general activist versus non-activist debate is re-examined in the light of the issues discussed in this and the previous chapter.

8.1 The Government Budget Identity in the New Classical Model

The irrelevance hypothesis, which has been presented above as the idea that predictable government policy will have no real effects, has been taken to imply that the government should follow a simple known rule for the behaviour of the money supply.[1] The reasoning is that, although the distribution of price forecast errors and output depends on the random component of the money supply, 'there is no way the authority can base a countercyclical policy on this particular non-neutrality, since there is no way the authority can regularly choose . . . [the random component] . . . in response to the state of economic affairs in order to offset other disturbances in the system' (Sargent and Wallace, 1975, p. 249). In other words, any exogenous shocks to the system are unpredictable, and, therefore, no random component of the money supply can be used systematically to offset them, as it will only increase uncertainty and the variance of output; so a simple known monetary policy rule should be followed to avoid introducing further shocks to the economy. Recognition of the government budget identity, however, makes clear that this argument is a *non sequitur*.

Consider the following government budget identity:

$$P_t G_t = T_t + \Delta M_t + \Delta B_t - r_t B_t \qquad (8.1)$$

where the Δ term signifies 'changes in' and bonds are, for simplicity, of the fixed-nominal-value, variable-interest-rate type used in the previous chapter. Taken in conjunction with a tax equation such as (7.6) (see note 4 of chapter 7), which assumes that nominal tax receipts depend upon the levels of nominal income and interest payments, the government budget identity makes clear that the government cannot pre-announce with certainty the values for all of its policy variables. Tax receipts will vary with income, and the government must allow something to vary to satisfy the government budget identity.

Two obvious alternative means of financing any imbalance on the government budget are to print more or less money than expected, or to sell more or fewer bonds than expected.[2] Since changing the money or bond stock in unforecastable ways leads to effects on aggregate demand, via their effects on the *IS* and *LM* schedules, it is not certain which policy would, on average, lead to more stable output behaviour. It is not clear that controlling the money supply regardless of shocks to the economy, and hence letting the bond stock vary unpredictably, would be the best policy for the government to follow. For instance, consider that for some reason there is a shock which unpredictably reduces aggregate demand and, hence, output. Tax receipts would fall and the government budget deficit would rise. Should this deficit be financed by printing money or by selling bonds? It might well be that printing money would cause aggregate demand to rise, partly offsetting the initial reduction in aggregate demand and helping to stabilize output. Therefore, the best policy might be to allow the money stock to adjust to satisfy the government budget identity. Whether this policy would indeed be better than letting the bond stock so adjust would, in fact, depend upon all the parameters of the economy and the variances of the various shocks which hit the economy. It is, then, a matter for empirical research to decide whether the government should deterministically fix the money supply or let it adjust to shocks.

Notice that this argument is not an argument for fine-tuning the economy in the traditional activist sense, and does not refute the irrelevance hypothesis that predictable policy has no real effects. One could well believe that the government should pre-announce consistent targets for all its policy variables, and, in the absence of shocks, should stick to those targets, but that, in the presence of shocks, the government should allow the money stock to adjust as an automatic stabilization policy. Such a policy would not increase the shocks to the economy, but would imply automatic countercyclical responses to the unavoidable shocks which do occur. Furthermore, when we remember the discussion in chapter 5 concerning the likely destabilizing effects of allowing the bond stock to adjust to finance any government budget imbalance, it seems all the more likely that the New Classical economists and the Monetarists might do better to favour fixing the bond stock (as in Friedman's original 1948 proposals) over fixing the money stock (as in Friedman's later proposals).

Thus, recognition of the government budget identity forces a modification of the implications of the irrelevance hypothesis and, also, of the New Classical and Monetarist policy conclusions. It does not, however, attack the fundamental theoretical stance of either school. The following section further modifies the New Classical model by arguing that the natural levels of variables may be affected by government policies; and section 8.3 looks at more fundamental criticisms of the model.

8.2 Real Effects of Anticipated Fiscal and Monetary Policies and New Classical Models

The irrelevance hypothesis has been presented as the argument that predictable government policy cannot affect real output and employment, but only nominal values. The natural rate of output was taken to be an exogenous constant independent of the setting of government policy variables. While the irrelevance hypothesis is often presented in this manner, it is easy to show that even fully anticipated policy changes can, in fact, influence real variables, even in New Classical models. As Buiter pointed out,

> It is trivial to show that fully anticipated changes in fiscal policy will
> have real effects. From the standard microeconomics of the utility-

maximising household, changes in tax rates will alter labour supply and saving behaviour (Fair, 1978, 1979). The theory of the firm tells us of the effects of the payroll tax on labour demand and of the influence of investment tax credits, depreciation allowances, etc., on capital formation. . . . Such real effects occur even in perfect foresight models, whether or not the state of the economy is characterised at each instant by a frictionless, market-clearing competitive Walrasian temporary equilibrium. Clearly, fiscal policy is 'non-neutral' even in the most classical of economic systems. (Buiter, 1980, p. 39)

Furthermore, Buiter (1980) argues that anticipated monetary policy will also have real effects in New Classical models. There are two major reasons for such effects to occur. First, different fully anticipated rates of growth of the money supply are associated with different anticipated rates of inflation, and hence with different anticipated real rates of return on money balances whose nominal rate of return is fixed at zero. Thus, equilibrium financial portfolios are affected, with consequent effects on real rates of return on other assets and on investment, the capital stock and the capital-labour ratio. Second, fully anticipated monetary policies will have other real effects if the private-sector agents hold bonds and these enter into private-sector behavioural arrangements. Barro (1974) has argued that bonds are not treated as wealth by private-sector agents, who 'discount' the future taxes required to service the bonds. However, it is not necessary that bonds be treated as wealth in order for anticipatable monetary policy to have real effects, but only that liquidity or distributional effects be present. And, in any case, there are good theoretical and empirical arguments against the idea that bonds are not treated as wealth (see Davies, 1985).

Thus, even predictable monetary policies or switching from tax financing to bond financing of given expenditure policies will almost certainly affect the microeconomic structure of the economy and the natural levels of real variables. The irrelevance hypothesis is not, however, destroyed by this demonstration. Rather, the hypothesis must be modified to say that predictable government behaviour affects real economic variables only to the extent that it alters the microeconomic structure of the economy and changes the natural levels of these variables. That is to say, predictable policies may well affect the natural levels of real economic variables and cause them to move in predictable ways; but any unanticipated dispersion of real variables about their natural levels (or about their expected path, if they are moving to new natural values) must still be due to unanticipated shocks, as in the simpler version of the irrelevance hypothesis presented earlier. In other words, although the government can now affect real variables, it is still left unable to fine-tune the economy in the face of random shocks. Indeed, Buiter's arguments on the non-neutrality of fiscal and monetary policy in market-clearing models may be thought of as echoing and developing Friedman's views about the natural rate of unemployment being dependent upon the 'structural characteristics of the labor and commodity markets' (1968, p. 8). Therefore, the New Classical economists could easily accept Buiter's arguments, and even argue that they are perfectly consistent with their own claims that unemployment should be reduced by structural or supply-side improvements, rather than by aggregate demand management.[3]

As far as stabilization policy is concerned, the introduction of the government budget identity discussed in the previous section must also be considered. Taken in conjunction, the arguments in this section and those in the last indicate that government policy can affect the natural levels of real variables, and that some government procedures will be better at stabilizing the economy than others. Thus, the government cannot fine-tune the economy, according to these arguments, but it still may have important roles to play even in New Classical models which allow for the arguments presented above.[4] It is now necessary to turn to more fundamental criticisms of the New Classical model.

8.3   Attacks on the Foundations of the New Classical Macroeconomics

The discussion of the irrelevance hypothesis so far has not questioned the two pillars of the New Classical macroeconomics, that is, the assumptions of rational expectations and of market clearing subject to those expectations. Relaxation of one or both of these assumptions changes the nature of the model significantly, and the most fundamental criticisms of the New Classical macroeconomics consist of arguments in favour of replacing these assumptions with alternatives which lead to different policy conclusions.

Asymmetric Information

However, before examining these criticisms, it is worth examining the argument that the government may have superior information to that possessed by private-sector agents, whether firms or workers. This case leaves the basic New Classical assumptions of rational expectations and market clearing intact, but provides the government with scope to exploit its informational advantage to adjust its policies (in response to information not yet available to the private sector) in order to stabilize economic behaviour and modify the shocks to the private sector. The irrelevance hypothesis no longer holds if the government has such an informational advantage, and it also breaks down in some models where one group of private agents has superior information to that available to other private agents and the government (see Minford and Peel, 1983, ch. 3).

Thus, this apparently slight modification to the New Classical model leads to fundamentally different policy conclusions from those above, and for reasons similar to those present in the other arguments in favour of activist intervention. Any argument for activist government intervention must assume that such intervention will improve social welfare, or in other words must assume that the outcome under non-activist policies would be socially inferior to that under activist policies. In the case of informational advantages, the argument is that the government, by using its own superior information (or responding appropriately to knowledge that some subset of the private sector has superior information), can implement an activist policy to improve upon the outcome that would occur if it followed a non-activist policy. The reason is obvious: private agents with inferior information might not actually be able to 'optimize' as well as the more knowing government. Similarly, if private-sector agents do not form expectations rationally, and make systematic errors, then the government may well have scope for implementing activist policies to improve upon the outcomes that would otherwise be achieved. On the other hand, even if all private agents form rational expectations, and have as much information as the government, but are able to respond more slowly than the government, then the government may be able to use its faster speed of response to implement successful activist policies, as in the contract-based New Keynesian models. Thus, if private agents have less information, are less rational, or are less quick to adjust to circumstances than the government, then the government may be able to implement activist policies to stabilize the economy.

The New Classical rejoinder to the case of informational advantages is that, if it is the government which has the superior information, then, rather than implement activist policies it should rapidly and widely disseminate this information to the private sector. If it did so, private agents would be able to make better-informed decisions and activist government policies would be unnecessary. On the other hand, if certain private-sector agents possess superior information of a macroeconomic nature to that of other agents, the government should insist that this be made available, at low cost, to other agents too. (But even if this is not enforced, it is likely that a market in such information will develop, or else that it will be transmitted indirectly via asset prices.) Thus, the New Classical position is that information advantages do not really provide grounds for supporting activist macroeconomic policies. The most significant attacks on the New Classical position, however, come from those who attack the assumptions of rational expectations or market clearing.

Rational Expectations: A Critical Assessment

The assumption of rational expectations, as the term has come to be used, is that economic agents have the information and knowledge of the economic system to permit them to form subjective expectations of the outcomes of the economic process that are equivalent to the predictions that would be derived from a full and proper knowledge of the true model of the economy. Several authors find this assumption to be so implausible that they do not deem it worthy of serious consideration. Nevertheless, many such authors will concede that the rational expectations hypothesis has been useful in forcing economists to recognize the key importance of expectations and to try to gain an understanding of how they are formed. It may even be conceded that it is important to recognize that people learn from the past and, in some circumstances at least, take into account government policy announcements and changes.

But, having conceded all that, it is still possible to argue that the man or woman in the street simply does not form rational expectations. Indeed, in the real world, where it is costly to acquire information and to process it, it may not really be rational to spend the time and trouble it would take to form a rational expectation; it may be better to make a quite crude guess.

This argument seems quite forceful, and the response that all agents do not need to form rational expectations but need only listen to the predictions of the economic forecasting models seems wide of the mark. Perhaps a better response is that, for the theory to work, it requires only that a few important individuals, such as government officials, business and labour leaders, form rational expectations. This line of defence is weakened once it is recognized that for most developed economies there are several competing forecasting models with widely different properties. Which one are the key individuals supposed to use, and what happens if they don't all use the same one? The last line of defence for the rational expectations hypothesis would appear to be that, like any other hypothesis about expectations or anything else, it is a simplification, an abstraction to be judged not by its realism, but by its effects on the performance of empirical models. However, it is still too early to come to any straightforward conclusions on this aspect; some writers believe the results to be more promising than others. (The interested reader is referred to, for example, Begg, 1982b, and Tobin, 1980, for further discussion.)

B. M. Friedman has pursued the question of the plausibility of the rational expectations hypothesis. The hypothesis that economic agents have full knowledge of the 'true' economic model and use this to form expectations excludes any discussion of the learning procedure followed by economic agents. It 'casts models in which it is used in a mold most commonly associated with long-run equilibrium economics' (B. M. Friedman, 1979, p. 25). Out of this long-run equilibrium position, Friedman argues, individuals continually learn through observation, and the model which they use to formulate their expectations evolves over time. The expectations generated by this procedure will not be 'rational' if that word is taken to imply expectations formed on the basis of the 'true' economic model.

The actual procedure that individuals use to formulate expectations is a matter for empirical as well as theoretical research, but it is open to question whether expectations could ever be expected to converge on rational expectations. In the real world, circumstances, and policy stances, shift and change, and individuals have to form expectations with little evidence available to provide them with much confidence. Friedman argues that under certain circumstances it may be more plausible to assume that individuals use adaptive rather than rational expectations. He concludes that

> Macroeconomic models based on the assumptions of the rational expectations hypothesis do not demonstrate the short-run ineffectiveness of policy, therefore, because they are not really short-run models. The information availability assumption of the rational expectations hypothesis implicitly places such models in a long-run equilibrium context in which their classical properties – including the neutrality of monetary policy – are not surprising. (B. M. Friedman, 1979, pp. 39–40)

Finally, the reader should note that a technical problem which occurs in many models with rational expectations is that of 'multiple equilibria'. In such cases there may be several or an infinite number of potential equilibria, any of which could occur if it was expected to occur. This means that even rational agents have no reason to expect any particular solution to occur, and so cannot decide upon a specific rational expectation. (For an example of this type of problem in an open economy context, see page 246 below.) Whilst some writers see this as providing a forceful objection to the use of rational expectations, others would argue that there are many instances where this problem does not arise, and that when it does arise it either indicates a deficiency elsewhere in the model, which should be corrected rather than abandoning the rational expectations assumption, or else that the real world is characterized by expectational confusion and that the assumption of rational expectations is doing a great service in bringing this to light and possibly providing a guide for policy to avoid or overcome the problem.

New Keynesian Models

New Keynesian models are those which accept the hypothesis that expectations are formed rationally, but reject the market-clearing assumption of the New Classical school.[5] Instead, New Keynesians argue that, in the short run at least, money wages and employment do not adjust to clear the labour market, given some level of price expectations. Rather, contractual arrangements in the labour market fix money wages for a certain period of time. As a result, money-wage adjustment is restricted during the life of the contract, and this may prevent private-sector adjustment to random shocks. If the government is able to adjust its policies in the face of random shocks more quickly than the private sector can renegotiate labour market contracts, then there may, once more, be scope for aggregate demand management. This conclusion holds even if, at the time of signing contracts, both employers and employees set a money wage which they believe will, in the absence of random shocks, clear the labour market; and it also holds when it is recognized that all labour market contracts are not set on the same day for the same length of time.

New Classical economists argue that the New Keynesians provide no micro-theoretic rationale for the existence of such contracts in a world of profit-maximizing employers and utility-maximizing employees. The New Keynesian rejoinder is that contractual wage-fixing is an observed key phenomenon in the real world, and that it is better to allow for this in model-building than to ignore it simply because no micro-theoretic explanation for such behaviour is yet available. New Keynesians also point out that the adjustments to the New Classical model to produce business cycles are often *ad hoc* in the sense that they are not derived from any underlying optimization behaviour. Furthermore, there is work going on to try to find a microtheoretic foundation for wage rigidities (see for example Lindbeck and Snower, 1986).

The New Keynesian contract-based model is illustrated using figure 8.1. Assume, for simplicity, that all labour contracts are signed on the same day and are of equal duration and that, during the life of the contract, labour supply is infinitely money-wage-elastic. Consider that, initially, aggregate demand is given by AD_1 and that wage bargaining results in the money wage W_1 (and the New Keynesian aggregate supply curve $NKAS_1$), which it is believed will clear the labour market given AD_1.[6] Should AD_1 persist, then, since labour market participants form rational expectations, the labour market will indeed clear, output will be at its natural level, y^*, and the price level will be P_1.

Now consider that, during the life of the labour market contract, there is a sudden and unexpected shift in the aggregate demand curve to AD_2. What is required to maintain labour market clearing is a renegotiation of the money wage to the lower level W_2, which would shift the New Keynesian aggregate supply curve to $NKAS_2$. This latter shift would reduce the price level to P_2, and maintain output at its natural level, y^*. But during the life of the labour market contract the money wage is fixed at W_1, and the New

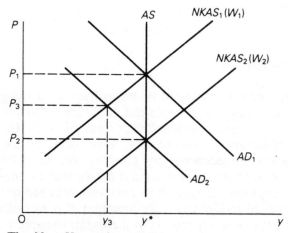

Figure 8.1 The New Keynesian model

Keynesian aggregate supply curve remains at $NKAS_1$. The money wage does not adjust to W_2, and prices do not adjust to P_2 with output remaining at y^*. Instead, the price level falls to P_3 at the intersection of AD_2 and $NKAS_1$, and output falls below its natural level to y_3. If, in such circumstances, the government is able to adjust its policies more quickly than the private sector can renegotiate money wages, there is scope for aggregate demand management, that is, deterministic Keynesian (or New Keynesian) fine-tuning policies, to respond to the initial aggregate demand shock and return the aggregate demand curve to AD_1. Such a policy, if successfully implemented, would be quicker and better than waiting for the labour market to adjust money wages to W_2. For instance, consider that the labour market contracts lasted for four periods, while the government could adjust its policies in response to last period's price and output levels. If the shock to aggregate demand occurred in the first period of life of the labour market contracts, then output would be depressed for four periods in the absence of aggregate demand management. However, if the government could adjust its policies (according to some known rule in relation to the previous period's price and output levels), it could return aggregate demand to a level consistent with full employment in the period after the shock occurred, and thereby avoid three periods of depressed output.

Thus, the New Keynesian contract-based analysis provides a rationale for government fine-tuning policies, and shows that the New Classical model depends upon both of its key assumptions – that is, market clearing and rational expectations – for its policy implications.

8.4 Conclusions

The New Keynesian argument is, basically, that a sluggish adjustment of money wages and prices can cause the economy to diverge from full employment for lengthy periods of time. In such cases fiscal and monetary policy changes, anticipated or not, can have real effects on the economy by affecting the level of aggregate demand. Furthermore, it was argued above that the natural levels of output, employment and other real variables are not invariant, even in Classical models, to fully anticipated policy changes.

If one accepts these arguments, it seems fair to agree with Buiter's conclusion that:

there is no reasonable case that deterministic monetary and fiscal policy rules cannot alter the cyclical fluctuations of the economic system or the nature of its trend growth path. . . . The recognition that monetary and fiscal policy give the government a handle on the real economy implies the existence of scope for both beneficial and detrimental policy behaviour. There is no presumption at all that a government that sits on its hands and determines the behaviour of its instruments by the simplest possible fixed rules is guaranteed to bring about the best of all possible worlds. (Buiter, 1980, pp. 47–8)

The above arguments, if true, apply to the New Classical macroeconomic model, and especially to the irrelevance hypothesis. Some writers, for example Hahn (1980) and Parkin and Bade (1982), seem to treat New Classical macroeconomics and Monetarism as synonymous. The reason for this treatment would seem to be that the New Classical model, in its extreme form, provides a theoretical basis for the Monetarist rejection of countercyclical policy. It is also often interpreted as providing a basis for the Monetarist policy prescription of fixing the rate of growth of the money supply, although, as section 8.1 of this chapter has shown, inclusion of the government budget identity in the New Classical model casts doubt upon the validity of that interpretation. Thus, the New Classical model does not provide a *sufficient* basis for Monetarism, but, equally important, it is not a *necessary* basis either. Therefore, even if the above arguments demolish the New Classical position, they do not demolish the Monetarist position and establish the case for demand management policies. As Mayer notes, 'this case requires a demonstration that such policies are correctly timed and of an appropriate magnitude, so that they are not themselves destabilising. Monetarists have argued at length that this is not the case' (1984, p. 129). Laidler put the same argument another way:

it is one thing to say that the world is so structured that policy can influence output and employment in the short run, and another thing altogether to say that policy-makers have enough knowledge to use that ability in a way that will be beneficial. . . . One can rest the monetarist case against activist policy on the proposition that markets always clear and that expectations are rational, but one can also rest it on the much more down-to-earth proposition that we are too ignorant of the structure of the economies we live in and of the manner in which that structure is changing to be able safely to implement activist stabilisation policy in the present environment, or in the foreseeable future. (Laidler, 1981, pp. 18–19)

It does not, therefore, seem to be appropriate to equate Monetarism with New Classical macroeconomics. The New Classical school may be characterized as assuming widespread economic knowledge on the part of both the government and private agents, but Monetarism might well be characterized better by the assumption of widespread ignorance. The former seems to assume that, barring unavoidable shocks, the *laissez-faire* economy works perfectly well and does not require government intervention; the latter can accept that the *laissez-faire* economy is far from perfect, but takes the view that activist intervention would only make matters worse, not better. In some ways, the New Keynesian model is closer to the New Classical model than is Monetarism, but by recognizing contractual rigidities it identifies a role for activist intervention.

Certainly the debate still hinges upon the same issues as those at stake between Keynes and the Classics – the dynamic efficiency of the competitive market economy, and the potential role for government intervention. It is hoped that this book has given readers some guidance as to the foundations of the alternative points of view, and some food for thought before forming their own opinions.[7]

Readers wishing to gain some flavour of more recent developments in the debate are referred to the survey article by Fischer (1988). Fischer argues that:

> two basic views of macroeconomic behaviour have persisted even as conceptual innovations and the application of more powerful analytical and empirical techniques have brought significant changes in macroeconomics. One view and school of thought, associated with Keynes, Keynesians and new Keynesians, is that the private economy is subject to co-ordination failures that can produce excessive levels of unemployment and excessive fluctuations in real activity. The other view, attributed to classical economists, and espoused by monetarists and equilibrium business cycle theorists, is that the private economy reaches as good an equilibrium as is possible given government policy. (Fischer, 1988, p. 294)

He points out that although such a two-fold division is 'inevitably a caricature' which cannot do full justice to such a complex field of study as macroeconomics, it 'nonetheless . . . captures the essence of macroeconomic controversies' (1988, p. 294).

The most recent developments follow the lines laid out for them by the history of the debate which has been reviewed in this book, as can be seen by examining, very briefly, two of the more interesting developments. On the Keynesian side there has been an impetus to provide microeconomic foundations for the ideas not just of sticky or rigid wages, as we have already discussed above, but also for sticky prices. In order to do this, researchers have begun to analyse models of imperfect or monopolistic competition, rather than the perfect competition with which Keynes worked. The reason for this development is that 'the Keynesian assumption that suppliers are always willing to sell more if demand at the existing price increases is a characteristic of a monopolistic equilibrium' (Fischer, 1988, p. 321). When allied to the idea that changing prices is costly for firms, the assumption of monopolistic competition can be used to show that an increase in aggregate demand could, in some circumstances, improve social welfare. This development may be viewed as an extension of the Clower–Leijonhufvud-inspired disequilibrium analysis introduced in chapter 4 above (to explain why prices are rigid in some circumstances), and also as a response to the New Classical argument that macroeconomic propositions should have microeconomic foundations (an argument that the New Classicals themselves do not always follow, and which some Keynesians would deny, see Blinder, 1987 for an interesting discussion of this and other issues). It is interesting to note that most of these New Keynesian models adopt the assumption of rational expectations, which provides a useful illustration of how the different schools respond to one another.

On the New Classical side, the most interesting development has concerned the rejection of the idea that imperfect information about current monetary variables could really explain business cycles or divergences from the natural rate of unemployment. In one sense this argument denies the relevance of the New Classical model, but in another sense it is just taking it one step further and saying that if imperfect information were the cause of such divergences, then rational agents would take steps to improve their sources of information. Thus, according to Fischer, 'It would be entirely possible to produce an on-line estimate of the current price level at low cost by providing terminals to businesses, which could enter price changes as they took place' (1988, p. 303). If cycles cannot originate with aggregate demand shocks, since agents are all assumed constantly to acquire accurate information on these and instantly readjust all prices, then where do they originate? The answer provided by the 'equilibrium real business cycle approach' is that they originate with productivity shocks hitting an economy in which markets are always in equilibrium. Such shocks then generate cycles through such factors as those mentioned in the discussion of the New Classical model in chapter 7 above, for example the costs involved in hiring or firing labour mean that the level of employment adjusts only gradually to any change in its equilibrium level, thus imparting a cyclical pattern even if the shocks causing the changes exhibit no such pattern.

It would seem that there is much potential for the different approaches to come together. The real business cycle theorists could explore the effects of monopolistic competition in their models, and the imperfect competition theorists could explore the effects of productivity shocks. Thus, although the controversy generates heat and passion on either side of the debate, it is to be hoped that it will ultimately enable a clearer understanding of macroeconomic problems and of the similarities, as well as the differences, between the various schools of thought.

The next, and final, part of this book will not introduce any fundamentally new views, but will show how some of the ideas and techniques developed above can be applied to models of the open economy.

Notes

1   This section is based upon Hillier (1985).
2   It is assumed throughout this discussion that government spending plans or tax rates are not suitable policies for continual adjustment to satisfy the government budget identity; the reader may ponder the difficulties involved, e.g., in trying continually to adjust spending plans which take time to decide upon, to organize and get started or stopped.
3   Several New Classical economists seem to go even further than Friedman, and not only eschew activist policies, but also advocate *laissez-faire* on the grounds that a decentralized economy will achieve a Pareto-optimal outcome, that is, one from which it will be impossible to make one individual better off without making another worse off (e.g. Barro, 1979). One might well argue that the government ought to intervene to redistribute income even if the *laissez-faire* outcome were Pareto-optimal. Furthermore, the conditions under which a *laissez-faire* economy will achieve Pareto optimality are unlikely to exist, so that there can be scope for non-activist policy intervention to improve upon the *laissez-faire* outcome (see Hahn, 1982).
4   See also Minford and Peel (1983, ch. 3) for the argument that explicit recognition of intertemporal decision-making may give some scope for stabilization policy.
5   For examples of such models, see the seminal papers by Fischer (1977) and Phelps and Taylor (1977).
6   The interested reader may care to try to derive the New Keynesian aggregate supply curve. This may be done by using a figure like figure 7.3 but with a vertical supply-of-labour curve for money wage W_1 in part (i) of the figure. The resulting aggregate supply curve should be

compared with the New Classical expectations-augmented aggregate supply curve.

7   We have not, however, in all of this, become involved in debates about the optimum size of the public sector, but only in the debate about macroeconomic stabilization policy. This is partly because the debate about the optimum size of the public sector would involve more microeconomic than macroeconomic issues, although we accept that both should be discussed together in this context; it is also partly because entering into such debate would involve more overtly political and moral issues and would require dealing with radical views on both the right and left of the political spectrum, which would take us far beyond the aims of this book.

Part VI

The Open Economy: The Consequences of Exchange Rate Regimes for Domestic Stabilization

9

The Open Economy: An Introduction

The analysis so far has been concerned with the determination of macroeconomic variables and the use of macroeconomic policy under the assumption of a closed economy, that is, an economy in which there is no dealing with residents of other countries. This and the following chapters introduce trade with other countries and international capital flows into the analysis. Leaving the open economy until this late stage reflects a judgement that the key theoretical issues in the macroeconomic debate, concerning the efficiency of the market economy and the scope for government intervention, can best be presented without the extra complications involved in dealing with an open economy. Nevertheless, in a world where international trade and capital flows have great practical significance, it is important to extend the analysis to deal with the open economy. This task is carried out below.

As a starting point, section 9.1 discusses the definition of the foreign exchange rate. Section 9.2 then presents the basic accounting conventions for recording international transactions. Section 9.3 discusses different exchange rate systems and section 9.4 introduces the theoretical treatment of the open economy by modifying the simple Keynesian multiplier model to allow for international trade under a system of fixed exchange rates. The analysis is greatly simplified by assuming that prices are fixed and there are no capital flows. Section 9.5 examines a similar model under a system of floating exchange rates. Subsequent chapters progressively develop the complexity of the models, in a manner comparable to the earlier closed economy chapters. Chapter 10 shows how to extend the *IS–LM* model to deal with open economy issues, and also introduces capital flows into the analysis. Chapter 11 stresses the relationship between stocks and flows, and shows that the implications of this relationship are just as great for the open economy as chapter 5 showed them to be for the closed economy. Finally, chapter 12 relaxes the fixed-price assumption to offer a fairly comprehensive model of the open economy.

9.1 Exchange Rates

The most elementary complication introduced by modelling international trade, in goods, services, or physical or financial assets, concerns the fact that the buyers and sellers are used to dealing in terms of different currencies. Consider the case of a French farmer selling apples in England: the farmer wishes to receive French francs whilst his English customers wish to pay with pounds sterling. In order for such transactions to take place it is necessary to be able to convert one currency into another, either directly or indirectly through the use of some internationally acceptable medium of exchange (such as gold or the US dollar).

The rates at which one currency may be converted into another are known as exchange rates, or, more strictly, nominal exchange rates. The exchange rate between any two currencies, say, dollars and sterling, may be expressed in one of two ways, either as the dollar price of a pound sterling or as the pound sterling price of a dollar. If two dollars trade for one pound, nothing of substance hinges upon whether the exchange rate is expressed as two dollars per pound or fifty pence per dollar, but a word of caution is needed. In Britain, it is common to express exchange rates as the foreign currency price of a unit of the domestic currency, sterling, whilst it is common in other countries to express exchange rates as the domestic currency price of a unit of foreign currency. Hence, under the British convention a rising exchange rate indicates a rising value of the domestic currency in terms of the foreign currency, but under the alternative convention a rising exchange rate would indicate a falling value of the domestic currency. It is, therefore, necessary to know how the exchange rate has been defined before interpreting statements involving phrases like 'a rising exchange rate'.

The real exchange rate, or terms of trade, is defined as the price, in terms of a common currency, of exports relative to the price of imports. An increase in the real exchange rate, therefore, is an unambiguous statement no matter how the nominal exchange rate is defined: an increase in the real exchange rate means that exports increase in price relative to imports and that fewer domestic goods or services need to be given up in exchange for a given volume of imports than before the increase in the terms of trade, and vice versa for a reduction in the terms of trade. Changes in the real exchange rate may be due to a change in the nominal exchange rate or to a change in the price of domestic or foreign goods or services.

9.2 The Balance of Payments

The objective of the balance of payments accounts is to record transactions between the residents and government of a country and the rest of the world over a given period of time. An item is entered as a credit when it increases the supply of foreign currency to private residents, businesses or government agencies in the country, and as a debit when it increases the supply of domestic currency to foreigners. Credit items enter the accounts with a plus sign and debit items with a negative sign. The balance of payments is usually divided into three major component parts.

1 *The Current Account* This records trade in goods, services, investment income and transfers. It is possible to subdivide the current account into categories representing each of these major subgroups. For example, the Trading Account, or balance of trade, shows all trade in goods, that is exports and imports of physical merchandise, with export values being entered as credits and import values as debits, i.e. export values enter the accounts with a plus sign and imports with a negative sign. Services involve charges for professional services such as banking and insurance, transport and tourist expenditures. Investment income includes such things as receipt or payment of interest on outstanding loans to or from foreigners, dividend payments, etc. Transfers include private transfers (e.g. gifts to or from overseas relatives) and government transfers (e.g. aid payments or British government payments to support the budget of the European Community).

2 *The Capital Account* This records all transactions involving the purchase or sale of assets between the domestic economy and the rest of the world, and lending to or borrowing from the rest of the world. When there is an inflow of capital from abroad, this is shown as a credit item because it makes foreign exchange available to domestic residents, even if this is caused by a domestic company borrowing from overseas sources. An outflow of capital is shown

as a debit item, since it makes domestic currency available to foreigners.

The capital account may also be subdivided, for example into long- and short-term accounts, where long-term covers assets with a life-to-maturity exceeding one year.

3 *The Official Financing Account* This records transactions by the central bank on behalf of the government. It includes changes in official reserves of gold and foreign currencies, government borrowing from abroad and transactions with the IMF. Transactions which involve an increase in the official reserves are shown as debit items, since they involve reducing the supply of foreign currency held by domestic residents, and transactions which reduce the official reserves are shown as credit items.

The overall balance of payments includes all outgoings (payments for imported goods and services, purchase of foreign assets, etc.) and all incomings (receipts for export sales, sales of domestic assets to foreigners, etc.), using the double-entry method of bookkeeping, which implies that each transaction involves precisely offsetting debit and credit entries and, hence, that the overall balance of payments must always balance. For example, an import of merchandise will be recorded as a debit on the current account, but the finance for this import purchase must be recorded somewhere else in the accounts – either as proceeds from export sales (a current account credit), as a loan from foreigners (a capital inflow resulting from the sale of a financial asset or IOU to foreigners, recorded as a capital account credit), or as a change in the reserves of foreign currency (due to the government providing importers with foreign exchange and, thereby, diminishing the reserve stock, which shows up as a credit on the official financing account).

While the overall balance of payments accounts must, by definition, always balance, it is not necessary that any of the sub-components balance. Furthermore, it is common to talk of a deficit or surplus on the overall balance of payments. A 'deficit (surplus) on the overall balance of payments' is used to refer to a deficit (surplus) on the sum of the current and capital accounts, requiring a fall (rise) in official reserves or an official international loan to balance the accounts; this convention will be followed below. Note that an 'overall balance of payments balance' in this sense is consistent with a current account deficit (surplus) matched exactly by a capital account surplus (deficit).

Finally, notice that all the transactions are recorded per period of time and, therefore, represent flow variables, although they may involve changes in the stock of international reserves or foreign financial assets held in the country, or even changes in the domestic money supply. The significance of the relationship between stocks and flows will be developed in the following chapters.

9.3 Exchange Rate Systems

There are several possible ways of organizing the foreign exchange market, the most important of which are listed below.

Fixed-but-adjustable Exchange Rates

This system prevailed in much of the world from 1944 to 1971, following the Bretton Woods conference in 1944. Participants at the conference sought to establish an international monetary system conducive to peaceful international trade. In order to do this, they agreed upon a pattern of exchange rates between the currencies of the participant nations and committed themselves to support this pattern. In other words, governments (or central banks) were committed to buying or selling currencies at fixed exchange rates to members of the private sector who wished to make international transactions.[1, 2]

Since private sector demands for, and supplies of, currencies do not necessarily always balance, the system implied that central banks had to intervene in the foreign exchange market to sell foreign currencies in exchange for the domestic currency at the fixed exchange rate whenever the supply of the domestic currency on the market exceeded demand for it, and vice versa. The amount of such possible intervention for deficit currencies, that is, currencies whose supply exceeds demand on the exchange market, is limited by the amount of reserves of gold and foreign currencies held by the government of the deficit currency, supplemented by the possibility of borrowing from the International Monetary Fund (IMF), which was set up in 1944 to monitor the system.

It was hoped that the system of fixed exchange rates would foster international trade by removing the risk imposed upon importers or exporters by fluctuations in exchange rates, which mean that deals struck in terms of a foreign currency are of uncertain value in terms of the domestic currency and, therefore, involve an extra degree of risk compared to deals struck in terms of the domestic currency. Deals involving imports and exports can be struck in terms of the domestic currency of one of the parties to the deal, but one of the parties must accept some exchange rate risk. (Although there are ways to insure against this risk on the financial markets, it is, even so, an extra complication and cost.) Furthermore, it was hoped that the system would avoid the competitive policies of exchange rate manipulation which had been employed during the 1930s to improve domestic employment by making the domestic currency cheap on the exchange market and giving an advantage to domestic exports. Such beggar-thy-neighbour policies were held to be partly responsible for the international depression of the 1930s. In cases of 'fundamental disequilibrium', however, with countries running persistent deficits or surpluses, it was accepted that some adjustment in exchange rates would be necessary, subject to international agreement via the IMF. Hence, the system is often known as the 'adjustable peg' system, since the parities at which currencies were pegged were adjustable.

The system was a compromise between unadjustably fixed exchange rates and freely floating exchange rates (to be discussed below). It suffered from several problems and collapsed in 1971 after persistent deficits by the United States, whose dollar was the key international reserve currency under the system. The problems included the lack of explicit criteria to define 'fundamental disequilibrium', the unwillingness of governments to follow domestic policies necessary to support fixed exchange rates (the constraints on domestic policies implied by fixed exchange rates will be made clear below), and the ease with which the system generated profits for currency speculators. For example, if sterling is currently fixed at $2.40 per £1 and the UK is persistently running deficits, then it is easy to expect a *devaluation* of sterling – that is, a reduction in its value from, say, $2.40 to $2.00 per £1. (A *revaluation* is an increase in the value of a currency.) By selling sterling in exchange for dollars, and then buying sterling after the devaluation of sterling, speculators can increase their sterling holdings. There is little risk involved in this activity, since when sterling is the deficit currency it is not likely to be revalued, so that for the speculators, the worst that can happen is that sterling holds its value and they incur the transaction costs of buying and selling currencies without making any speculative profit or loss. The existence of forward markets may exacerbate the problems caused by such speculative forces. Deals in forward markets involve contracts to trade in currencies in the future, say sixty or ninety days, at an exchange rate specified in advance. If devaluation is expected the price of the currency will fall on the forward markets and reinforce the reluctance of speculators to hold it.

The European Monetary System or EMS is an adjustable peg system, although member currencies are allowed to fluctuate with respect to one another within defined bands and float together against non-member currencies.

Freely Floating or Flexible Exchange Rates

Under freely floating exchange rates governments do not intervene at all in the exchange market. The exchange rate is allowed to adjust continuously to achieve an overall balance of payments, without the need for official financing transactions. The case for freely floating exchange rates is that domestic fiscal and monetary policies are freed from the constraints implied by support for fixed exchange rates, and that market forces should set the exchange rates at appropriate levels. The case against them is that, left to itself, the exchange market may be highly unstable, and speculative forces may result in highly volatile exchange rates and, hence, hinder international trade by increasing the uncertainty associated with dealing with foreigners. For example, a UK exporter agreeing a US dollar price for some deal to be completed in the future, will be uncertain about the sterling value of the deal if he is uncertain about the future value of the sterling–dollar exchange rate. He can, of course, hedge against this uncertainty by entering the futures market for currencies, but this is an extra, and possibly costly, complication which may deter him from the export market.

Under floating rates it is usual to talk of *appreciation* and *depreciation* of exchange rates rather than revaluation and devaluation, as under the adjustable peg system.

Managed or Dirty Floating Exchange Rates

Under this system, exchange rates are allowed to adjust on a day-to-day basis, but governments may intervene from time to time to try to smooth out adjustment. This is the system that has prevailed in many countries since the collapse of the adjustable peg system. Intervention is, however, a difficult operation, since even internationally co-ordinated central bank actions can prove fruitless in the face of massive private sector capital flows. Such intervention can, however, be successful if it is correctly timed and provides a convincing signal to the markets that the authorities are willing to take action to support a feasible exchange rate or set of exchange rates.

9.4   The Simple Keynesian Multiplier Model of a Small Open Economy under Fixed Exchange Rates

The first open-economy macroeconomic model to be examined is the small open-economy version of the Keynesian multiplier model. Although this model is extremely simple, it provides a clear illustration of the effects of open-economy considerations, and provides a useful starting point from which to progress to more complicated models.

Consider the domestic economy to be the UK, and the rest of the world to be one giant economy with which the UK trades. Let the exchange rate, e, measured in dollars per pound sterling, be fixed but adjustable. Assume that domestic output has a fixed price in terms of sterling of £P per unit, and the output of the rest of the world, which is some good different to the domestic good, has a fixed dollar price of $\$P^*$ per unit. Assume, for simplicity, that there are no dealings on the capital account. The model under these assumptions is shown in figure 9.1, where the units on the axes are in pounds sterling.

Part (i) of the figure shows the famous Keynesian cross diagram extended to allow for exports, X, to be an extra source of demand for domestic output, and imports, F, to be part of spending by domestic residents which does not increase demand for domestic output. The equilibrium condition is no longer that y equal $(C + I + G)$ as in the closed economy model, but rather that y equal $(C + I + G + X - F)$, as shown leading to the level of income y_0.

Part (ii) of figure 9.1 plots exports and imports against domestic income. The upward-sloping F line (which need not necessarily pass through the origin) indicates that, with foreign and domestic prices and the exchange rate fixed, the demand for imports rises with domestic income. The horizontal X line, on the other hand, shows the demand for exports to be independent of the level of domestic income. Exports are assumed to be dependent upon the level of real income in the rest of the world, foreign and domestic prices and the exchange rate, all of which are assumed to be fixed independently from whatever happens in the small domestic economy. The horizontal X line, thus, embodies the small economy assumption that the level of real income in the rest of the world is independent of domestic income, because as domestic income and import demand rise this has a negligible effect on income in the rest of the world and, hence, no impact upon the demand by the

Figure 9.1 The Keynesian multiplier model of a small open economy under fixed exchange rates (all units in pounds sterling)

rest of the world for the exports of the small domestic economy. Since the X and F lines intersect above y_1, and since to the right of y_1 import demand exceeds export demand, while to the left of y_1 export demand exceeds import demand, then only at y_1 is the current account in balance. To the right of y_1 there is a current account deficit, and to the left a surplus. The vertical line *BOCA* in part (i) of the figure then indicates that a balance on current account occurs only at y_1. Simple as it is, the model in figure 9.1 is very useful. First, it shows how exports and imports need to be taken into account in determining the flow equilibrium condition. Second, it shows that there may be a conflict between internal and external policy targets. Consider that the domestic government wishes to achieve the level of income y_0, which it believes to be consistent with full employment. It can achieve this internal target by adjusting the level of government spending on real goods and services, G, and has done this correctly in figure 9.1 to achieve y_0. However, with the fixed exchange rate, e, this implies running a persistent deficit on current account, as shown in part (ii) of the figure. Such a deficit cannot be allowed to continue for ever, for the government would eventually run out of international reserves and would be unable to support the exchange rate e by borrowing from abroad indefinitely. The government, if it wishes to support the exchange rate e, must sacrifice its policy variable, G, to that end; an independent fiscal policy is not consistent with a rigid fixed exchange rate system. G must be reduced until the $C + I + G + X - F$ line in figure 9.1 (i) is pulled down to intersect the 45° line above y_1 and balance on current account is achieved.

The policy of adjusting G up or down is known as an 'expenditure changing policy', since it drives expenditure up or down as it is varied. Reliance on expenditure changing policy alone when attempting to achieve both internal and external targets will not allow both targets to be achieved simultaneously. This illustrates a result due to Tinbergen (1952) that, in order to achieve n targets or goals, a government usually needs at least n policy instruments, although satisfying this condition will not always guarantee success. In this case, reliance on the one policy would generate what might be called a stop-go cycle in which output is pushed up and down between y_0 and y_1 as first the policy is adjusted to achieve internal balance, then external balance, then internal balance, and so on. Such a simple picture may quite well represent UK experience in the 1950s and early 1960s, when the balance of payments alternated with domestic output and employment levels as the prime target of policy. The exchange rate was fixed and prices were relatively stable during this episode of UK economic history, so the simple model may not be too unrealistic, although in practice monetary policy as well as fiscal policy was used to affect the level of aggregate demand in the UK economy. Monetary policy will be introduced into the analysis in the following chapter.

In order to achieve both internal and external targets simultaneously, it is necessary to use an additional policy tool, and, importantly, to use a tool which causes expenditure switching, that is, one which for any level of domestic income affects the gap between imports and exports. Such policies might include direct controls on imports, tariffs on imports, subsidies to exports, and so on. In principle, it is possible to consider taxation as an additional policy in this context. An increase in the rate of income tax may lower the general level of expenditure in the domestic economy and, thereby, lower the demand for imports, and if coupled with an increase in government expenditure concentrated on domestic production this may alter the mix of expenditure between imports and domestic production and, thereby, reconcile the conflict between the internal and external targets. Such a policy mix might be very difficult to bring about, however, and might imply an unacceptably high level of government expenditure. Therefore, tax policy is best viewed as a supplement to government expenditure policy in this context, both policies being part of fiscal policy. Let us, instead, consider an adjustment in the exchange rate as the expenditure switching policy needed to enable the simultaneous achievement of both internal and external targets.

Adjustments to the exchange rate work by affecting the terms of trade TT, which may be defined as the price, in terms of a common currency, of exports relative to the price of imports. Using sterling as the common currency, and defining e to be the dollar price of sterling, yields TT equal to £P, the sterling price of exports, divided by £P^*/e, the sterling price of imports; that is, TT equals Pe/P^*. Exactly the same value for TT would be obtained if the dollar were used as the common currency, although the formula would look a little different. With P and P^* given, a devaluation of sterling will lower the terms of trade and make imports relatively more expensive (in sterling terms) on the UK market than before the devaluation, and exports relatively cheaper (in dollar terms) on the overseas market. The effect of a devaluation, therefore, will be to shift the X line upwards and the F line downwards in a figure such as figure 9.1 (ii), assuming that demand for imports falls as they become dearer, while that for exports rises as they become cheaper.[3,4]

The government can, now, achieve its internal and external targets simultaneously, but it must carefully combine its expenditure switching and expenditure changing policies if it is to do so. The arguments may be illustrated using figure 9.2 for the case of a devaluation (a similar analysis may easily be applied for the case of a revaluation). Assume that the government's internal target is to achieve an income level of y_0, and that it initially does so, at the exchange rate e, with a level of government spending of G. Thus, in part (i) of the figure the initial $C + I + G + X - F$ line is given by $(C + I + G + X - F)(e)$ and achieves y_0. However, with an exchange rate of e, exports and imports are given in part (ii) of the figure by $X(e)$ and $F(e)$. A balance on current account would, thus, be achieved at y_1 and so the *BOCA* line is drawn vertically above y_1 in part (i). The government, therefore, is achieving its internal target of y_0, but at the expense of a deficit on current account.

In order to achieve both internal and external targets simultaneously, the government must adjust the exchange rate, but, less obviously, it must also adjust its fiscal policy as will be shown. First of all the government must obtain agreement with the nation's trading partners for a devaluation of the currency by just enough, given knowledge of the relevant price and income elasticities, to move the intersection of the X and F lines to above y_0. In figure 9.2 (ii) this is shown to be achieved by a devaluation of the exchange rate to e', giving the lines $X(e')$ and $F(e')$. This devaluation

Figure 9.2   Simultaneous use of devaluation and fiscal policies to achieve internal and external balance

improves the international competitiveness of the nation's producers; that is, it lowers the terms of trade and lowers the relative price of the domestic output on the international market, so that exports rise and imports fall for any level of domestic income. The effect of this, however, is to cause the $C + I + G + X - F$ line to move upwards to $(C + I + G + X - F)$ (e'), in turn causing income to rise to y_2 and a deficit still to occur on current account. It is necessary, therefore, to adjust fiscal policy at the same time as the exchange rate is adjusted, if y_0 and a balance on current account are to be achieved together. Thus the $C + I + G + X - F$ line must be pulled back down to intersect with the 45° line in part (i) of the figure: this can be done, for an exchange rate of e', by reducing the level of government expenditure from G to G' as shown.[5]

Thus, simultaneous achievement of the internal and external targets would require a careful co-ordination of devaluation and a restrictive fiscal policy. In practice the restrictive fiscal policy would probably be justified by the monetary authorities arguing that, for the devaluation to succeed, it was necessary to ensure that domestic output be made available for export and not for home consumption, and also that it was necessary to prevent the devaluation from generating domestic inflation, which would offset the boost to the competitiveness of domestic producers given by the devaluation if it were allowed to occur.

Finally it should be noted that the actual adjustment of exports and imports to a devaluation is complicated by the fact that the response of supply and demand to the price change is slow. Thus, initially exports rise very little in response to their new lower price, whilst imports hardly fall even though they have become more expensive. This can mean that the balance on current account initially moves into a larger deficit position after a devaluation, and only improves once the relative price changes begin to cause demands to respond. A figure of the current account plotted over time would, in such a case, look like a letter J, and so this dynamic response to devaluation is often known as the J-curve effect. A successful combination of fiscal policy and devaluation would, therefore, require not only accurate knowledge of the parameters of the economy, but also strong nerves in the face of the initial current account deterioration.

Useful as it is, the Keynesian multiplier model of this section does have important weaknesses. For instance, it assumes that there are no capital account flows, which is unrealistic, and it therefore gives too much weight to current account imbalances.

There may be little, if anything, wrong with current account imbalances if they are financed by capital account flows. For example, a developing nation borrowing on capital account to finance current account deficits may well be doing the right thing if the imports are being used to develop natural resources and generate the finance to pay off the loans within an agreed time-scale. Also, the model neglects any stock effects and does not take account of the money market. The Monetarist approach to the balance of payments emphasizes that, eventually, balance of payments imbalances affect the domestic money stock and, thereby, produce forces which move the economy towards a balance on the balance of payments. It will be useful, therefore, to introduce the money stock into the argument. This is done in the next chapter using an *IS–LM* model, but before moving on to that more advanced model, it is worthwhile to examine the simple Keynesian multiplier model under flexible exchange rates.

9.5　The Simple Keynesian Multiplier Model of a Small Open Economy under Floating Exchange Rates

Consider the same model as in the previous section, but now let the exchange rate *e* be freely floating. In this case the exchange rate will be determined by the forces of supply and demand on the foreign exchange market. Assuming that the foreign exchange market works perfectly, the government need no longer worry about achieving a balance on current account. If at some exchange rate the demand for sterling on the foreign exchange market differs from the supply, then the exchange rate, that is the price of sterling, should automatically adjust until supply and demand are brought into equality with one another. The supply of sterling on the foreign exchange market is offered in exchange for foreign currency by UK residents wishing to buy imports, and the demand for sterling is by foreigners offering foreign currency in exchange for sterling with which to buy UK exports, so that equality of the supply and demand for sterling implies that the current account is in balance with the demand for exports equal to the demand for imports. In other words, the exchange rate should automatically adjust to bring about a balance on current account as well as on the foreign exchange market. In order to explain this process more fully, and to examine the relationship between fiscal policy and the exchange rate, it is necessary to extend the diagrammatic apparatus set up in the previous section.

The above arguments may be illustrated using figure 9.3. The figure looks quite complicated, but its interpretation is really quite straightforward. Consider quadrants (i) and (iv) first. Quadrant (i) shows two $C + I + G + X - F$ lines, both drawn for the common levels of government expenditure, G_0, and investment, I, but for different exchange rates, e_0 and e_1. At the exchange rate e_0 the equilibrium level of income would be y_0. Quadrant (iv) shows two pairs of X and F lines, one pair for the exchange rate e_0, and one for e_1. It is easy to see that for the exchange rate e_0 and income level y_0, the value of imports would exceed the value of exports, F_0 being greater than X_0 (both in sterling values). Thus, with government expenditure set at level G_0, equilibrium in quadrant (i) would not be consistent with a balance on current account in quadrant (iv) if the exchange rate were e_0. Under a fixed exchange rate system this would, in the short-run, imply that the central bank would be running down reserves (or borrowing from abroad) in

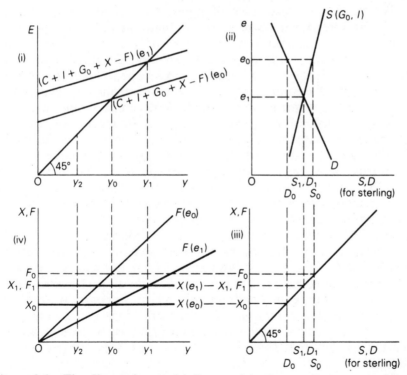

Figure 9.3 The Keynesian multiplier model of a small open economy under flexible exchange rates

order to provide the funds to pay for the excess value of imports over exports, and, in the long-run, that action must be taken to eliminate the deficit. However, under perfectly floating exchange rates the central bank would not intervene to provide the funds to finance such a deficit, which would not prevail even in the short-run. Instead, the exchange rate would adjust away from e_o until the values of export and import demands were brought into equality with one another. In the case of a deficit the exchange rate would fall. Let the new lower exchange rate consistent with a balance on the current account for the government expenditure level of G_0 be e_1. The depreciation to e_1 causes the X and F lines to move to $X(e_1)$ and $F(e_1)$ respectively in quadrant (iv), and the rise in exports and fall in imports for any income level causes the $C + I + G + X - F$ line to move upwards to $(C + I + G_0 + X - F)(e_1)$ in quadrant (i). (The slope of the $C + I + G + X - F$ line in quadrant (i) would also change, but this is not shown.) The new equilibrium income level in quadrant (i) is y_1, which is shown to be consistent with a balance on current account in quadrant (iv).

The remaining quadrants of figure 9.3 extend the analysis to cover the foreign exchange market. Quadrant (iii) has exports, X, and imports, F, measured on the vertical axis and the foreign exchange market supply, S, and demand, D, for the domestic currency, sterling, on the horizontal axis. The demand for sterling on the foreign exchange market is derived from the demands of the rest of the world for UK exports. With an exchange rate of e_0, export demand is for X_0 worth of exports (measured in sterling), as shown in quadrant (iv). Hence at e_0 the demand for sterling on the foreign exchange market, D_0, equals X_0. With common scales on the vertical and horizontal axes of quadrant (iii), the 45° line may be used to convert X_0 into D_0 by reading X_0 across from quadrant (iv) to quadrant (iii). The value for D_0 may then be transferred upwards into quadrant (ii), which shows the demand for sterling against the corresponding exchange rate, D_0 against e_0 in this case. This yields one point on the demand curve for sterling; another such point may be found by carrying out a similar exercise for the exchange rate e_1. Joining the locus of all such points would yield the D curve in quadrant (ii), which slopes downwards as shown under the assumption that, other things being equal, the demand for exports would rise as their price on the foreign market fell (remember that their price in terms of domestic currency is fixed).

The supply of the domestic currency, sterling, to the foreign exchange market is derived from the demand for imports by the domestic economy, the UK in this case. With an exchange rate of e_0, and government and investment spending of G_0 and I respectively, import demand is for F_0 worth of imports (measured in sterling), as shown in quadrant (iv). This value may be converted into the supply of sterling, S_0, equal to F_0, by reading across from quadrant (iii) to quadrant (iv) and using the 45° line. The value for S_0 may then be transferred upwards into quadrant (ii), which shows the supply of sterling against the corresponding exchange rate, S_0 against e_0 in this case. This yields one point on the supply curve of sterling; another such point may be found by carrying out a similar exercise for the exchange rate e_1. Joining the locus of all such points would yield the S curve in quadrant (ii). The S curve is drawn such that the supply of the domestic currency to the foreign exchange market falls as the domestic currency depreciates and imports become relatively expensive on the domestic market. This is not necessarily the case, but will depend upon the price and income elasticities of the demand for imports.[6, 7] Since the demand for imports at any exchange rate depends upon the level of domestic income, and this in turn depends upon the exogenous levels of investment and government expenditure, the position of the S line is dependent upon the levels of government expenditure and investment too, which is indicated by the G_0, I terms in the brackets accompanying the S line in the figure. For example, an increase in the level of government expenditure would cause an increase in domestic income at any exchange rate, and hence an increase in import demand and an increase in the supply of sterling on the foreign exchange market. The S line would, therefore, move right-wards if G were increased, so that an increase in G would reduce the market clearing value of the exchange rate on the foreign exchange market. The reader may verify this by working through the effects of an increase in G on the diagram, starting with the effects on the $C + I + G + X - F$ lines for e_0 and e_1.

Taken as a whole, figure 9.3 shows that with a level of government expenditure of G_0 the equilibrium level of income will be y_1, and that the exchange rate consistent with a balance on current account at this level of income will be e_1. If the exchange rate were at any other level, such as e_0, quadrant (ii) of the figure shows that the forces of supply and demand would cause the exchange rate to adjust, in this case downwards, towards equilibrium at e_1. This exchange rate adjustment would cause domestic output to adjust towards y_1 as the aggregate demand for domestic output responded to the exchange rate.

It is possible to show that if the government wished to achieve a level of domestic income in excess of y_1, it could do so by increasing G, but it would have to accept that this would bring about a devaluation of the domestic currency: the increase in G would cause income to rise and, hence, the current account to worsen (as import demand rises with income), therefore a reduction in the exchange rate would be needed to restore balance to the current account.

The interested reader ought to be able to work out the effects on the equilibrium levels of domestic income of changes in the level of real income in the rest of the world, or of changes in the domestic or foreign price levels, by working through the effects of such changes on the lines in the figure. Notice that the figure may also be used for analysis under the assumption of fixed exchange rates. For instance, if the fixed exchange rate is e_0 and the level of government expenditure is G_0, the level of domestic income will be y_0 and there will be a current account deficit of $(F_0 - X_0)$, or equivalently of $(S_0 - D_0)$. This excess supply of sterling to the foreign exchange market will require the central bank, the Bank of England in this case, to purchase sterling to the value of $(S_0 - D_0)$ to support the exchange rate e_0. In exchange for this sterling, the Bank of England would have to provide dollars and, hence, its reserves of foreign currency would fall (unless it restored them by borrowing from abroad). If the government wishes to persist with its expenditure level of G_0 then it must seek agreement, under the adjustable peg system, to devalue the currency to e_1, which would not only improve the current account position, but also cause income to rise to y_1.

The above analysis makes clear that under floating exchange rates the government need not concern itself with achieving a current account balance. It can set expenditure at any level it wishes, and let the exchange rate adjust to bring about a balance on current account. However, if the government wishes to target a level for the exchange rate, then, just as under a fixed exchange rate system, it would have to adjust the level of government expenditure to that end. Imagine it wished to achieve the exchange rate e_0, then it would have to adjust the level of government expenditure until the level of domestic income generated import demand equal in value to export demand at e_0. The required level of income is shown to be y_2 in part (iv) of figure 9.3; achieving it would require reducing government expenditure to lower the $C + I + G + X - F$ line for the exchange rate e_0 until it intersected the 45° line above y_2 in quadrant (i).

In the absence of an exchange rate target, the freedom to let the exchange rate adjust to bring about a balance on the current account means that the government can achieve an internal target level of income by adjusting government expenditure without having to worry about the balance on current account or obtain agreement to adjust the exchange rate as under a fixed exchange rate system. This does not, however, mean that it can totally neglect the external sector of the economy, since the choice of the appropriate level of government expenditure to achieve an income level target must take into account the effect of changes in government expenditure on the exchange rate, and the repercussions of the resultant effects on exports and imports on the level of aggregate demand for domestic output. Indeed such effects enhance the power of fiscal policy since, from an initial position of current account balance, an expansionary fiscal policy would cause a depreciation which would boost the competitiveness of domestic products on both home and overseas markets, whilst a contractionary fiscal policy would cause an appreciation, and so damage competitiveness. Nevertheless, it would be easier under flexible exchange rates to adjust government expenditure by trial and error to achieve a given income target, whilst letting the exchange rate adjust to maintain current account balance, instead of having to repeatedly seek agreement for devaluation (or revaluation) as under fixed-but-adjustable exchange rates.

Such benefits of the floating exchange rate system must in practice be weighed against any damage done to international trade by the extra uncertainty created by fluctuating exchange rates. Also depreciation of the exchange rate may create inflationary pressures in the domestic economy, since it pushes up the price of imports. Therefore, the freedom to let the exchange rate adjust on the foreign exchange market is not gained without accepting a potential cost. Indeed it is possible to argue that a fixed exchange rate system provided a beneficial constraint on governments, concern over the balance of payments preventing them from following over-expansionary aggregate demand policies and, hence, preventing them from generating inflation (see Laidler, 1978 and 1986). Experience with floating exchange rates has involved considerable volatility of exchange rates, and has disappointed some of the proponents of the floating rate system. However the world has experienced several important economic shocks since the system was introduced, most notably the oil price rises in the 1970s, and governments have, at times, pursued widely divergent policies in response to them. In such circumstances, no pattern of exchange rates could have been expected to hold steady, and a fixed-but-adjustable exchange rate system may have fared little better: frequent exchange rate adjustments would have been required since governments seemed unwilling to sacrifice domestic policies to support stable exchange rates. In a stable world without large shocks and with stable government policies, the flexible exchange rate system may have fared much better. With such stability the benefits of a fixed-but-adjustable exchange rate system would seem much less, and without it such a system might have collapsed in any case.

Thus, the simple Keynesian model of the small open economy is a useful introduction to the macroeconomics of the open economy, and can help in understanding the links between the exchange rate system, government policies and macroeconomic variables in the real world. It is, however, a very simplified model. The following chapters develop models of the small open economy which allow analysis of a broader set of issues. The next chapter introduces the supply of money into the analysis by dealing with an open-economy version of the *IS–LM* model, which it is shown, also facilitates the introduction of capital flows into the picture.

Notes

1   This does not imply that governments placed no restrictions in the way of international transactions, indeed they often felt a need to do so, for example by limiting how much foreign currency a holidaymaker could buy before going abroad on holiday, and how much domestic currency he could take with him.

2   Obviously, in a world of many currencies the agreed parities had to be mutually compatible; for example, the rates between sterling and the dollar, and the dollar and the franc must be compatible with the rate between sterling and the franc. In simple numbers, if \$2 bought £1 and \$1 bought 1 fr. then 2 fr. must buy £1 – any other franc–sterling rate would imply that people could make money simply by buying and selling currencies to and from central banks. For example, consider how to make money if \$1 bought £1, \$1 bought 1 fr., and 2 fr. bought £1. For very small movements away from the agreed parities arbitrage transactions were not profitable, given dealing costs, hence exchange rates were, in fact, allowed to vary by 1 per cent on either side of the agreed values or parities.

3   Strictly, since £*P* is given, the demand for exports, measured in pounds sterling, must rise as long as the quantity sold rises. However, the sterling demand for imports could rise when sterling is devalued, since the sterling price of imports rises and, depending upon the price elasticity, this could more than offset the reduction in quantity of imports demanded. Thus, it can be argued that the current account balance will improve (that is, a deficit will decline or a surplus will increase) for any income level only if the price elasticities of demand

for imports and exports are sufficiently large. It is assumed in the text that the condition for this to be the case is satisfied.

4 Notice that since we are dealing with a two currency world we have to consider only one exchange rate. In the real world, with many currencies, it is possible for a currency to rise in value in terms of some currencies whilst falling in value in terms of others (especially under floating exchange rates). It is, therefore, common to discuss the effective or trade-weighted exchange rate. This takes into account the importance in trade, for the country concerned, of the different currencies for which its currency may be converted, to provide a kind of average expression of the relative value of its currency. Similarly, it is possible to set up a measure of the effective or trade-weighted terms of trade.

5 Actually the new line $(C + I + G' + X - F)$ (e') would have a different slope than the old line $(C + I + G + X - F)$ (e), but this is not shown, to avoid cluttering the diagram.

6 Since income rises, from y_0 to y_1 in quadrant (iv), as the exchange rate falls, this will tend to moderate the fall in import demand as a result of their price rise. Furthermore, since imports rise in price in sterling terms as the exchange rate falls, then a demand for fewer imports could involve an increase in expenditure on them, and that expenditure is the supply of sterling to the foreign exchange market.

The reader may show for himself that, given a downward sloping demand for sterling curve, the exchange rate will move towards its equilibrium value, from any disequilibrium value, so long as the exchange rate falls (rises) when there is excess supply of (demand for) sterling, and the supply curve is upward sloping or more steeply downward sloping than the demand curve. Alternatively, under an adjustable peg system such conditions would guarantee that a devaluation of the currency would lead to a smaller deficit or larger surplus on the current account, and vice versa for a revaluation.

7 Notice that the supply of sterling curve could be interpreted as the demand for dollars curve, since sterling is only supplied to the foreign exchange market by those who wish to obtain dollars in order to buy imports (in the real world these actions are, of course, usually carried out indirectly by banks and importers, and the consumers of imports do not actually go to the foreign exchange market themselves). Similarly, the demand for sterling curve may be interpreted as the supply of dollars curve. Also notice that although the supply and demand curve diagram in quadrant (ii) may be interpreted in a similar way to standard microeconomic supply and demand diagrams, the underlying derivation of the supply curve is rather different than in the standard microeconomic case. Specifically, the supply curve shows how the supply of sterling varies with its price (the exchange rate) after taking into account changes in income associated with changes in the exchange rate, whereas the supply curves drawn in standard microeconomic textbooks usually assume income to be given.

10

The *IS–LM–BP* Model of a Small Open Economy

This chapter performs three important tasks using the *IS–LM–BP* model of the small open economy. One task is to introduce the money supply into the analysis, another is to introduce capital flows. Section 10.1 presents the model under the assumption of a fixed-but-adjustable exchange rate system, whilst section 10.2 examines the floating exchange rate version of the model. In each case the simplifying assumptions of a fixed level of income and interest rate in the rest of the world, and constant domestic and overseas price levels, are maintained. Section 10.3 performs the third task, which is to introduce exchange rate expectations into the model.

10.1 Fixed-but-adjustable Exchange Rates

The closed-economy *IS–LM* model requires only minor modifications to make it suitable for open-economy analysis. Consider, first, the *IS* curve. The equilibrium condition for the goods market, namely, that planned injections equal planned withdrawals, is easily amended by recognizing that export demand is an injection into aggregate demand for domestic output, and import demand is a withdrawal. The equilibrium condition therefore becomes

$$S + T + F = I + G + X \tag{10.1}$$

where the export, X, and import, F, functions are considered to be identical to those discussed in the previous chapter. The effect of this is to increase the gradient of the *IS* curve in comparison to the closed-economy case, as may be explained with the help of figure 10.1.

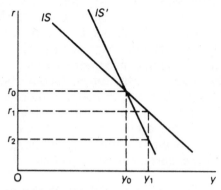

Figure 10.1   A comparison of *IS* curves for the closed and open economies

Figure 10.1 shows two *IS* curves, *IS* for the closed-economy case and *IS'* for the open-economy case. Consider the two economies to have identical savings, investment and taxation functions, and to have the same level of real government expenditure. They differ only in that one is closed and one is open. The relationship between the two curves may be explained as follows. Let y_0 be the level of income for which the open economy achieves a balance on current account for some exchange rate, say e_0. That is, at y_0, X equals F, where both X and F are measured in terms of the domestic currency. At the interest rate r_0, for which planned injections equal planned withdrawals given y_0, it, therefore, follows from equation (10.1) that

$$S + T = I + G \qquad\qquad (10.2)$$

Equation (10.2) is the equilibrium condition for the goods market in the closed economy (and is identical to equation (2.13) presented in chapter 2 on the closed economy). Therefore, the point $r_0 y_0$ is on the *IS* curves for both the closed and open economies.

Now consider an increase in the level of income to y_1, and, for the open economy, hold the exchange rate constant. In the closed economy this will cause an increase in withdrawals, since savings S, and taxation, T, may both be assumed to rise with income, necessitating a fall in the interest rate to r_1 to maintain goods market equilibrium by inducing a rise in investment to match the rise in withdrawals. For the open economy, however, the rise in withdrawals is greater as income rises to y_1, since in this case imports F, as well as savings, S, and taxation, T, rise. Equilibrium in the goods market will, therefore, now only be restored by a bigger fall in the interest rate, to r_2, to generate the bigger rise in investment needed to match the bigger rise in withdrawals (given that exports, X, and government expenditure, G, are both assumed to be independent of changes in either income, y, or the interest rate, r). Similarly, a given reduction in income below y_0 requires a bigger rise in the interest rate to maintain goods market equilibrium for the open-economy *IS* curve, than is needed for the closed-economy curve. Thus the open-economy *IS* curve is steeper than the closed-economy *IS* curve, and they intersect at the level of income which achieves current account balance for the open economy.

Changes in the exchange rate will affect the position of the *IS* curve for the open economy. A devaluation or depreciation of the domestic currency may be assumed to cause exports, X, to rise and imports, F, to fall for any given level of domestic income, thus reducing withdrawals and increasing injections. Restoring equality between injections and withdrawals will then require either an increase in income, to cause withdrawals to rise, or an increase in the interest rate, to cause injections to fall, or some mixture of both. In other words, the *IS* curve will shift away from the origin in response to a devaluation or depreciation. Similarly, the position of the open-economy *IS* curve depends on other factors held constant in the above discussion, such as the domestic and foreign price levels, changes in which would affect both export and import functions. Of course, the factors discussed in the closed-economy model earlier in this book, such as the level of government expenditure, G, still continue to have their usual impact on the *IS* curve in the open-economy case.

Appendix 10.1 presents a diagrammatic derivation of an open-economy *IS* curve, similar to the derivation for the closed-economy case in appendix 2.1. Using the diagrammatic apparatus presented in the appendix, the interested reader ought to be able to work out the effects upon the position of the *IS* curve of changes in any of the factors just mentioned.

Now consider the *LM* curve in the open-economy case. The extension that is necessary within the *IS–LM–BP* model is to recognize that the domestic money supply is altered by overall balance of payments deficits or surpluses unless specific government policy action is taken to offset such effects. Imagine the domestic economy to be running a surplus on the overall balance of payments. This means that domestic residents are receiving more foreign currency from the sales of exports plus net capital flows than they are spending on imports. Assume that the domestic residents do not hold foreign currency, but sell it to the government in exchange for domestic currency at the fixed exchange rate. The result of the overall balance of payments surplus is, thus, to increase the reserves of foreign currency held by the domestic government, and to increase the domestic money supply in the hands of domestic residents. Similarly, an overall balance of payments deficit causes a decline in government reserve holdings and a decline in the domestic money supply.

The effects of overall balance of payments imbalances on the domestic money supply may be offset by appropriate open-market operations, that is, by the sale of bonds to withdraw the extra money from circulation when there is a balance of payments surplus, and vice versa. Such a policy is known as 'sterilization', and the alternative policy of allowing imbalances on the overall balance of payments to have an impact on the domestic money supply is known as 'non-sterilization'.

It would now be possible to use the *IS–LM* model to examine open-economy issues before going on to introduce capital flows into the picture. However, it is worthwhile to postpone using the model until capital flows have been introduced. This will avoid some repetition and, since capital flows are important in the real world, enable the discussion to be based around the more realistic version of the model. In any case, the reader ought to be able to work out the implications of excluding capital flows from the analysis once he has understood the workings of the model including them.

Capital flows may be introduced into the model by assuming that capital is injected into the domestic economy from overseas if the domestic interest rate is above that in the rest of the world, and vice versa. The logic behind modelling the capital account in this way is, quite simply, that investors transfer their funds from one country to another in response to the relative yields their investments will produce.[1,2] The workings of the capital account under this assumption may be illustrated using figure 10.2.

The vertical axis of figure 10.2 shows the domestic interest rate, and the horizontal axis shows the net capital account position, *NK*. Two capital account lines are drawn. The upward sloping line represents a situation of imperfect capital mobility. It shows that if the interest rate on assets invested in the domestic economy, r, is equal to r^*, the interest rate in the rest of the world (which is assumed to be given exogenously), capital neither flows into nor out of the domestic economy. If the domestic interest rate diverges

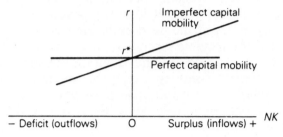

Figure 10.2   The capital account

from that in the rest of the world then capital flows in or out, depending on whether r exceeds or falls below r^*.

The greater the response of capital flows to a given interest differential, the nearer to the horizontal becomes the capital account line. In the extreme case of perfect capital mobility, the capital account line becomes horizontal at the interest rate r^*. In this case investors treat domestic and foreign assets as perfect substitutes for one another, so that any difference between the domestic and foreign interest rates would induce such enormous capital flows that the difference would be eliminated immediately.[3] For example, if the interest rate in the domestic economy rose above that in the rest of the world there would be such an inflow of capital that the domestic interest rate would immediately be returned to the same level as in the rest of the world, as the domestic money supply rose in response to the capital inflow and caused the domestic interest rate to fall.

In the real world capital is, indeed, highly mobile, especially between the developed market economies. The extreme case of perfect capital mobility, therefore, may provide a reasonable approximation to reality. The reader may wonder then why it is that in the real world interest rates so obviously differ from one economy to another? The answer is that, especially in a world of flexible exchange rates which frequently change, it is necessary to recognize that expectations of exchange rate changes are as important as interest differentials in driving the capital account. The reason for this is that an investor deciding where to allocate his funds to achieve the best return must consider not only the interest payments he will receive on those funds, but also any capital gains or losses brought about by changes in the interest rate or the exchange rate. Investors, therefore, have an incentive to form expectations about interest rate or exchange rate changes in an attempt to maximize total returns on their funds. The role of expectations about exchange rate changes will be dealt with in section 10.3 below; for now they may be safely neglected since they do not affect the comparative static results to be derived in this, and the following, section.

The importance of adding capital flows to the model stems from the fact that they make it possible to achieve an overall balance of payments balance without having a balance on current account. It becomes possible to support a given exchange rate without having to accept whatever level of domestic income is consistent with a balance on current account for that exchange rate. A current account deficit (or surplus) may now be financed out of an equal capital account surplus (or deficit) – all that is needed is that the domestic interest rate be adjusted to ensure the appropriate level of capital inflows (or outflows) is achieved. This argument is illustrated using figure 10.3.

Figure 10.3 shows two lines, *BP* and *BP'*, in interest-income space, and also shows a *BOCA* line. The interpretation of the *BOCA* line is simple and follows that given in the previous chapter. It is drawn vertically above the level of income, y_0, for which the current account is in balance given the exchange rate e_0. Interpretation of the *BP* lines is only slightly more complicated. They show the relationship between the level of domestic income and the domestic interest rate necessary for the overall balance of payments to balance, the line *BP* representing the case of imperfect capital mobility and the line *BP'* representing the case of perfect capital mobility. Consider the line *BP* first. It passes through the point

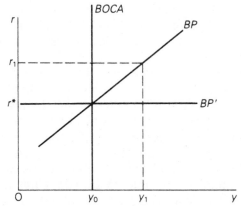

Figure 10.3   The *BP* curve

r^*y_0, since at y_0 the current account is in balance, therefore overall balance requires a capital account balance too, which occurs when the domestic interest rate equals that in the rest of the world, r^*. Now consider the higher level of domestic income, y_1. At this level of income, given the exchange rate e_0, the current account will be in deficit since imports will have risen as income rose from y_0 to y_1, but exports will have remained constant. Therefore, an overall balance of payments balance now requires a capital account surplus just big enough to offset the current account deficit. From figure 10.2 it is clear that this requires that the domestic interest rate be higher than r^*, say r_1. The point r_1y_1 is, therefore, on the *BP* line. Similarly for levels of income below y_0, it is clear that an overall balance of payments requires capital account deficits to offset current account surpluses, so that the domestic interest rate falls below r^* as income falls below y_0 along the *BP* line. Thus the *BP* line slopes upwards from left to right for the case of imperfect capital mobility.

From the above discussion, it is clear that the slope and position of the *BP* curve depend upon the interaction of the import and export demand functions as drawn in the previous chapter and the current account line drawn in figure 10.2. Any of the factors which shift any of these lines will cause the *BP* line to shift. For instance, a devaluation of the exchange rate which caused the export and import functions to shift and the *BOCA* line to move rightwards, would move the *BP* line rightwards too. For instance, if y_1 became the level of income consistent with a balance on current account, then r^*y_1 would be on the new *BP* line. Other factors which would move the *BP* line rightwards would be a reduction in the domestic price level or a rise in the foreign price level, a rise in the income level in the rest of the world, or a fall in the interest rate in the rest of the world.[4] Opposite changes would, of course, move the *BP* line leftwards. Appendix 10.2 provides a diagrammatic derivation of the *BP* line, and the interested reader ought to try to work out for himself why the *BP* line would move in the ways just stated, and check his reasoning by carefully tracing through the effects of the changes mentioned using the diagrammatic framework.

The line *BP'* for the perfect capital mobility case is horizontal at the interest rate r^*, under the assumption that any divergence between the domestic and rest-of-the-world interest rate would be eliminated by enormous capital flows. In other words, the domestic economy is assumed to be able to borrow (that is run a capital account surplus) or lend (that is run a capital account deficit) exactly enough to offset any current account imbalance without the domestic interest rate moving away from r^*. The position of the *BP* line in this case depends only on the interest rate in the rest of the world, r^*; the line moves up or down as r^* moves up or down.

Notice that current account imbalances are no longer necessarily a problem now that they may be financed by offsetting capital account imbalances. They may be looked upon in a similar way to an individual running up an overdraft at the bank, that is as borrowing which may be helpful so long as it does not become too big a debt to be paid off in the future. Indeed, just as an individual might be happy to run up an infinite overdraft were it not for the fact that some day he would be expected to pay it off, then a nation might be happy to run current account deficits forever – which after all means that it is receiving more from overseas in the form of imports than it is paying for by its exports – were it not for the fact that it will at the same time be running up debts on the capital account, or spending its reserves of foreign currency.

Thus a current account deficit is only a problem when it implies that the deficit nation is getting into debt at a greater rate than is desirable, given that the debt must be serviced in the future. On the other hand, a current account surplus is not necessarily desirable since it implies that the surplus nation is swopping its current output of goods and services for assets, which may be looked upon as similar to saving by an individual – obviously in some circumstances saving is desirable, but it is possible to save too much and spend too little, especially if the saving is in foreign currency denominated assets which might fall in value if the foreign currency depreciates. In conclusion, an imbalance on the current account may only be deemed to be a problem if it is different than the optimal, or most desirable, imbalance given a nation's planned allocation of consumption and investment expenditure over time; an imbalance cannot be deemed necessarily to be a problem. The reader should note that it is not possible to define a current account deficit to be a problem when it is used to finance consumption but all right when it is used to finance investment; rather whether it is a problem or not depends on whether it is helping the nation to reallocate expenditure patterns in a better manner than in the absence of the deficit, or not.

With these preliminaries understood, it is now possible to bring the *IS*, *LM* and *BP* lines together to form the *IS–LM–BP* model of a small open economy under fixed-but-adjustable exchange rates. A number of interesting points may be illustrated using the model. Consider, first of all, an argument stressed by the Monetarist approach to the balance of payments: that overall balance of payments imbalances eventually affect the domestic money supply and thereby produce forces which automatically move the economy towards overall balance of payments balance. There is, according to this argument, no need for deliberate policy or exchange rate adjustment to secure overall balance on the balance of payments: any imbalance would automatically be self-righting. The argument may be illustrated using figure 10.4 (although the Monetarist argument was often put in terms of models where prices adjust, rather than income adjusting as here. See, for example, Johnson, 1972b.)

Figure 10.4 shows two *BP* lines, one for the case of perfect capital mobility and one for the case of imperfect capital mobility. Notice that the line *BP*, for the case of imperfect capital mobility, is drawn less steeply than the *LM* curves shown. This is to reflect the idea that, even with imperfect capital mobility, capital flows are more sensitive to interest rate changes than is the demand for money. Reversing this idea would reverse the relative steepness of the slopes of the lines and would have implications for some of the discussion to follow below, as could easily be checked by simply redrawing the lines and tracing through the arguments.

Imagine the economy to be operating, initially, at point A in the diagram, at $r_0 y_0$ for a given exchange rate e_0, and consider capital to be imperfectly mobile. The line *BP* indicates that for the overall balance of payments to balance at an income level of y_0, the domestic interest rate would need to be r_1. However, at point A the interest rate is r_0, which is less than r_1. Thus, net capital inflows will be less than those required to produce an overall balance of payments balance; instead there will be a deficit. Similar arguments

Figure 10.4　Automatic balance of payments adjustment

could be used to show that all points below the BP line represent overall balance of payments deficits, whilst all points above the line represent overall balance of payments surpluses. Running an overall balance of payments deficit under a fixed exchange rate system implies that the domestic central bank must be losing international reserves, that is running down its stocks of foreign currency or gold, or increasing its borrowing from overseas. The impact of the overall balance of payments deficit on the domestic money supply could be offset by a policy of sterilization in the short-run, but eventually the central bank would run out of reserves and find itself unable to borrow from abroad, if it tried to keep the economy at point A in the face of persistent overall balance of payments deficits. Therefore something will have to be done to resolve the situation.

The Monetarist approach to the balance of payments argues that all that needs to be done to restore balance to the overall balance of payments at the given exchange rate e_0 is for the central bank to end its policy of sterilization. Sterilization is, in any case, not feasible in the long-run in the face of persistent imbalances, and should only be used to offset erratic short-term balance of payments fluctuations. Once sterilization ends, the overall balance of payments deficits will automatically reduce the domestic money supply and cause the LM curve to move leftwards. This leftward movement will continue as long as the overall balance of payments deficits continue, that is until the LM curve has been moved to LM_1, and the $IS–LM$ intersection is on the BP curve at point B. At point B, like any other point on the BP curve, the overall balance of payments is in balance, in this case with a current account surplus offsetting the capital account deficit, following from the domestic interest rate being less than the rate in the rest of the world, r^*.

The story would be very similar under conditions of perfect capital mobility, except that under those conditions sterilization would not be possible even in the short-run. In the absence of capital controls currency would flood out of the domestic economy if it ever tried to operate at a point like A in figure 10.4, with an interest rate below that available to investors in the rest of the world. The domestic money supply would rapidly shrink and move the LM curve leftwards to a point, C, of $IS–LM$ intersection on the line BP^1. This intersection must, in this case, be at the interest rate r^* and requires a bigger leftward shift of the LM curve, to LM_2, than for the imperfect capital mobility case.

The preceding discussion highlights the argument that the money supply has an important role to play in open economy analysis, and shows that under fixed exchange rates there will, in the absence of sterilization, be forces operating automatically to restore balance to the overall balance of payments. The next chapter will qualify this latter point, but for the moment even total acceptance of both points does not necessarily imply that the government should refrain from sterilization and let automatic adjustment of the money supply cure any balance of payments problem. What if the government has an internal target of the income level y_0 in figure 10.4? Clearly the automatic solution to the balance of payments problem would be unsatisfactory, since the resulting income level, y_1 or y_2 depending on the relevant BP line, would be below the target value. However, unlike the model in the previous chapter, the present model allows simultaneous achievement of internal and external balance without any need to adjust the exchange rate. The appropriate aggregate demand policies are illustrated using figure 10.5.

To avoid clutter, figure 10.5 is drawn for the case of imperfect capital mobility only. The analysis under perfect capital mobility is very similar and may be easily worked out once figure 10.5 has been understood. Imagine the economy to be operating at point A in the figure at the intersection of the IS_0, LM_0 and BP lines. The interest rate is r_0, the income level is y_1 and the overall balance of payments is in balance. However, point A is not consistent with the government's internal target of the income level y_0. The significance of capital flows for the analysis is that y_0 can be achieved without devaluing the exchange rate to offset the worsening of the current account (either a smaller surplus or bigger deficit) as

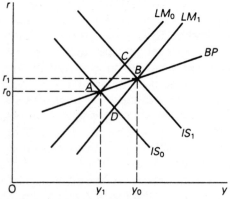

Figure 10.5   Internal and external balance

imports rise when income moves from y_1 to y_0. There is no need to devalue the exchange rate since, instead, the domestic interest rate may be increased to r_1 to keep the economy on the *BP* line. The rise in the interest rate causes the capital account to improve (either a bigger surplus or smaller deficit) to offset exactly the worsening of the current account. All that aggregate demand management must do is move the *IS–LM* intersection from *A* to *B* on the *BP* line. Note that this argument would not follow if capital flows were excluded from the analysis, in which case simultaneous achievement of internal and external targets would, as in the previous chapter, require devaluation.

Notice that the movement from *A* to *B* requires an adjustment of both fiscal policy, to move the *IS* curve to IS_1, and of the domestic money supply, to move the *LM* curve to LM_1. This illustrates the use of two policies, fiscal and monetary, to achieve two targets. Success of the joint use of the two policies is possible since they have differential impacts on the two targets, that is for a given change in income they offer different changes in the domestic interest rate and, hence, in the balance of payments. Therefore, appropriate adjustment of the two policies allows simultaneous achievement of internal and external targets. It is important to point out, however, that in this model the government may use fiscal policy on its own as an effective instrument to achieve both internal and external targets simultaneously, whilst monetary policy used on its own will eventually be totally ineffective.

The relative efficacy of fiscal and monetary policy may also be illustrated using figure 10.5. Consider fiscal policy first. Starting from point *A*, an expansionary fiscal policy which moves the *IS* curve to IS_1, under a policy of sterilization to hold the domestic money supply constant, will initially move the economy to point *C*. At point *C* the economy will be running an overall balance of payments surplus. Eventually, although obviously it is easier to run a surplus and build up reserves than it is to run a deficit and run down reserves, the government will have to cease sterilizing and let the domestic money supply rise. This will cause the *LM* curve to drift rightwards until it reaches LM_1, by which time the *IS–LM* intersection will have moved to point *B* on the *BP* curve, and the overall balance of payments will once again balance. Thus, fiscal policy is effective in the short-run with sterilization, and even more effective in the long-run when the domestic money supply is allowed to adjust. This money supply adjustment reduces the domestic interest rate associated with a fiscal expansion and so moderates the crowding-out of private investment normally associated with fiscal policy, which, in turn, increases the impact of the policy on income.[5] It also follows that a government wishing to move from *A* to *B* along the *BP* line could actively adjust both its fiscal and monetary policies to shift the *IS*, *LM* curves to IS_1 and LM_1, or it could actively adjust its fiscal policy only, and let the domestic money supply adjust passively to the resultant balance of payments forces on it. Thus adjusting fiscal policy carefully and letting the domestic money supply adjust to external forces can achieve an income target and an overall balance of payments balance simultaneously.

Now consider a government which tried to use monetary policy without at the same time adjusting its fiscal policy. Starting from point *A* again, an expansionary monetary policy which shifted the *LM* curve to LM_1 would cause the *IS–LM* intersection to move to point *D*. At point *D* the economy would be running an overall balance of payments deficit. The effect of this deficit on the domestic money supply may be sterilized in the short-run, but eventually the domestic money supply would have to be allowed to shrink, as continued sterilization would cause the country to run out of reserves of international currency as the overall deficits drained them overseas. Once sterilization ceased the domestic money supply would go on shrinking until the *LM* curve returned to LM_0 and the economy to point *A*. Thus, monetary policy is effective in the short-run with sterilization, but totally ineffective in the long-run unless it is accompanied by changes in the exchange rate or fiscal policy.

Similar conclusions for the effectiveness of fiscal or monetary policy follow under conditions of perfect capital mobility, except in that case sterilization is not possible even in the short-run. It follows that fiscal policy is very powerful even in the short-run, and even more so than indicated above, since the interest rate does not rise at all, so that there is no crowding-out of investment as a result of the policy. On the other hand, monetary policy on its own becomes totally ineffective even in the short-run.

The ineffectiveness of monetary policy, brought about by the impact of overall balance of payments imbalances on the domestic money supply, indicates that under fixed exchange rates the domestic government loses control over its monetary policy unless it is willing to sacrifice either fiscal policy or the exchange rate to its monetary policy. That is to say, in figure 10.5 a government wishing to adjust its monetary policy to shift the *LM* curve from LM_0 to LM_1 must be prepared either to adjust fiscal policy to maintain the overall balance of payments in balance, that is move the *IS* curve to IS_1 given the line BP, or else to adjust the exchange rate. Under imperfect capital mobility, adjusting the exchange rate would move both the IS and BP lines. The appropriate adjustment necessary to support the new monetary policy would require devaluing the exchange rate to such a level that the new IS and BP lines, which would both move rightwards after a devaluation, intersected one another somewhere along LM_1, in between points B and D. (Under perfect capital mobility, devaluation would move the IS curve but not the BP line, but the argument would not otherwise be affected.)

Given the above discussion the reader ought to be able to work out the effects of such things as a devaluation of the exchange rate, or a change in any of the factors held constant above, that is the domestic and foreign price levels, and the foreign income level and interest rate. It is also possible to show that, under imperfect capital mobility, the government may, in the long-run, choose values for any two of the following list of variables, providing that it knows all the parameters of the $IS–LM–BP$ model and is willing to accept the appropriate values for the remainder of the list: fiscal policy (that is expenditure and/or taxation policy), monetary policy, the domestic income level, the domestic interest rate, and the exchange rate. Under perfect capital mobility the domestic interest rate becomes equal to the foreign interest rate and the government may no longer exercise any choice or control over it. The analysis above has shown how the government may choose to achieve an exchange rate target and an income level target, and the analysis of how to achieve any other combination of targets would be similar. It would, however, be excessively tedious to present the analysis for each possible pair of targets here. It will be more instructive to go on to consider the $IS–LM–BP$ model under floating exchange rates in the next section, and then go on to further develop the model in the next chapter.

10.2   Flexible Exchange Rates

The switch from fixed to flexible exchange rates has considerable policy implications in the $IS–LM–BP$ model. As the discussion in the previous chapter made clear, the government no longer needs to worry about supporting a fixed exchange rate, or to gain international agreement for exchange rate adjustment. Furthermore, the conclusions reached in the previous section about the efficacy of fiscal and monetary policy must be amended, and for the case of perfect capital mobility, reversed.

The reason for revising policy conclusions is to be found in the behaviour of the domestic money supply and the *LM* curve. Under fixed exchange rates the domestic money supply adjusts, in the short-run under perfect capital mobility and in the long-run under imperfect capital mobility, to overall balance of payments imbalances, but under flexible exchange rates such imbalances do not occur. Under flexible exchange rates the central bank does not intervene in the foreign exchange market to buy or sell currency to support the exchange rate, instead it stands back and lets the exchange rate adjust to equate supply and demand for the domestic currency. The overall balance of payments is, therefore, in the absence of central bank intervention, always balanced and the domestic money supply is not subjected to changes arising from balance of payments imbalances.

In terms of the *IS–LM–BP* diagrams, under fixed exchange rates the *LM* curve shifts, eventually at least, until it cuts the *IS* curve where it cuts the *BP* line, which makes fiscal policy powerful and monetary policy ineffective. Under flexible exchange rates, domestic monetary policy determines the position of the *LM* curve, and it is the *IS* and, under imperfect capital mobility, the *BP* curves which must shift until all three lines intersect at a common point. The *IS* and *BP* shifts are brought about by exchange rate changes and mean that under flexible exchange rates monetary policy regains its effectiveness, whilst fiscal policy is weakened and, under perfect capital mobility, becomes completely ineffective. These policy conclusions may be clarified with the aid of figures 10.6 and 10.7 below.

Figure 10.6 shows how monetary policy is effective under flexible exchange rates. Imagine the economy to be initially in equilibrium at point A on the curves LM_0, and $IS(e_0)$ and $BP(e_0)$ for the exchange rate e_0. Since the *BP* line slopes upwards this implies that capital mobility is imperfect; the perfect mobility case will be dealt with later. Now consider that the government decides to carry out an open market purchase of bonds to increase the domestic money supply and move the *LM* curve to LM_1. If the exchange rate remained at e_0 the *LM* shift would imply a movement of the *IS–LM* intersection from point A to point B, with a rise in income to y_1 brought about as a result of the rise in investment expenditure as the interest rate fell from r_0 to r_1. However, point B lies below the *BP* (e_0) line and would imply an overall balance of payments deficit as a result of imports rising with income and the capital account deteriorating as the interest rate fell. The economy will not, however, move to point B and the balance of payments deficit will not

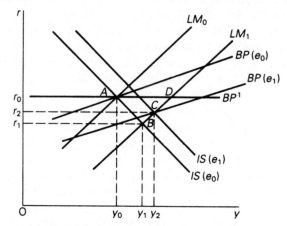

Figure 10.6 Monetary policy under flexible exchange rates

occur, but instead the exchange rate will depreciate to remove the balance of payments deficit. The depreciation will cause the *IS* and *BP* curves to move rightwards. The new equilibrium exchange rate, e_1, will be that which causes the *IS* and *BP* curves to intersect at a point like *C* on the curve LM_1. At the new exchange rate, e_1, the overall balance of payments is balanced and the power of monetary policy has been increased by the movements in *IS* and *BP* which it brings about. Notice that the interest rate, r_2, at point *C* is higher than the interest rate, r_1, at point *B*, therefore the positive impact of monetary policy on investment expenditure is lessened by the depreciation of the currency, although not eliminated, since r_2 is, like r_1, less than r_0. However, the effects of the smaller rise in investment are more than offset by the expansionary effects upon income of the depreciation of the exchange rate.

Notice that under imperfect capital mobility the point *C* would certainly involve a lower interest rate than point *A*, since the *BP* curve must, under the usual assumptions about the response of exports and imports to depreciation, move rightwards further than the *IS* curve in response to a depreciation and, hence, given the slopes of the two lines the interest rate must fall. The strength of the rightwards shifts can be seen by considering how far to the right of point *A* must lie the points on the new $IS(e_1)$ and BP (e_1) lines for the interest rate r_0. In each case the depreciation causes exports to rise and imports to fall for the initial income level, so that the new *IS* point for r_0 needs income to rise to restore equality between injections and withdrawals, whilst the new *BP* point requires income to rise to cause imports to rise to restore the current account to the same level of surplus or deficit as at point *A* (the capital account and investment being held constant by the constant interest rate). Equality between injections and withdrawals is restored for a lower increase in income than is required to restore the current account position, since the latter relies entirely on imports rising to match the rise in exports and fall in imports at the initial income level, whilst the former relies on imports plus savings plus taxes rising to match the rise in exports and initial fall in imports.

Also notice that if capital were perfectly mobile, then the domestic interest rate would be fixed at the world rate of interest and the *BP* line would be horizontal at that rate of interest. Therefore, monetary policy under perfect capital mobility works entirely through its effects on the exchange rate; even so it is more powerful than under imperfect capital mobility.[6] Let the world rate of interest be r_0 in figure 10.6 and the relevant *BP* line be BP^1. In this case the effect of a monetary expansion which shifted the *LM* curve from LM_0 to LM_1 would require a bigger depreciation of the exchange rate to restore the overall balance of payments to balance at point *D*. The interest rate cannot fall below r_0 in equilibrium and the higher equilibrium interest rate, compared to the imperfect capital mobility case, requires a higher level of domestic income to restore equality between the supply and demand for money. The higher level of income is achieved by a bigger depreciation, giving a bigger boost to the competitiveness of domestic industry.

The impact of fiscal policy under floating exchange rates is illustrated using figure 10.7.

Imagine the economy to be initially in equilibrium at point *A* for the exchange rate e_0 at the intersection of the lines LM_0, $IS(e_0)$ and $BP(e_0)$. Since the *BP* line slopes upwards this implies that capital mobility is less than perfect; the perfect mobility case will be dealt with later. Now consider that the government carries out an expansionary fiscal policy, say a bond-financed increase in government expenditure. If the exchange rate remained at e_0, this policy would shift the *IS* curve to $IS^1(e_0)$ and the *IS–LM* intersection to point *B*, with income and the domestic interest rate rising to y_1 and r_1 respectively. Point *B* lies above the *BP* line, and would imply an overall balance of payments surplus (as a result of the interest rate and net capital account inflows rising faster than necessary to offset the rise in imports as income rises). The economy will not, however, move to point *B*, and the overall balance of

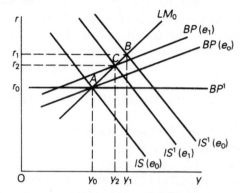

Figure 10.7 Fiscal policy under flexible exchange rates

payments surplus will not occur; instead the exchange rate will appreciate to remove the surplus. The appreciation will cause the IS and BP curves to move leftwards. The new equilibrium exchange rate, e_1, will be that which causes the IS and BP curves to intersect at a point like C on the curve LM_0. Notice that the horizontal distance between the old and new BP lines, $BP(e_0)$ and $BP(e_1)$, exceeds that between the old and new IS^1 lines, $IS^1(e_0)$ and $IS^1(e_1)$, for reasons similar to those used to explain the relative size of the IS and BP line shifts in response to a depreciation, earlier in this section. Comparing point C with point B, it is clear that the power of fiscal policy to expand income has been reduced by the appreciation which is a by-product of the policy. Although the crowding-out of investment is moderated since the interest rate rise is moderated, the power of fiscal policy is reduced because the associated appreciation reduces the competitiveness of domestic industry, crowds-out exports and encourages imports.

If capital mobility were perfect and the relevant BP line in figure 10.7 was the line BP^1, then, again starting from point A and carrying out an expansionary fiscal policy, point C would no longer represent the new equilibrium, but would be a point of enormous capital inflows and overall balance of payments surplus. A new equilibrium would require a much bigger appreciation of the exchange rate to pull the IS curve back to the intersection between the original IS, LM and BP^1 lines at point A, since neither the LM nor BP curves shift in response to depreciation in this case. Thus, the IS curve at the new equilibrium exchange rate, say, e_2, would need to be pulled back so far as to make fiscal policy totally ineffective in this case. Since the interest rate is pegged at the same rate as that in the rest of the world, r_0 in figure 10.7, there would be no crowding-out of investment. What makes fiscal policy ineffective in this case is the crowding-out of exports and encouragement of imports due to the appreciation of the exchange rate.[7]

10.3   Expectations and the Foreign Exchange Market

The analysis so far has focused upon interest rate differentials between the domestic economy and the rest of the world as the driving force behind the capital account. This is fine for the comparative static analysis carried out above; however, in any dynamic analysis, it becomes necessary to recognize that expectations of exchange rate changes are as important as interest differentials in driving the capital account. The reason for this has been mentioned earlier: an investor deciding where to allocate his funds to achieve the best return must consider not only the interest payments he will receive on those funds, but also any capital gains or losses brought about by changes in the interest rate or the exchange rate. Investors, therefore, have an incentive to form expectations about interest rate or exchange rate changes in an attempt to maximize total returns on their funds. Imagine that the financial assets which give rise to capital account flows are of the fixed nominal value, variable interest rate type, and that they are denominated in terms of either domestic or foreign currency. In this case there will be no capital gains or losses associated with interest payments, but there may still be capital gains or losses due to exchange rate changes. In terms of the domestic currency, the return on an asset denominated in the domestic currency is simply the interest yield, but the return on an asset denominated in the foreign currency is the interest yield plus a capital gain or loss due to any exchange rate change. For instance, if the interest rate on foreign currency denominated assets were 5 per cent per annum, and domestic currency depreciated by 5 per cent over the year, then the total yield of the asset in terms of the domestic currency would be 10 per cent; that is, a 5 per cent interest yield plus, in terms of the domestic currency, a 5 per cent capital gain. Another way of looking at this would be in terms of the total return measured in terms of the foreign currency, in which case the return on the foreign currency denominated asset would be 5 per cent, whilst that on the domestic currency denominated asset would be its interest yield, say 10 per cent, less the rate of depreciation of the domestic currency, 5 per cent, which gives a total yield of 5 per cent in terms of the foreign currency compared with 10 per cent in terms of the domestic currency.

The impact of such considerations can be seen most clearly under the flexible exchange rate model, and under the following simplifying assumptions. First, assume that the risk of default on foreign or domestic currency denominated assets is zero, and that they are viewed as perfect substitutes for one another by investors who are risk-neutral and continuously place their funds in those assets which they expect to yield the highest total return; that is, assume perfect capital mobility. In this case investors or speculators will be indifferent between holding assets denominated in domestic or foreign currencies only when the interest differential between domestic and foreign denominated assets is just offset by the expected rate of appreciation or depreciation of the domestic currency. In other words, perfect capital mobility now means that speculators are indifferent between assets denominated in either the domestic or foreign currencies when both offer the same total return (measured in terms of either currency). In terms of the above example, the total return on both assets is equal at 10 per cent in terms of the domestic currency (or 5 per cent in terms of the foreign currency) and speculators would be indifferent as to which type of asset they held. For speculators to be so indifferent the following condition must hold:

$$r^* = r + \dot{e} \qquad\qquad\qquad (10.3)$$

where r^* is the nominal interest rate on foreign currency denominated assets, r is the nominal interest rate on domestic currency denominated assets, and $\dot{e}$ is the expected proportional rate of change per annum of the exchange rate. Remember that the exchange rate is defined as the foreign currency price of a unit of domestic currency, so that $\dot{e}$ is positive if the domestic currency appreciates, and negative if it depreciates.[8]

Assume that the exchange rate is a spot price set on an efficient auction market which continuously clears to equate supply and demand, in which case the exchange rate will continuously adjust to satisfy equation (10.3). In equilibrium $\dot{e}$ will be zero, so equation (10.3) implies that under perfect capital mobility the foreign and domestic nominal interest rates will be equal in equilibrium, which is the condition that has been used in the comparative static analysis above. Out of equilibrium, however, equation (10.3) makes clear that even under conditions of perfect capital mobility the domestic and foreign nominal interest rates may diverge.

Finally, assume that the domestic nominal interest rate always adjusts to clear the domestic money market, that out of equilibrium the level of domestic output adjusts positively but slowly in response to excess demand, that speculators form rational expectations of exchange rate changes (or strictly, have perfect foresight, which is the deterministic counterpart of rational expectations) and that, as usual, the foreign and domestic price levels, and the foreign interest rate and real income levels are all held constant. The assumption of perfect foresight implies that, except for times at which new policies are announced, the behaviour of the economy is perfectly predicted by speculators. Under these, and the other assumptions already made, the significance of expectations may be illustrated using figure 10.8 to examine the results of a sudden and unexpected monetary expansion by the domestic monetary authorities.

Part (i) of figure 10.8 shows the now familiar *IS–LM–BP* diagram, but where *BP* is denoted by *LRBP*, to show that it is now only in the long-run equilibrium that the domestic and foreign nominal interest rates must be equal. Consider that initially the domestic economy is in equilibrium at point A in part (i) of the diagram, at the intersection of the $IS(e_0)$, LM_0 and *LRBP* lines. Parts (ii) to (v) of the diagram show the paths of the domestic interest rate, r, the exchange rate, e, aggregate demand, AD, and domestic real income, y, respectively, over time. Initially, until time t_0, these variables take equilibrium values of r^*, e_0, y_0, and y_0 respectively. Now let the government, at time t_0, disturb this equilibrium by carrying out a previously unannounced and unanticipated expansionary monetary policy, which causes the *LM* curve to shift to LM_1. The comparative static analysis of that policy is identical to that presented earlier using figure 10.6. The new equilibrium level of income will be given by the point on the new *LM* curve for which the domestic interest rate equals r^*, that is y_1 at point D in part (i) of the figure, and this new level of income will be achieved by a depreciation of the domestic currency, to e_1 in this case, which moves the *IS* curve outwards to intersect with the LM_1 and *LRBP* curves at point D. Assume that this new equilibrium is achieved by time t_1, as is illustrated by the time taken for r, e, AD and y to achieve their new equilibrium values of r^*, e_1, y_1 and y_1, respectively, in parts (ii) to (v) of the diagram. The time paths of these variables between time t_0 and time t_1 are, however, quite interesting and capable of explanation given the assumptions made above.

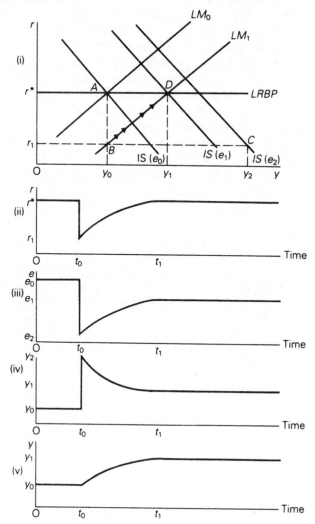

Figure 10.8 Monetary expansion and exchange rate overshooting

Consider what happens at the instant the domestic money supply is increased, and remember that this increase had not been forecast by members of the domestic or foreign private sector (the reason for this assumption will be discussed later) even though, once the policy has been carried out, perfect foresight ensures that the behaviour of economic variables, including capital gains or losses, is perfectly predicted by private sector members. In part (i) of the diagram, the LM curve moves from LM_0 to LM_1, but output adjusts slowly to any resulting increase in aggregate demand and so can be considered, initially, to remain at y_0. The domestic interest rate must, therefore, adjust downwards to r_1 to clear the domestic money market at point B in part (i) of the figure; it is, therefore, shown to jump from r^* to r_1 in part (ii) of the figure. In response to the domestic interest rate being lower than the foreign interest rate, speculators will wish to adjust their portfolios of domestic and foreign assets and will affect the demands and supplies of domestic currency on the foreign exchange market, which will cause the exchange rate to change. Like the interest rate, and unlike domestic output, the exchange rate may be assumed to jump to whatever level is necessary to clear its market. The important point to note, however, is that it does not jump to e_1, but falls even further than e_1, to e_2, as shown in part (iii) of the figure. The reason for this is that since the domestic interest rate at r_1 is below the foreign interest rate, speculators, in keeping with equation (10.3), will only be willing to hold domestic currency denominated assets if they expect an appreciation of the domestic currency. Therefore, the domestic currency is placed under pressure by speculators until it falls past, or overshoots, its new long-run equilibrium level. From the level of e_2 the exchange rate can rise over time towards its new equilibrium level of e_1. With an exchange rate of e_2 the IS curve in part (i) of the figure is pushed all the way out to $IS(e_2)$, which shows that with the low interest rate of r_1 and the low exchange rate of e_2 the level of aggregate demand for domestic output will be y_2, which is further illustrated in part (iv) of the figure. The aggregate demand for domestic ouput at y_2 exceeds the supply at y_0, and this is assumed to cause the supply of domestic output to begin to rise above y_0 as shown in part (v) of the figure. As the domestic income level rises above y_0, this causes the domestic interest rate to begin to rise above r_1, whilst equation (10.3) is still satisfied as the rate of appreciation of the currency becomes less rapid (as indicated by the slope of the line in figure 10.8 (iii) becoming less steep as time passes between t_0 and t_1). The appreciation of the domestic currency and the rise in the domestic interest rate combine to reduce the level of aggregate demand for domestic output below y_2, as shown in part (iv) of the figure where AD heads toward y_1 as time elapses. In terms of part (i) of the figure, the reduction in AD would be brought about by an inward movement of the IS curve from $IS(e_2)$ towards $IS(e_1)$, and a movement up the IS curve as the interest rate rose. This process will continue with e, r and y rising and AD falling until they all achieve their new equilibrium values.

The above analysis is important in showing how the foreign exchange market may be highly volatile in response to policy changes. In the above case monetary policy changes caused the exchange rate to jump initially to a new low level, and then to rise back to partially offset that initial jump. Fiscal policy would not have such interesting effects in the above model; it would simply affect the level of the exchange rate, which would immediately jump to its new level.

A similar analysis may be used to show that pre-announced and, therefore, anticipated policies can begin to have effects from the date of their announcement rather than the date of their execution. This may be understood by first noting that in the above analysis of an unanticipated monetary policy, the holders of domestic currency denominated assets suffer sudden and unexpected capital losses when the policy is introduced and the exchange rate falls (and, similarly, holders of foreign currency denominated assets make capital gains). Therefore, had the policy been announced in advance, speculators would have responded in advance to reallocate their asset portfolios, thus causing the domestic currency to fall in value on announcement of the policy, rather than waiting for execution of the policy. Similarly, other variables would respond to the exchange rate change and would all change before the policy causing those changes was actually enacted. The time paths of the variables would, however, differ from those shown in figure 10.8. The exchange rate would fall on announcement of the policy and then continue to depreciate. The fall in the exchange rate would cause aggregate demand to rise above y_0, and so cause y to increase. The rising income level, before the enactment of the expansionary monetary policy, would cause the domestic interest rate to rise above r^*; equation (10.3) would be satisfied because the higher domestic interest rate would be offset by the depreciation of the domestic currency. Once the expansionary monetary policy was enacted, the domestic interest rate would fall instantly below r^* and the currency, whose exchange rate would by now have overshot its new equilibrium value, would start to appreciate and the interest rate to rise towards r^*. At the same time, income would continue to rise towards its new equilibrium value and aggregate demand would begin to be dampened down as the exchange rate and domestic interest rate continue to rise, until eventually the new equilibrium values for all the variables were achieved. Thus, a pre-announced policy has different dynamic implications than an unanticipated policy, but the final stages of the time paths of the variables involved are similar in each case, and the eventual equilibrium levels are identical. It is, therefore, important to distinguish between anticipated and unanticipated policies when considering their dynamic impact.

Since variables like output and the exchange rate can begin to react to policy changes even before these policy changes take place, it is likely that straightforward empirical relationships between, for example, the actual growth of the money supply and the change in the exchange rate will be difficult to find. This reinforces the argument made in the closed-economy context using the government budget identity: dynamic analysis indicates that empirical relationships may be difficult to unravel.

Also notice that, once rational expectations are introduced, it is possible for there to be more than one solution to the model. For instance, if the government, from some initial equilibrium like that represented by point A in figure 10.8 (i), announced that at some time in the future it would increase the domestic money supply if the domestic interest rate had risen above r^*, but would hold it constant if the interest rate remained at r^*, then two solutions would be possible. One solution would be for the economy to remain at A, in which case the money supply would not be increased and remaining at A would be a viable solution. On the other hand, another viable solution might be for the economy to move away from A and the interest rate to rise, as above, in response to the expected increase in the domestic money supply, which would, indeed, be forthcoming. This raises several interesting questions; the most obvious is how individuals are supposed to decide on which of the possible outcomes to expect. Another is how, if at all, can the government influence the outcome or avoid the problem in the first place? In the example here it could avoid the problem by not making announcements of policies which are conditional with respect to the behaviour of the economy.

Finally, notice that although the above discussion has focused on the role of expectations under flexible exchange rates, they could equally play an important role under fixed-but-adjustable exchange rates. Rather obviously, if a currency were expected to be devalued (or revalued) under the fixed-but-adjustable exchange rate system, then speculators would have a considerable incentive to move their funds out of (or into) assets denominated in that currency, thus exacerbating the existing pressure on the currency and making the devaluation (or revaluation) all the more likely. In such circumstances speculators may force devaluation (or revaluation) on a government which might otherwise have tried to avoid such exchange rate adjustment. Clearly, such a government would tend to criticize this speculation, especially as the speculators need take little risk. Speculators can be quite sure which way a currency is likely to move if it is going to move (a devaluation may be expected for the currency of a country with a current account deficit and a revaluation for the currency of a country with a current account surplus), therefore the worst outcome, for them, is likely to be that the adjustment does not take place, in which case all they lose is the transaction costs involved in reallocating their portfolios. On the other hand, such criticism may be unfair if the speculation and the eventual exchange rate adjustment are really a consequence of government policy.

In conclusion, this chapter has introduced the money supply, the capital account, and expectations into the analysis. The resulting model offers several interesting insights into the behaviour of the small open economy, and has important policy implications. It will be useful, however, to extend the model to see how these insights and implications are amended by introducing the government budget identity and supply-side considerations into the analysis. The first of these two tasks is carried out in the next chapter, which also discusses the feasibility of the assumption, implicit in the present chapter, that persistent current account imbalances may be financed by offsetting capital account flows.

Appendix 10.1
A Diagrammatic Derivation of the *IS* Curve in the Small Open Economy

Figure 10.9 derives the open-economy *IS* curve diagrammatically for given values of the exchange rate, foreign and domestic prices and income in the rest of the world, and assuming exports and imports to be determined as in chapter 9.

The figure may be interpreted as follows. Quadrant (iv) shows the relationship between planned injections and the domestic rate of interest under the assumptions that planned investment varies inversely with the rate of interest, and that government spending and exports are given independently of the rate of interest (and also of the level of domestic income). The line $I + G + X$, therefore, shows total planned injections for any level of the domestic interest rate. The line $I + G$ is shown for comparison with

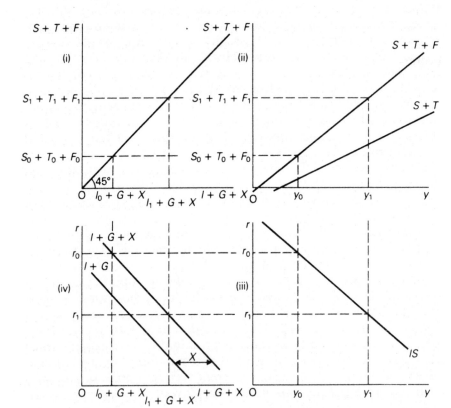

Figure 10.9 Derivation of the open-economy *IS* curve. (i) Equilibrium condition. (ii) Withdrawals function. (iii) *IS* curve. (iv) Injections function

the closed-economy case. The horizontal distance between the $I + G$ and $I + G + X$ lines is simply the level of exports, X; the lines are parallel since X is independent of r.

Quadrant (ii) shows the relationship between planned withdrawals and the level of income under the assumptions that planned imports and planned savings vary positively with the level of domestic income, and that taxation is given exogenously. The line $S + T + F$, therefore, shows total planned withdrawals for any level of domestic income. The line $S + T$ is shown for comparison with the closed-economy case. The vertical distance between the $S + T$ and $S + T + F$ lines is simply the level of imports, F; it increases as y increases, since F increases as y increases.

All points on the 45° line in quadrant (i) represent goods market equilibrium in the sense of equality between planned injections and planned withdrawals. The *IS* curve in quadrant (iii) may now be derived. Consider the rate of interest, r_0, which induces planned injections of $I_0 + G + X$ in quadrant (iv). Follow the vertical dotted line about $I_0 + G + X$ upwards to quadrant (i). When planned injections are $I_0 + G + X$ it is necessary for equilibrium that planned withdrawals equal $S_0 + T_0 + F_0$. Following the horizontal dotted line from $S_0 + T_0 + F_0$ in quadrant (i) to quadrant (ii) shows that planned withdrawals of $S_0 + T_0 + F_0$ will result if income is y_0. Planned withdrawals will, therefore, equal planned injections if the interest rate is r_0 and the income level is y_0. The intersection in quadrant (iii) of the dotted lines from r_0 in quadrant (iv) and from y_0 in quadrant (ii), therefore, provides a point on the open-economy *IS* curve. Similarly, it is possible to show that planned injections equal planned withdrawals when the interest rate is r_1 and the level of income is y_1. This provides another point on the open-economy *IS* curve. Repetition of this procedure would yield the *IS* curve shown in quadrant (iii).

The reader ought to be able to derive the closed-economy *IS* curve for comparison with the open-economy curve (after re-reading appendix 2.1, if necessary, to revise the derivation of the closed-economy curve), and also to work out how changes in the parameters of the model or the exogenous variables would affect the open-economy *IS* curve. Specifically, the reader should consider how the curve would change in response to a change in the exchange rate, which would affect the level of exports and the level of imports for any given level of domestic income. It should also be easy to show that points below the *IS* curve represent excess demand in the goods market, and that points above represent excess supply.

Appendix 10.2
A Diagrammatic Derivation of the *BP* curve in the Small Open Economy

Figure 10.10 derives the *BP* curve diagrammatically under conditions of imperfect capital mobility for given values of the exchange rate, foreign and domestic prices and income in the rest of the world.

The figure may be interpreted as follows. Quadrant (i) shows exports, X, imports, F, and the current account position $(F - X)$ plotted against domestic income, assuming exports and imports to be determined as in chapter 9. When $(F - X)$ is greater than zero there is a current account deficit, and when $(F - X)$ is less than

Figure 10.10   Derivation of the *BP* line. (i) The current account. (ii) Overall balance of payments. (iii) The capital account. (iv) The *BP* line.

zero there is a current account surplus. Only at y_B is there a balance on the current account. All values are measured in terms of the domestic currency.

All points on the 45° line in quadrant (ii) represent a balance on the overall balance of payments, with the current account position exactly offsetting the capital account position.

The capital account is shown in quadrant (iii). It shows the net capital account position to be in surplus when the domestic interest rate, r, exceeds that in the rest of the world, r^*, in balance when r equals r^*, and in deficit when r is less than r^*.

The *BP* line in quadrant (iv) may now be derived. Consider the income level, y_0, which induces a current account deficit of $(F - X)_0$ in quadrant (i). Follow the horizontal dotted line about $(F - X)_0$ across to quadrant (ii). With a current account deficit of $(F - X)_0$, balance on the overall balance of payments requires an offsetting capital account surplus of NK_0. Following the vertical dotted line from NK_0 in quadrant (ii) to quadrant (iii) shows that a capital account surplus of NK_0 will be produced if the domestic interest rate is r_0. The intersection in quadrant (iv) of the dotted lines from r_0 in quadrant (iii) and y_0 in quadrant (i), therefore, provides a point on the *BP* line. Similarly, it is possible to show that when domestic income is y_B and the domestic interest rate is r^* there is overall balance in the balance of payments, since both current and capital accounts are themselves in balance at $y_B r^*$. Repetition of this procedure would yield the *BP* line shown in quadrant (iv).

The reader ought to be able to work out how changes in the parameters of the model or the exogenous variables would affect the *BP* line. Specifically, the reader should consider how the line would change in response to a change in the exchange rate, which would affect the level of exports and the level of imports for any given level of domestic income. It should also be easy to show that points below the *BP* line represent overall balance of payments deficit, and points above represent overall balance of payments surplus.

Notes

1 It ought to be clear that 'investments' here refers to financial assets and not real, physical investment, I, although in practice, of course, some of these financial flows will be used to purchase direct or indirect claims on real capital or land.
2 It should be noted that, in reality, the response of capital flows to a given interest differential may vary over time. Consider, for example, the response of capital flows to an increase in the domestic interest rate from r^* to a new level above that in the rest of the world. There may be an initial surge of capital inflows as a result of this, as investors reallocate their portfolios and move capital into the domestic economy. Once this initial reallocation has been carried out, however, the inflow of funds may be considerably reduced, so that maintaining a high rate of inflows may require further increases in the interest rate, possibly to unsustainably high levels.
3 The reason for the terminology of perfect and imperfect capital mobility ought to be clear. Perfect capital mobility exists when foreign and domestic assets are perfect substitutes, and imperfect capital mobility when they are imperfect substitutes.
4 Actually some of these changes could have an ambiguous effect, depending on the appropriate price and income elasticities of the demand for exports and imports. The stated effect is, in that case, the one thought most likely.

5   The result that the long-run multiplier for fiscal policy is greater than the short-run multiplier is dependent upon the assumption that the slope of the *BP* line is less steep than that of the *LM* curve. The reader may care to work out the long-run versus short-run comparison when the *BP* line has the steeper slope. Several of the other policy conclusions reached in this, and the following chapters, are similarly dependent upon this assumption.

6   The comparison of the strength of monetary policy, or any of the other policies discussed in this chapter, between the closed and open economies is left as an exercise for the reader.

7   The new *IS* curve, say $IS^1(e_2)$, would intersect the LM_0 and BP^1 lines at point *A*, but would not be identical to the line $IS(e_0)$ which also passes through point *A*, since the two *IS* lines would have different slopes. The reader may check, using the diagrammatic approach given in appendix 10.1, that changing the exchange rate tends to change the slope as well as position of the *IS* curve, since it changes the slope of the *F* function.

8   Strictly, equation (10.3) holds exactly only under continuous compounding of interest and appreciation/depreciation and under the assumption of zero transaction costs.

11

Stock–Flow Equilibrium in the Open Economy

Chapter 5 introduced the idea, in a closed-economy context, that for the economy to be in a position of rest, both stocks and flows need to be in unchanging equilibrium. The interrelationships between stocks and flows, and the implications for the dynamic behaviour of the economy, were analysed by introducing wealth effects and the government budget identity into the model. Such considerations are just as important for the open economy as for the closed economy, and it is the task of this chapter to introduce them into the analysis. This is done in two stages. First, section 11.1 examines the relationships between stocks and flows which emanate from the balance of payments and are, thus, peculiar to the open-economy model. This is done without taking any account of the government budget identity, and shows that, in many ways, the balance of payments plays a role in models of the open economy similar to that played by the government budget identity in models of the closed economy. Section 11.2 introduces the government budget identity into the open economy, and discusses how it interacts with the balance of payments to determine the dynamic behaviour of the economy.

11.1 The Balance of Payments and Stock–Flow Equilibrium

Fixed Exchange Rates

The previous chapter focused on equilibrium in the overall balance of payments, in considering the equilibrium of the *IS–LM–BP* model. This focus may, however, be shown to be appropriate only in the short run. In the long run it is not feasible to maintain current account imbalances financed by equal and offsetting capital account imbalances. Long-run stock–flow equilibrium requires the absence of imbalances on both the current and capital accounts, not just on their sum.[1]

The short-run nature of the *IS–LM–BP* equilibrium presented in the previous chapter may be seen quite easily using figure 11.1 and taking into account the interrelationships between stocks and flows. Figure 11.1 represents a small open economy under a fixed exchange rate system and conditions of imperfect capital mobility. Initial short-run equilibrium is at point A in part (i) of the figure at the intersection of the lines *IS*, *LM* and *BP* for the exchange rate e. Since point A is to the right of the *BOCA* line, clearly there is a current account deficit being financed by a capital account surplus: the domestic interest rate at r_0 exceeds the rest-of-the-world interest rate, r^*, and enables the domestic economy to run the capital account surplus necessary to finance the current account

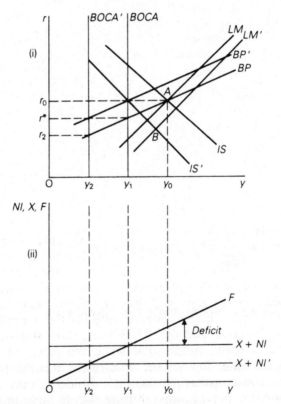

Figure 11.1 The *IS–LM* model and stock–flow effects under fixed exchange rates and imperfect capital mobility

deficit without official reserves being depleted.[2] The analysis should not, as in the previous chapter, stop at this point; it is necessary to go on to examine the repercussions of the balance of payments position on the future path of the economy.

The equilibrium at point A implies an increase in net borrowing from overseas. This may involve sales by domestic residents of any overseas assets they had acquired in the past, or the purchase of domestic assets by foreigners, but, either way, net investment income from abroad will decline in the future as a result of the asset flows due to the present capital account position. The effect of the fall in net investment income will show up in the current account in the future, and is shown in part (ii) of the figure as a downward shift of the $X + NI$ line, to $X + NI'$, where NI is net investment income from abroad and is explicitly included in the current account from now on. The effect of this is to move the level of income consistent with a balance on the current account leftwards to y_2 from y_1, and, consequently, to move the $BOCA$ line leftwards to $BOCA'$ in part (i) of the figure. Also, since for any level of income the current account deficit is larger (or surplus smaller for low levels of income), the corresponding capital account surplus necessary to achieve an overall balance must be higher too (or deficit smaller for low levels of income); this will require a higher interest rate than in the past, so that the BP line moves upwards to BP'. This latter shift may be understood more easily with the aid of an example. Consider the income level y_2. When the $X + NI$ line was given by $X + NI$, y_2 was consistent with a current account surplus, so that overall balance of payments balance required a capital outflow, which required the domestic interest rate to lie below r^* at r_2; the point r_2y_2 was on the BP line. Now, however, that the $X + NI$ line has moved to $X + NI'$, y_2 is consistent with a balance on the current account, so that a balance on the overall balance of payments requires a balance on the capital account too. A balance on the capital account requires the domestic interest rate to equal that in the rest of the world, so that the point r^*y_2 now lies on the new BP' line. Similarly, any other income level now requires a higher interest rate for the overall balance of payments to balance, and the BP' line is, thus, shifted away from the BP line. Finally, notice that since the stock of net foreign investment and the flow of net investment income from abroad have fallen, consumption by domestic residents may fall for any level of domestic income, thus shifting the IS curve in to IS', and, similarly, the demand for money may fall, thus shifting the LM curve to LM'.[3]

The result of the above movements is to move the *IS–LM* intersection to point *B* below the new *BP'* line, with a reduction in the domestic interest rate and, depending on the strengths of the *IS* and *LM* shifts, a fall in domestic income too. At point *B* there is an overall balance of payments deficit so that official reserves will be depleted, and, if the effect of the deficit on the domestic money supply is not sterilized, the domestic money supply will begin to decline. Exactly to where the economy moves from point *B* depends on the actions taken by the government. It may be that endogenous reductions in the domestic money supply and in the net foreign asset position of the economy eventually move the economy to a new equilibrium at some low level of income consistent with a balance on the current and capital accounts, or the government may take action to devalue the exchange rate if it wishes to support the income level of y_0.

It is clear that although in the short-run it is possible to finance current account deficits with capital account surpluses, and vice versa, in the long run the effects of the interactions between balance of payments flows and the stock of net foreign investment, and the consequent repercussions on the domestic money supply and economic behaviour, must be taken into account and will cause changes in the economy. Under fixed exchange rates either income must be allowed to adjust (downwards in the case here) to a level consistent with a current and capital account balance for a given exchange rate, or else the exchange rate must be adjusted if an income level target is to be attained. In any case, full stock–flow equilibrium requires monetary and fiscal policies to produce a combination of domestic income and interest rate consistent with simultaneous equilibrium on both the current and capital accounts of the balance of payments. This conclusion is much nearer to that derived using a simple model in chapter 9 than to that derived in chapter 10 using the *IS–LM–BP* model, but neglecting the relationships between stocks and flows.

Notice that, strictly, full stock–flow equilibrium, as chapter 5 stressed, also requires the government budget to be balanced, and the absence of open-market operations, but, for simplicity, the effects of government budget imbalances or open-market operations are ignored until the next section of this chapter.

Figure 11.2 shows how devaluation and fiscal and monetary policy may be used to take the economy from a point like point *B* in figure 11.1 above to a stock–flow equilibrium consistent with an internal income level target. The economy is initially at position *B* in part (i) of the figure, with an overall balance of payments deficit

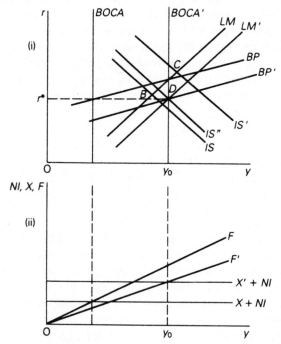

Figure 11.2 Devaluation, slack money and tight fiscal policy to achieve internal and external balance

and a current account deficit too, as may be deduced from the positions of the relevant *BP*, *BOCA*, *X + NI* and *F* lines in the figure. The government wishes to achieve an income level of y_0 and a balance on the current and capital accounts. In order to do this it must devalue the domestic currency to cause the *BOCA* and *BP* lines to shift to *BOCA'* and *BP'* respectively in part (i) of the figure, and the *X + NI* and *F* lines to shift to *X' + NI* and *F'* in part (ii). At the new exchange rate it is now possible to achieve long-run equilibrium at the income level y_0, providing that fiscal and monetary policies are adjusted to achieve an intersection of the *IS*, *LM*, *BP* and *BOCA* lines at r^*y_0. Assume that the devaluation moves the initial *IS* curve to *IS'* whilst leaving the *LM* curve unchanged. The new *IS'*, *LM* intersection, therefore, occurs at point *C* in part (i) of the diagram. In this case the appropriate fiscal policy would be contractionary (to partially offset the expansionary effects of the devaluation in the goods market) and the appropriate monetary policy would be expansionary (to equate the domestic interest rate with that in the rest of the world): thus, policy moves the *IS'* line to *IS''* and the *LM* line to *LM'*, and the government's goals are achieved at point *D* in part (i) of the figure.[4] Notice that even though there is imperfect capital mobility, the need for both current and capital accounts to be in balance simultaneously in long-run equilibrium means that in the long run the domestic interest rate is constrained to be equal to that in the rest of the world.

Flexible Exchange Rates

Considerations similar to those presented above in the context of a fixed exchange rate system are just as pertinent under a system of flexible exchange rates, as may be illustrated using figure 11.3.

Figure 11.3 represents a small open economy under conditions of perfect capital mobility and a flexible exchange rate system. Initial short-run equilibrium is at point *A* in part (i) of the figure, at the intersection of the *IS*, *LM* and *LRBP* lines for the initial exchange rate *e*. Since point *A* is to the right of the *BOCA* line there is a current account deficit, being financed by a capital account surplus.

Figure 11.3   The *IS–LM–BP* model and stock–flow effects under flexible exchange rates and perfect capital mobility

The short-run nature of an equilibrium such as point *A* is easily seen by tracing through the effects of the balance of payments flows on the stock variables in the economy, and the consequent effects of stock changes on flow variables. Thus, the capital account surplus involves a reduction in the stock of net foreign investment held by the members of the domestic economy. This reduces the net wealth position of the members of the domestic economy and also their net disposable income for any given level of domestic income; hence, for the initial exchange rate *e*, the *IS* and *LM* curves may move to *IS'* and *LM'* respectively, causing their intersection to move to point *B* in part (i) of the figure, with a reduction in the domestic interest rate and, depending on the strengths of the *IS* and *LM* shifts, a fall in the level of domestic income. Also, as before, the decline in net foreign investment income may be seen to move the *X* + *NI* line down to *X* + *NI'*, and the *BOCA* line to *BOCA'*.

Clearly, point *A* is only a short-run equilibrium. However, point *B* is not even a short-run equilibrium under floating exchange rates and perfect capital mobility. If the government does not adjust its policies then the domestic currency will depreciate, causing the *IS* curve to move outwards until it intersects the new *LM'* line at point *C* and restores the balance on the overall balance of payments. As *X* and *F* respond to the depreciation the *F* line moves, and also the *X* + *NI'* and *BOCA* lines move back towards, or beyond, *X* + *NI* and *BOCA* respectively. Point *C* would not necessarily represent full stock–flow equilibrium, since it need not necessarily be consistent with current and capital account balance, but persistent depreciation could, potentially at least, eventually bring the economy to a full stock–flow equilibrium at a simultaneous intersection of the *IS*, *LM*, *LRBP* and *BOCA* lines, and at a higher level of domestic income than the initial level of y_0. Alternatively, the government could act to support the initial exchange rate of *e* by following a tight monetary policy to move the *LM* line away from *LM'* to bring about intersection with the *IS'* (which holds for the initial exchange rate) and *LRBP* lines at *D* in part (i) of the figure. Again, *D* would represent only a short-run equilibrium, with a current account deficit and capital account surplus, but a persistent pursuit of a tight monetary policy could, potentially at least, bring about a full stock–flow equilibrium, although this time this would occur at a level of income lower than the initial level of y_0. Clearly, stock–flow considerations, and policy choices, are important for the dynamic behaviour of the economy.

Perhaps the implications of stock–flow considerations may be shown most starkly by considering the effects of a fiscal expansion from an initial position of simultaneous current and capital account balance, as is illustrated using figure 11.4. The figure shows a small open economy under floating exchange rates and perfect capital mobility. Initial stock–flow equilibrium is at point A at the intersection of the IS (e_0), LM, $LRBP$ and $BOCA$ (e_0) lines in part (i) of the figure. Thus, at the initial equilibrium the current and capital accounts are simultaneously in balance.

Now consider that the initial equilibrium is disturbed by an expansionary fiscal policy, which at the initial exchange rate of e_0 would move the IS curve to IS' (e_0). The new IS' (e_0) and LM intersection occurs at point B. Point B involves a domestic interest rate above r^*, the rate available in the rest of the world, and, since capital is perfectly mobile, international investors would seek to purchase financial assets denominated in the domestic currency. Under a system of fixed exchange rates this would cause currency to flood into the domestic eonomy and the domestic money supply to rise; but under floating exchange rates these two effects do not occur; instead, the domestic currency appreciates until international

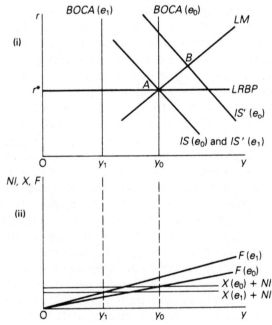

Figure 11.4   A fiscal expansion

investors no longer wish to purchase financial assets denominated in the domestic currency. This occurs when the exchange rate has moved to e_1, causing the *IS* curve to shift back to *IS'* (e_1), moving the *IS–LM* intersection back down the *LM* curve to point A.[5] At point A the domestic interest rate has returned to r^* and the domestic income level to y_0. The fiscal expansion affects only the composition of output, but not its level, the increase in government expenditure perfectly crowding out net exports via the appreciation of the domestic currency.

The analysis so far ought to be familiar to the reader; it is essentially a repetition of the analysis of the previous chapter. It is necessary now, however, to point out that point A is no longer consistent with a simultaneous equilibrium on current and capital accounts. The current account has moved into deficit as a result of the appreciation of the currency, which is shown by the movements of the X and F lines to X (e_1) in part (ii). Clearly, the deficit on the current account and the offsetting capital account surplus indicate that asset supplies are changing: the domestic economy is losing assets to the rest of the world and this will, in turn, imply a reduction in net investment income from overseas and further shifts downwards of the $X + NI$ line, unless offset by future depreciation of the domestic currency.

Once again, recognition of the effects of asset flows points out the short-run nature of a seemingly well established conclusion. Indeed, in this case it may even alter the short-run prediction of an appreciation of the currency in response to a fiscal expansion. The movement to a full stock–flow equilibrium from point A after the fiscal expansion could involve a tightening of monetary and fiscal policy, to move the *IS–LM–LRBP* intersection leftwards in the figure towards the *BOCA* (e_1) line (which might, itself, be moving leftwards as a result of the falling net investment earnings from overseas). Alternatively, the government of the domestic economy may not wish to accept the reduction in domestic income implied by the above scenario, and might, instead, slacken future monetary policy in order to cause the exchange rate to depreciate and move the full equilibrium (should it ever be attained) to a level of income higher, rather than lower, than y_0. Such an equilibrium might require slackening or tightening fiscal policy, depending on the government's objectives for the composition of output. If this future slackening of monetary policy were anticipated at the time of the initial fiscal expansion, then the domestic currency might well depreciate, rather than appreciate, in response to the initial fiscal expansion, since rational investors would take the future depreciation into account in making their current choices about where to allocate their funds. The effects of a fiscal expansion on income and the exchange rate are, therefore, ambiguous. They depend upon the expectations of private investors about future policy responses, as well as upon the actual future policy responses themselves. Any detailed modelling of the transition to a new equilibrium would require the careful introduction of expectations into the analysis and would be very complicated, even if an acceptable way of modelling expectations and market psychology could be found. This brings to mind Keynes's comment (in a different, but similar context) that

> an uninterrupted process of transition . . . to a new long-period position can be complicated in detail. But the actual course of events is more complicated still. For the state of expectation is liable to constant change, a new expectation being superimposed long before the previous change has fully worked itself out; so that the economic machine is occupied at any given time with a number of overlapping activities, the existence of which is due to various past states of expectation. (1936, p. 50)

Before going on to the next section, which introduces the government budget identity as another source of stock–flow relationships, it is worth pointing out here that although the above analysis has tended to focus upon the difficulties facing countries with current account deficits, the arguments also apply, although not quite symmetrically, to countries with current account surpluses. A country running a current account surplus is obviously in a somewhat different position than one with a deficit, since rather than wonder how to finance its borrowing or eliminate its deficit, it has to consider what to do with the proceeds of the surplus. It could, undoubtedly, run current account surpluses for many years whilst buying up assets overseas, but these asset flows and their consequent net investment income flows need to be taken into account in just the same way as they were taken into account for the deficit country cases discussed above. Furthermore, it is unlikely that such a process could go on forever, for that would imply that a country with a current account surplus would be happy to go on indefinitely giving its goods and services to foreigners in exchange for assets and/or debt which will never be repaid. Ultimately, countries with current account surpluses wish to see adjustment towards a balanced position, since running such surpluses is akin to extending credit to one's trading partners, and this process will not go on indefinitely. Creditors eventually want something in exchange for the credit they have extended.

11.2 The Government Budget Identity in the Open Economy

The dominant theme of the previous section was that stock–flow relationships emanating from the balance of payments must be taken into account in determining the behaviour of an open economy; full or stock–flow equilibrium requires that both stocks and flows be unchanging, with demands and supplies for each being matched. Models which do not recognize this requirement for full equilibrium ignore important aspects of the dynamic behaviour of the system being modelled, and may provide misleading answers. This theme is extended in the present section, which points out that the government budget identity is another important source of stock–flow relationships in the open, just as in the closed, economy. A full stock–flow analysis of the open-economy model requires simultaneous consideration of the government budget identity and the balance of payments.

The interaction of the government budget identity and the balance of payments may be illustrated quite clearly with the aid of figure 11.5. The figure shows a small open economy under conditions of imperfect capital mobility and fixed exchange rates. The initial $IS–LM$ intersection occurs at point A in part (i) of the figure at r^*y_1. The rate of interest of r^* is equal to that in the rest of the world, so the capital account of the balance of payments may be taken to be in balance. The overall balance of payments and the current account are, however, in deficit since r^*y_1 lies below the BP line and to the right of the $BOCA$ line in part (i) of the figure. The current account deficit is clearly shown in part (ii); it exactly matches the overall deficit (since the capital account is in balance). Point A, thus, implies that the current account deficit is being financed by a reduction in the reserves held by the domestic government: to pay for the excess value of imports over exports, private sector individuals acquire foreign currency by purchasing it from the government with domestic currency (or in so far as the government is purchasing imports it does so by using its reserves), and this causes domestic reserves of foreign currency to decline. Ignoring the government budget identity for the moment, it is possible to see that this process, unless offset by a deliberate policy of sterilization, would also imply a reduction in the domestic money supply held by domestic residents (they give some to the government in exchange for foreign currency which they then spend on imports). Hence, in the absence of sterilization, the money supply would fall

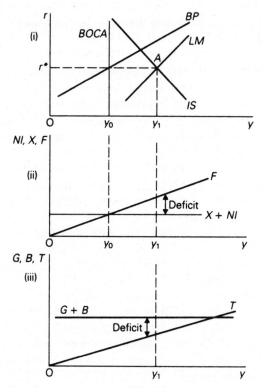

Figure 11.5 The government budget identity and the balance of payments

and cause the *LM* curve to shift leftwards (and also the *IS* curve if there are wealth effects on consumption).

Since sterilization cannot continue forever, it is possible to argue that the government need take no discretionary action to cure the balance of payments deficit other than to stop sterilization. The induced movements of the *LM* curve will, it is argued, remove the overall balance of payments imbalance. This type of argument, which features heavily in the Monetarist approach to the balance of payments, was given in the previous chapter; there are, however, a number of problems with it. First of all the government may wish to achieve the domestic income level of y_1, so that discretionary action would be needed to achieve a balance of payments equilibrium and y_1 simultaneously, since the endogenous process involving reductions in the domestic money supply would bring about a level of income lower than y_1. Secondly, the endogenous process might produce an *IS–LM–BP* intersection off the *BOCA* line. In this case the new equilibrium would not satisfy the requirements necessary for a full stock–flow equilibrium as outlined in the previous section. Further changes would occur endogenously, whilst discretionary changes might be needed to bring about full stock–flow equilibrium. Thirdly, the argument neglects the government budget identity.

In the special case shown in figure 11.5 the effects emanating from the government budget identity offset those emanating from the balance of payments disequilibrium, and make discretionary policy essential for the attainment of a full stock–flow equilibrium, Part (iii) of figure 11.5 shows a government budget deficit which is of exactly the same size as the current account deficit shown in part (ii). If the government budget deficit is financed by printing money, the drain of money from the private sector implied by the overall balance of payments deficit is, in the absence of open market operations, entirely offset by the inflow of money to finance the budget deficit. In such circumstances, the equilibrium associated with point A in part (i) of the figure is consistent with full private sector stock–flow equilibrium: private sector wealth stocks are unchanging, since there are no net capital account flows (and hence no effects on net investment income from abroad) and the supplies of money and bonds held by the domestic private sector remain constant, and flow equilibrium is achieved since point A is on the *IS* curve. Thus, the imbalances on the government budget and the balance of payments may offset one another; even though, on their own, each imbalance would create dynamic forces on the economy, together they produce no such forces in the special case under examination here.[6] Obviously, in other cases the pressures arising from imbalances on the government budget and the balance of payments may not offset one another, and may even reinforce one another.

Even for the special case under consideration here the above does not imply that the short-run equilibrium shown in figure 11.5 can persist indefinitely. The private sector may be in full stock–flow equilibrium in figure 11.5, but the government is not. Effectively, the government in figure 11.5 is selling its reserves of foreign currency in exchange for domestic currency. The foreign currency is used to pay for the current account deficit, whilst the government returns the domestic currency to the private sector to pay for the government budget deficit. Alternatively, the government may be viewed as printing money to pay for its budget deficit, but buying it back with foreign reserves. Whichever way one chooses to look at it, the private sector is in full stock–flow equilibrium but the government sector is not, since the supply of foreign currency reserves which it holds is declining and will, if the situation is not remedied, eventually be exhausted. The point is not that the equilibrium associated with point *A* can persist; it cannot. But since there are no endogenous dynamic forces at work to disturb private sector stock–flow equilibrium, adjustment towards a full stock–flow equilibrium, for both the government and private sectors simultaneously, requires the use of discretionary government policy and/ or exchange rate adjustment. Another way of saying this would be to say that in equilibrium the government of a small open economy under fixed exchange rates cannot set its fiscal and monetary policies independently from the value of the exchange rate.

The above argument has general application and holds outside the special case being considered at present. Full stock–flow equilibrium for both the government and private sector requires that there be simultaneous balances on the government budget, the current and capital accounts of the balance of payments, and in the goods and money markets, and also that there be no open market operations or other impulses to disturb this equilibrium. In other words, the *IS–LM–BP* and *BOCA* lines must all intersect at one common point for which the level of income generates a balanced government budget.

The requirements for full stock–flow equilibrium for the flexible exchange rate case are exactly the same as the above. Out of equilibrium the dynamic forces emanating from the balance of payments tend to work on the exchange rate rather than on the domestic money supply under floating exchange rates. On the other hand, the forces emanating from the government budget identity may affect the domestic money supply.

The model implied by the arguments presented above is rather complicated, since it shows the need to take into account several factors at one time, although individually these factors are themselves not too complicated. The benefits of the approach are that it points out the varied and sometimes offsetting forces at work on the economy, and that it can be used to analyse a whole host of possibilities. It can be applied to analyse fiscal and monetary policy under fixed or floating exchange rates, perfect or imperfect capital mobility, and to analyse the longer run implications of various combinations of imbalances on the balance of payments and the government budget. Rather than to attempt to go through all the possibilities here, the next chapter will examine just two cases under floating exchange rates, both of which involve a current account deficit, but one of which deals with a government budget surplus and the other a government budget deficit. Furthermore the discussion will introduce one more complication into the analysis: the aggregate supply side of the model will be introduced and the domestic price level will no longer be assumed to be constant.

Notes

1   The focus on the current account is similar to the view expressed by Thirlwall that 'in the long run a country cannot grow faster than the rate of growth of output consistent with balance-of-payments equilibrium on current account' (1986, p. 251). The present text, however, abstracts from considerations of economic growth which feature heavily in Thirlwall's arguments. Equally, the importance placed upon stock–flow effects is similar to the monetary approach to the balance of payments. See, for example, Johnson (1972b), who wrote that 'deficits and surpluses [on the balance of payments] represent phases of stock adjustment in the money market and not equilibrium flows and should not be treated in an analytical framework that treats them as equilibrium phenomena' (p. 1560). This is essentially the argument being made in the present chapter, but, unlike Johnson, the present chapter uses a Keynesian model rather than a Monetarist one and does not focus so exclusively on the money market.

2   The reader should, as a revision exercise, work out why r^* is the interest rate at which the *BOCA* and *BP* lines intersect.

3   The reason for these shifts is that the net wealth position and the net disposable income of domestic residents have both fallen for any given level of domestic income. Also notice that, strictly, the F line in part (ii) of the figure might move downwards for similar reasons, but this movement is neglected here for the sake of simplicity.

4   It is assumed that the expansionary monetary policy involves purchasing government debt from domestic residents, so that NI is unaffected. If NI were affected this would move the BP line and would need to be taken into account when choosing the appropriate devaluation.

5   IS' (e_1) is shown as being the same line as IS (e_0). In practice the slopes of the two lines would differ, but, to avoid cluttering the diagram, this detail is not shown.

6   A case similar to this was, as far as I know, first used by McKinnon (1969). It has also been used by Currie (1976) and Hillier (1982).

Prices, Exchange Rates and Policy

This final chapter presents a model which draws together several of the ideas presented in the earlier chapters, as well as introducing price flexibility and aggregate supply considerations. It will be shown that it is always necessary to trace the repercussions of some change in one part of the model throughout the whole model, and that what seems to be an easy solution to one problem may well turn out to have unpleasant implications elsewhere.

Complex as the model in this chapter may seem, it should be remembered that it is an abstract model designed to focus on a limited number of issues by assuming away other complications. Thus real world policy-makers deserve some sympathy for the difficult nature of the task they undertake, even though one may wish to subject their policies to critical appraisal.

Section 12.1 presents the basic model in full stock–flow equilibrium using a four part diagram. The individual parts of the diagram are each discussed and their interlinkages mentioned, which involves some review of earlier material and some new arguments. Sections 12.2 and 12.3 then present versions of the model out of full stock–flow equilibrium and relate the ideas presented in this chapter to the difficult choices facing policy-makers in the real world.

12.1 The Model in Equilibrium

Figure 12.1 represents a small open economy in full stock–flow equilibrium. Part (i) of the figure shows the $BOCA$, IS, LM and $LRBP$ lines, which all intersect at the common point A or r^*, y_0. The IS curve is drawn for the exchange rate e_0 and price level P_0. The price level helps to determine the position of the IS curve under the assumption that it affects the real value of nominal asset

Figure 12.1 A small open economy in full stock–flow equilibrium

stocks (money and bonds) as discussed in chapter 5 above. The position and slope of the *IS* curve, of course, depends on many other things too (for example, the level of real government expenditure, G, the income propensity to consume, and so on), but it is useful, for the arguments which follow, to emphasize the dependence on e and P by denoting the *IS* curve as $IS (e_0, P_0)$ in the figure. Similarly, for all the other curves in the diagram, only those factors worthy of special emphasis here are denoted in brackets accompanying the curves. The *LM* curve is shown to depend upon the price level, since changes in the price level affect the real supply of money for any given nominal supply and also, via wealth effects, affect the demand for money too. The *BOCA* line is shown to depend upon the exchange rate and the price level, since, other things being equal, changes in each of those variables affect the international competitiveness of the output of the economy and, hence, the demand curves for exports, *X*, and imports, *F*, as shown in part (ii) of the figure. The vertical axis in part (ii) measures the real values of exports and imports, where, as in the last chapter, the current account explicitly takes account of net investment income from abroad, *NI*.

Finally, in part (i), the *LRBP* line is horizontal at r^*, the interest rate prevailing in the rest of the world, to indicate perfect capital mobility, since that is probably easier to deal with than the case of imperfect capital mobility and is, in any case, a reasonable approximation for many developed economies. In long-run equilibrium, under either fixed or floating exchange rates, constant asset stocks require a balanced capital account with the domestic interest rate r equal to r^*. This requirement holds for any exchange rate or price level, and so neither e_0 nor P_0 appears in brackets alongside *LRBP*.

The point *A* in part (i) of the figure is potentially consistent with full stock–flow equilibrium. Since point *A* is on the *IS* curve the flow of goods, y_0, will, if supplied, be matched exactly by demand. Since point *A* is at the intersection of the *BOCA* and *LRBP* lines, both the current and capital accounts are in balance and no asset changes (for the government or private sector) are being generated by the balance of payments. However, whether point *A* will be a full stock–flow equilibrium point cannot be discerned solely from part (i) of the diagram – it is also necessary to check parts (iii) and (iv). Part (ii) need not be checked since the relevant evidence it offers has already been used in determining the position of the *BOCA* line in part (i). Part (iii) represents the government budget identity familiar from chapters 5 and 11. It is worth remembering that *T* represents real tax revenues and that *G* represents real government expenditure on goods and services. *B* represents nominal interest payments and is, therefore, divided by P_0 to translate it into real terms. Thus, the government budget position is now shown to depend upon the price level (as mentioned in note 6 of chapter 5). A reduction in the price level will increase the real value of interest payments and so increase the deficit or reduce the surplus for any real income level, and vice versa for an increase in the price level. The government budget is shown to be balanced for the income level y_0, so there will be no forces emanating from it to disturb the equilibrium of the economy away from point A in part (i). If the budget were out of balance, then either asset stocks or policy would have to change and the equilibrium at point A would be disturbed.

Part (iv) shows three lines which all intersect at point B, or P_0y_0. The aggregate demand curve AD is derived from the underlying IS and LM curves as in chapter 3 above, but now for a given level of the exchange rate, e_0 in this case. The position of the AD curve could be affected by any of the factors which affect the underlying IS or LM curves, one of which, emphasized in brackets here, is the exchange rate. A depreciation of the exchange rate, as explained in chapter 10, would, other things being equal, increase the demand for domestic output by increasing its international competitiveness, or, in other words, by making it relatively cheaper than foreign output, thus moving the AD curve rightwards. The long-run aggregate supply curve, $LRAS$, is shown to be vertical above y_0, implying that y_0 is the exogenously given natural level of output for the domestic economy, regardless of the domestic price level or the exchange rate. This is a rather strong assumption, for instance it neglects the argument that the natural level of output depends upon the actual historical path of output, but it is, nonetheless, a convenient assumption for present purposes.[1] The short-run aggregate supply curve, $SRAS$, is shown to be upward sloping since output supply may be disturbed away from the natural level in the short run for the types of reason discussed in chapters 6, 7 and 8 above. $SRAS$ is assumed to depend upon the underlying money wage, W_0, and exchange rate, e_0. A rise in the money wage would cause $SRAS$ to move upwards by increasing labour input costs, and an appreciation of the exchange rate would cause it to move downwards by reducing the costs of imported inputs (such as raw materials). It will be convenient, for sections 2 and 3 below, to assume that, when the intersection of the AD and $SRAS$ curves is not on the $LRAS$ curve, output is given by the level at the intersection of the AD and $SRAS$ curves, and that the $SRAS$ curve moves slowly towards the intersection of the AD and $LRAS$ curves as the money wage adjusts upwards if output exceeds y_0, or downwards if output is below y_0. (Readers may wish to critically appraise this latter assumption using the arguments of the earlier chapters of this book, especially chapters 2 and 4.) This slow movement may be considered to be due to underlying adaptive expectations, or overlapping multi-period nominal wage contracts in the labour market which prevent rapid adjustment towards the natural level of output (and employment) once output has been disturbed away from y_0.

Since the *LRAS*, *SRAS* and *AD* curves all intersect at point *B*, this shows that, for the exchange rate, e_0, money wage, W_0, and price level, P_0, the aggregate demand for domestic output is equal to its long-run and short-run supply. There are no forces operating to move the *AD* curve, since none are operating to move the *IS* or *LM* curves, and no forces are operating to move the *SRAS* curve, since output and employment are already at their long-run or natural levels. The price level, money wage, exchange rate, and level of output are, therefore, all consistent with full stock–flow equilibrium in each part of the diagram, and the diagram as a whole shows an economy in full stock–flow equilibrium. The economy could be operating under fixed or floating exchange rates. Under floating exchange rates there would be no pressure to cause the currency to appreciate or depreciate, whilst under fixed exchange rates there would be no pressure to change any private asset stocks or the level of government held reserves of international currencies.

The conditions for full stock–flow equilibrium are quite stringent. The price level, money wage, exchange rate and level of domestic output must be consistent with a current account balance, the domestic interest rate must equal that in the rest of the world (to give a capital account balance), there must be a balanced government budget, and aggregate demand and short-run aggregate supply must equal the natural level of output. Furthermore, there must be no open market operations. If any one of these conditions were not satisfied then there would be forces operating to move one or more of the lines in one or more of the parts of the figure, and a complicated dynamic process would be set in motion, which might or might not move the economy to a new long-run equlibrium position. For instance, if only the government budget in part (iii) of the figure were out of balance with, say, a money financed deficit, this would have repercussions throughout the whole model. The increase in the money supply would cause the *LM* curve to move rightwards, an effect which would be mitigated but not wholly offset by wealth effects on the demand for money, and the *IS* curve also would move rightwards if wealth effects are present in the consumption function. These shifts would cause the *AD* curve in part (iii) of the figure to move rightwards too, thus causing the price and output levels to change, with repercussions on the *IS*, *LM*, *SRAS*, $X + NI$, *F*, and $G + B/P$ lines, and so on. Keeping track of such a complex dynamic process requires carefully noting all the interactions in the model, and tracing the repercussions of each change. Rather than attempt to deal with each and every disequilibrium possibility and each and every policy option, the model will be applied to two special cases in the following sections.

Before applying the model, there are two final points worth making in this section. First it should be noted that equilibrium in the open economy is very fragile, it may be disturbed by shocks generated abroad or at home. Open economies are affected by events and policies happening in the other economies with which they deal. For example, an expansionary fiscal policy in one country may well have profound effects in another country tied to it by significant trading links. Such effects are omitted from our discussion by assuming the world income, interest rate and price level to be given, and by making the assumption that we are modelling a small open economy. Nevertheless, it is easy to see how interdependencies can be important in the real world (by, for example, imagining what would happen in the model if events in the rest of the world caused the world interest rate to rise) and to see how they lead to calls for international co-ordination of macroeconomic policies.[2]

Secondly, notice that out of equilibrium an important influence upon the rate of change of the exchange rate is the difference between the domestic rate of inflation and the rate of inflation in the rest of the world. The basic idea is that if, for example, domestic inflation exceeds that in the rest of the world, then the domestic currency will depreciate in order to maintain the competitiveness of domestic production. This relationship, known as the Relative Purchasing Power Parity theory, holds only approximately, since in the short run there are several important influences upon inflation and the exchange rate, and they distort any simple relationship. For example, it is possible to imagine a country with a current account surplus moving towards equilibrium with inflation faster than in the rest of the world, and an appreciating exchange rate: both factors damage the competitiveness of domestic production, but both may help to restore equilibrium by reducing domestic output towards its natural level and at the same time helping to eliminate the current account surplus.

12.2 Twin Deficits

Figure 12.2 shows a small open economy under floating exchange rates in a world of perfect capital mobility. The current values for

Figure 12.2 Twin deficits

the domestic price level, money wage, output level, interest rate and exchange rate are P_0, W_0, y_0, r_0 and e_0 respectively. Notice that, even though capital mobility is perfect, r_0 exceeds r^*, which implies an expectation that the domestic currency is expected to depreciate (see chapter 10). The economy is operating away from full stock–flow equilibrium since it is running deficits on both the current account and the government budget.

In some ways the situation is quite satisfactory: y_0 is the long-run or natural level of output, so there is no serious unemployment problem, and the excess of imports over exports allows high levels of domestic consumption and investment. Assuming that the government budget deficit is bond-financed, with little affect on the *IS* and *LM* curves, the situation may be able to persist for quite a while. Assume, as an extreme but convenient case that the domestic private sector is able to get the foreign currency it needs to finance the current account deficit by selling domestic currency to foreigners, and that the foreigners then use this currency to purchase the bonds being sold by the domestic government to finance its budget deficit, the government then spending that currency, along with its tax receipts, on domestically produced goods and services, and so returning the domestic currency to the domestic private sector. There will, hence, be little pressure on private sector stock–flow equilibrium, and the *IS*, *LM*, *AD* and *SRAS* curves may all remain approximately as drawn, so that the situation shown in figure 12.2 can persist for quite a while. However, interest payments on the growing national debt will move the $G + B/P$ line upwards in part (iii) of the figure, and the $X + NI$ line downwards in part (ii) of the figure (since net investment income from abroad will decline as foreigners purchase domestic government bonds). This latter shift will, in turn, cause the *BOCA* line to move leftwards. Thus, although the situation shown in figure 12.2 may persist for quite a while, all the time it does so it is worsening the imbalances on the current account and on the government budget. Eventually, these imbalances will force the government to take action, or else foreigners will begin to doubt the value of purchasing the bonds being produced by the government, and so reduce their demand for domestic currency on the exchange market, causing a fall in the value of the domestic currency and/or a drain on the reserves of foreign currency held by the domestic government.

Removing the twin deficits is, however, no easy task and involves running the risk of unpopular inflation on the one hand, and unemployment on the other. Current account deficits in the real world are often accompanied by calls for 'protectionist' measures

such as tariffs or quotas on imports. But these policies are dangerous since they may lead to reprisals in a trade war which damages
all the combatants, and, in any case, there are arguments for
encouraging, not discouraging trade, not only because it allows
economic gains by allowing nations to specialize in producing certain goods and services, but also because it helps promote growth
in less developed economies which benefit from having a relatively
cheap labour supply (even though this may be, to some extent, to
the disadvantage of more developed economies with more expensive labour – this argument does, of course, involve a value judgement since it involves assessing whether the loss to some is worth
incurring in return for the gain to others).

It will be assumed here that protectionist measures will not be
introduced, so that removing the current account deficit requires
improving the competitiveness of domestic production. That is to
say, domestic production must be made relatively cheaper than
foreign production, either by a depreciation of the domestic currency, or by a fall in the price of domestic output, or some combination of both. Assume that bringing about a fall in the domestic
price level would require a massive reduction in aggregate demand
and huge unemployment in the short run, so that this policy is
ruled out. This means that the exchange rate must depreciate
instead. The trouble with this is that, on the one hand, it may
worsen the current account in the short run as exports and imports
take time to adjust to the change in relative prices, and, on the
other hand, depreciation pushes up the price of imports, creating
pressure on the price level in the domestic economy by causing
both the aggregate demand curve and the short-run aggregate
supply curve to move upwards (as import costs rise and push up
the price of raw materials, or as wage bargainers push for higher
money wages).

There is a danger that depreciation could spark an inflationary
recession if it causes *AD* to move rightwards and *SRAS* to move
leftwards at too great a speed. Alternatively, it could first boost
inflation and output if the strength of the *AD* movement is much
greater than that of the *SRAS* movement, but this could then be
followed by recession as policymakers respond to the inflation
with contractionary aggregate demand policies. This problem is
worsened if foreigners decide to dump assets denominated in the
domestic currency, because they fear the depreciation and inflation
will eat into their value, thus forcing the value of the domestic
currency down too far. A controlled depreciation is difficult to carry
out, but a country facing the problems illustrated in figure 12.2 may

have no choice other than to attempt it. Whether this should be called an activist or non-activist policy is a difficult, but largely pointless, question. It is non-activist in the sense that eventually it involves letting market forces determine the exchange rate necessary to achieve current account balance, but it will require a firm political will to carry it through, as well as some discretionary or activist policies to remove the other deficit, that on the government budget.

Removing the government budget deficit could be left to inflation to do, since the $G + B/P$ line falls as the price level rises. Because, in this case, depreciation may be accompanied by some inflation, the cure for the current account deficit helps lessen the government budget deficit. But some discretionary action to reduce government expenditure or increase taxes will probably be needed too. Both policies may be unpopular and both risk reducing aggregate demand by too much, so that output falls below y_0 and unemployment rises; but the risk of inaction is just as great, depreciation, inflation and unemployment all caused, proximately, by a crisis of confidence in the domestic currency.

Removing the twin deficits and restoring full stock–flow equilibrium, whilst avoiding excessive inflation and unemployment is, thus, a difficult and dangerous task. But, theoretically at least, it is possible that depreciation, accompanied by moderate inflation, could restore the competitiveness of domestic production, whilst a tightening of fiscal policy could restore the government budget to balance and at the same time moderate the boost to aggregate demand given by depreciation, so that the twin evils of unemployment and inflation could be avoided.

The above scenario is, in some ways, similar to that which faced the USA in the second half of the 1980s, even though the small country assumption is inappropriate for the USA. Countries dependent on the USA for export markets were keen to avoid an excessive depreciation of the US dollar and encouraged tightening fiscal policy to remove the budget deficit, whilst the USA in return encouraged its trading partners to take action to boost their demand for US exports, both as a way of moderating the size of depreciation required to remove the trade deficit and to offset the effects on aggregate demand of any tightening of fiscal policy in the USA. This episode of recent economic history is interesting, but to discuss the extent and success of any policy co-ordination would be beyond the scope of the present book. What is clear, however, is that modern economies do not exist in isolation, and are mutually dependent upon one another.

12.3 A Budget Surplus with a Trade Deficit

Figure 12.3 shows a small open economy under floating exchange rates in a world of perfect capital mobility. The current values for the domestic price level, money wage, output level, interest rate and exchange rate are P_0, W_0, y_0, r_0 and e_0 respectively. Notice

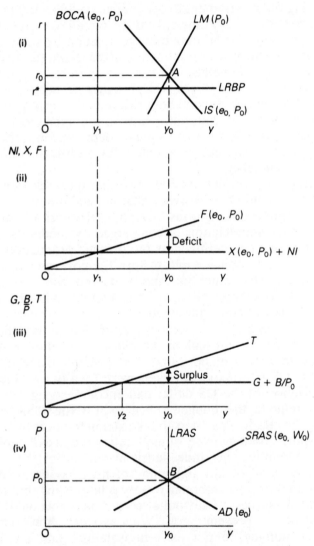

Figure 12.3 A budget surplus and a current account deficit

that even though capital mobility is perfect, r_0 exceeds r^*, which implies that the domestic currency is expected to depreciate. Parts (i), (ii), and (iv) of the figure are essentially the same as their counterparts in figure 12.2. The economy is again operating away from full stock–flow equilibrium, but this time it is running a deficit on the current account, accompanied by a surplus on the government budget, so that part (iii) of the figure differs from its counterpart in figure 12.2.

At first sight the problem facing the government of the economy depicted by figure 12.3 might appear to be easier than that facing the government of the economy depicted by figure 12.2, since the government is running a surplus on its budget. If this is true it is only because measures taken to reduce a government budget surplus, for example cutting tax rates or increasing government expenditure, are usually more popular than measures designed to reduce a government budget deficit, for example increasing tax rates or reducing government expenditure. However, the government of the economy depicted by figure 12.3 faces a difficult task, and its budget surplus could prove to be just as big a problem as a deficit. In the long run the government wishes to have a balanced government budget, rather than a deficit or surplus.[3]

The government will not wish to run a surplus for ever. The surplus, as shown in part (iii) of the figure, means that the government is receiving more money in the form of tax receipts than it needs to pay for its expenditure on goods and services and interest payments on its debt. The government may decide to hold on to this surplus, which means reducing the amount of money in circulation, or it may return the money to circulation by using the surplus to buy back its debt. Clearly, neither of these two options may be carried on for ever, one implies that the money supply in circulation will shrink to zero, the other that the amount of bonds in private hands will fall to zero. In the latter case the government would have to start buying up privately-held assets if it wished to keep returning to private circulation the excess money collected in taxes. These options may be useful in the short run, but in the long run the government will wish to eliminate its surplus by cutting tax rates or increasing government expenditure.

The government of the economy depicted by figure 12.3 must eventually reduce taxes or increase spending to remove the government budget surplus. The trouble with this is that either action causes a boost to aggregate demand, which part (iv) of the figure shows to be already adequate to generate aggregate supply at the desirable long-run or natural level, y_0. Removing the budget surplus will, therefore, prove to be inflationary. At the same time, boosting aggregate demand and the domestic price level will increase the demand for imports and reduce the demand for exports, thus worsening the current account position, which will in any case worsen as interest payments have to be made on the debt to foreigners incurred by financing current account deficits from capital account surpluses. In order to cure the current account deficit the domestic currency must depreciate. This will, however, push up the cost of imports (of finished goods, of raw materials and inputs to domestic production, and of services) and so worsen the problem of inflation. Indeed, inflation may proceed so rapidly as to offset any competitive gains accruing from depreciation, and make the current account deficit very difficult to remove, possibly leading to a highly restrictive aggregate demand policy in the future, which might only swap the current account and inflation problem for excessively high unemployment.

Clearly the situation depicted in figure 12.3 is laden heavy with dangers, and whatever seems to be a good policy with respect to the budget position seems to be a bad one with respect to the balance of payments. In many ways it resembles the problem facing the United Kingdom at the time of writing (spring 1989), although, of course, there are many factors special to the United Kingdom omitted from our analysis (for example, the forecast decline of tax revenues from the proceeds of the exploitation of the North Sea oilfields). Nevertheless, the figure helps to explain the diverse recommendations made to the United Kingdom government. Some commentators advised the government to slacken its monetary policy to bring about depreciation of the exchange rate to improve competitiveness, whilst combining this with a tight fiscal policy to offset the boost given to aggregate demand and inflation by the depreciation. Others focused on the budget surplus and recommended immediate tax cuts or expenditure increases, arguing that the balance of payments posed no problem, since it was not due to government profligacy but was just the outcome of voluntary and optimal private sector actions with UK residents borrowing from overseas. Yet other commentators supported a tight monetary policy to maintain a high interest rate and exchange rate and thereby prevent aggregate demand pressure from rising, whilst at the same time maintaining the budget surplus and reducing the amount of government debt (which would help to reduce government outlays in advance of the forecast decline in tax receipts as North Sea oil reserves became depleted). This seems to be a feasible policy only in the short run, and its proponents seem to imply a desire to allow a steady depreciation of the currency, moderate inflation and a steady reduction in the government budget surplus in the long run, which may, however, prove difficult to bring about since an expected steady depreciation may precipitate sales of the currency on the foreign exchange market and result in a rapid depreciation instead. Some economists argued that trying to control the exchange rate was a foolish policy; instead they claimed that the exchange rate should be left to the foreign exchange market, a tight fiscal and monetary policy being followed to control domestic demand and inflation.[4] The high interest rate–strong exchange rate policy seemed, nevertheless, to be the government policy at the time of writing this book. Readers will, possibly, know if the government persisted and succeeded with this policy.[5]

Certainly there are no easy options facing the government of an economy like the one shown in figure 12.3, and the government needs to be aware of the long-run as well as the short-run implications of its policies. It is hoped that the reader of this book will be able to appreciate the difficulties facing real world policy-makers, whilst also being able to critically evaluate their policies from a theoretical viewpoint.

Notes

1 For a readable introduction to the idea of hysteresis (and several other ideas relevant for open-economy modelling not dealt with here, such as the distinction between tradables and non-tradables (the distinction is self-explanatory, although its implications are less obvious)) see Morley, 1988.

2 For an introduction to such topics the reader is referred to Dornbusch and Frenkel (1979), chapters 5, 6 and 9.

3 This conclusion holds in a no-growth context. Once allowance is made for economic growth it may be the case that the government wishes to run a persistent budget deficit, partly financed by money and partly by bonds to satisfy growing private sector demands for financial assets.

4 Other criticisms of the high interest rate policy were that it discouraged investment and harmed growth prospects, acted as a rather inequitable tax which hit only those in debt, and by pushing up mortgage payments and the cost-of-living index (which in the UK includes mortgage payments) created inflationary wage pressures. Domestic industry, therefore, could be faced with high interest rates making borrowing expensive, low demand at home, a high exchange rate making their goods uncompetitive on the international market, and unions pushing for high wage increases. The policy, therefore, risks creating a recession if pushed too far.

5 Since writing the text of this chapter the then British Chancellor of the Exchequer resigned from office. His action was at least in part precipitated by criticisms of this policy by an adviser to the Prime Minister.

Bibliography

Alpine, R. L. W. (1985) 'A Pedagogical Note on Bond Financing of Government Expenditure', *Journal of Economic Studies*.

Artis, M. J. and Currie, D. A. (1981) 'Monetary Targets and the Exchange Rate: A Case for Conditional Targets'. In W. A. Eltis and P. J. N. Sinclair (eds), *The Money Supply and the Exchange Rate*, Oxford University Press.

Barro, R. J. (1974) 'Are Government Bonds Net Wealth?', *Journal of Political Economy*.

Barro, R. J. (1979) 'Second Thoughts on Keynesian Economics', *American Economic Review, Papers and Proceedings*.

Begg, D. K. H. (1982a) 'Rational Expectations, Wage Rigidity and Involuntary Unemployment: A Particular Theory', *Oxford Economic Papers*.

Begg, D. K. H. (1982b) *The Rational Expectations Revolution in Macroeconomics: Theories and Evidence*, Philip Allan, Deddington, Oxford.

Benassy, J. P. (1982) *The Economics of Market Disequilibrium*, Academic Press, New York.

Blaug, M. (1978) *Economic Theory in Retrospect* (3rd edn), Cambridge University Press.

Blinder, A. S. (1987) 'Keynes, Lucas and Scientific Progress', *American Economic Review*.

Blinder, A. S. and Solow, R. M. (1973) 'Does Fiscal Policy Matter?', *Journal of Public Economics*.

Brown, A. J. (1955) *The Great Inflation, 1939–1951*, Oxford University Press, London.

Brunner, K. (1976) 'A Fisherian Framework for the Analysis of International Monetary Problems'. In M. Parking and G. Zis (eds), *Inflation in the World Economy*, Manchester University Press.

Brunner, K. (1981) 'The Case Against Monetary Activism', *Lloyds Bank Review*.

Brunner, K. Cukierman, A. and Meltzer, A. H. (1983) 'Money and Economic Activity, Inventories and Business Cycles', *Journal of Monetary Economics*.

284 Bibliography

Brunner, K. and Meltzer, A. H. (1969) 'The Nature of the Policy Problem'. In K. Brunner (ed.), *Targets and Indicators of Monetary Policy*, Chandler, San Francisco.

Brunner, K. and Meltzer, A. H. (1972) 'Money, Debt and Economic Activity', *Journal of Political Economy*.

Buiter, W. H. (1977) '"Crowding Out" and the Effectiveness of Fiscal Policy', *Journal of Public Economics*.

Buiter, W. H. (1980) 'The Macroeconomics of Dr Pangloss: A Critical Survey of the New Classical Macroeconomics', *Economic Journal*.

Burrows, P. (1979) 'The Government Budget Constraint and the Monetarist-Keynesian Debate'. In S. T. Cook and P. M. Jackson (eds), *Current Issues in Fiscal Policy*, Martin Robertson, Oxford.

Cagan, P. (1956) 'The Monetary Dynamics of Hyperinflation'. In M. Friedman (ed.), *Studies in the Quantity Theory of Money*, University of Chicago Press.

Christ, C. F. (1968) 'A Simple Macroeconomic Model with a Government Budget Restraint', *Journal of Political Economy*.

Clower, R. W. (1965) 'The Keynesian Counter-revolution: A Theoretical Appraisal'. Chapter 5 in F. H. Hahn and F. Brechling (eds), *The Theory of Interest Rates*, Macmillan, Basingstoke. Reprinted in R. W. Clower (ed.), *Monetary Theory*, Penguin, Harmondsworth (1969) – page numbers in the text refer to the reprint.

Cohen, C. D. (ed.) (1982) *Agenda for Britain 2: Macro Policy*, Philip Allan, Deddington, Oxford.

Currie, D. A. (1976) 'Some Criticisms of the Monetary Analysis of Balance of Payments Correction', *Economic Journal*.

Cuthbertson, K. and Taylor, M. (1987) *Macroeconomic Systems*, Basil Blackwell, Oxford.

Davidson, P. (1983) 'The Dubious Labor Market Analysis in Meltzer's Restatement of Keynes' Theory', *Journal of Economic Literature*.

Davies, G. (1985) *Governments Can Affect Employment*, Employment Institute, London.

Debreu, G. (1974) 'Excess Demand Functions', *Journal of Mathematical Economics*.

Dornbusch, R. (1976) 'Expectations and Exchange Rate Dynamics', *Journal of Political Economy*.

Dornbusch, R. and Frenkel, J. A. (eds) (1979) *International Economic Policy: Theory and Evidence*, Johns Hopkins University Press, Baltimore and London.

Eltis, W. A. and Sinclair, P. J. N. (eds) (1981) *The Money Supply and the Exchange Rate*, Oxford University Press.

Fair, R. (1978) 'A Criticism of One Class of Macroeconomic Models with Rational Expectations', *Journal of Money, Credit and Banking*.

Fair, R. (1979) 'On Modelling the Effects of Government Policies', *American Economic Review, Papers and Proceedings*.

Feldstein, M. (1982) 'Government Deficits and Aggregate Demand', *Journal of Monetary Economics*.

Fischer, S. (1977) 'Long-term Contracts, Rational Expectations, and the Optimal Money Supply Rule', *Journal of Political Economy*.

Fischer, S. (1988) 'Recent Developments in Macroeconomics', *Economic Journal*.

Fisher, I. (1926) 'A Statistical Relation Between Unemployment and Price Changes', *International Labor Review*. Reprinted posthumously as 'I Discovered the Phillips Curve', *Journal of Political Economy* (1973).

Friedman, B. M. (1979) 'Optimal Expectations and the Extreme Information Assumptions of "Rational Expectations" Macromodels', *Journal of Monetary Economics*.

Friedman, M. (1948) 'A Monetary and Fiscal Framework for Economic Stability', *American Economic Review*. Reprinted in M. G. Mueller (ed.), *Readings in Macroeconomics*, Holt, Rinehart and Winston, New York (1966).

Friedman, M. (1953) 'The Methodology of Positive Economics'. In *Essays in Positive Economics*, University of Chicago Press.

Friedman, M. (1959a) 'Statement on Monetary Theory and Policy'. In *Employment, Growth and Price Levels* (Hearings before the Joint Economic Committee, 1st session, 25–28 May 1959), US Government Printing Office, Washington. Reprinted in R. J. Ball and P. Doyle (eds), *Inflation*, Penguin, Harmondsworth (1969) – page numbers in the text refer to the reprint.

Friedman, M. (1959b) 'The Demand for Money: Some Theoretical and Empirical Results', *Journal of Political Economy*.

Friedman, M. (1962) *Capitalism and Freedom*, University of Chicago Press.

Friedman, M. (1968) 'The Role of Monetary Policy', *American Economic Review*.

Friedman, M. (1970) 'The Counter-revolution in Monetary Theory', Institute of Economic Affairs for the Wincott Foundation, Occasional Paper no. 33, London.

Friedman, M. (1972) 'Comments on the Critics', *Journal of Political Economy*.

Friedman, M. (1977) 'Inflation and Unemployment', *Journal of Political Economy*.

Goodhart, C. A. E. (1975) *Money, Information and Uncertainty*, Macmillan, Basingstoke.

Gowland, D. H. (1985) *Money, Inflation and Unemployment*, Wheatsheaf Books, Brighton, Sussex.

Greenaway, D. and Shaw, G. K. (1983) *Macroeconomics*, Martin Robertson, Oxford.

Grossman, H. I. (1972) 'Was Keynes a "Keynesian"? A Review Article', *Journal of Economic Literature*.

Grossman, H. I. (1980) 'Rational Expectations, Business Cycles, and Government Behaviour'. Chapter 1 in S. Fischer (ed.), *Rational Expectations and Economic Policy*, Chicago University Press.

Haache, G. (1979) *The Theory of Economic Growth: An Introduction*,

Macmillan, Basingstoke.

Hahn, F.H. (1980) 'Monetarism and Economic Theory', *Economica*.

Hahn, F. H. (1982) 'Reflections on the Invisible Hand', *Lloyds Bank Review*.

Hahn, F. H. (1984) *Economic Theory and Keynes's Insights*, University of Cambridge Economic Theory Discussion Paper no. 72.

Hansen, A. (1949) *Monetary Theory and Fiscal Policy*, McGraw-Hill, New York.

Hicks, J. R. (1937) 'Mr Keynes and the Classics: A Suggested Interpretation', *Econometrica*.

Hicks, J. R. (1967) 'Monetary Theory and History: An attempt at Perspective'. Chapter 9 in *Critical Essays in Monetary Theory*, Clarendon Press, Oxford. Reprinted in R. W. Clower (ed.), *Monetary Theory*, Penguin, Harmondsworth (1969) – page numbers in the text refer to the reprint.

Hillier, B. (1977) 'Does Fiscal Policy Matter? The View from the Government Budget Restraint', *Public Finance/Finances Publiques*.

Hillier, B. (1980) 'A Note on Bond Finance and Stability in a Simple Income–Expenditure Model: A Comment', *Public Finance/Finances Publiques*.

Hillier, B. (1982) 'Progressive Interdependence and Economic Integration: (B) The Case of Monetary Union'. In D. Dosser, D. H. Gowland and K. Hartley (eds), *The Collaboration of Nations: A Study of European Economic Policy*, Martin Robertson, Oxford.

Hillier, B. (1985) 'Rational Expectations, the Government Budget Constraint, and the Optimal Money Supply Rule', *Journal of Macroeconomics*.

Hutchison, T. W. (1977) 'Keynes versus the "Keynesians" . . .?', Institute of Economic Affairs, London.

Johnson, H. G. (1964) *Money, Trade and Economic Growth*, Allen and Unwin, London, Chapter 5. Reprinted in part in R. W. Clower (ed.), *Monetary Theory*, Penguin, Harmondsworth (1969) – page numbers in the text refer to the reprint.

Johnson, H. G. (1972a) 'Panel Discussion, World Inflation'. In E. Clasen and P. Salin (eds), *Stabilisation Policies in Interdependent Economies*, North-Holland, Amsterdam.

Johnson, H. G. (1972b) 'The Monetary Approach to the Balance of Payments', *Journal of Financial and Quantitative Analysis*.

Kahn, R. F. (1931) 'The Relation of Home Investment to Unemployment', *Economic Journal*.

Kaldor, N. and Trevithick, J. (1981) A Keynesian Perspective on Money', *Lloyds Bank Review*.

Keynes, J. M. (1936) *The General Theory of Employment, Interest and Money*, Macmillan, London.

Keynes, J. M. (1937) 'How to Avoid a Slump', *The Times*, London, January, 12th, 13th and 14th.

Keynes, J. M. (1940) *How to Pay for the War*, Macmillan and Harcourt Brace, London.

Laidler, D. (1978) 'How to Maintain Stability – a Monetarist View', *The Banker*.

Laidler, D. (1981) 'Monetarism: An Interpretation and an Assessment', *Economic Journal*.

Laidler, D. (1986) 'International Monetary Economics in Theory and Practice'. In J. Sargent (ed.), *Postwar Macroeconomic Developments*, University of Toronto Press.

Laidler, D. and Parkin, M. (1975) 'Inflation: A Survey', *Economic Journal*.

Leijonhufvud, A. (1967) 'Keynes and the Keynesians: A Suggested Interpretation', *American Economic Review*. Reprinted in R. W. Clower (ed.), *Monetary Theory*, Penguin, Harmondsworth (1969) – page numbers in the text refer to the reprint.

Leijonhufvud, A. (1968) *On Keynesian Economics and the Economics of Keynes: A Study in Monetary Theory*, Oxford University Press, New York.

Lindbeck, A. and Snower, D. (1986) 'Efficiency Wages Versus Insiders and Outsiders', Centre for Economic Policy Research Discussion Paper no. 133.

Lipsey, R. G. and Parkin, J. M. (1970) 'Incomes Policy: A Re-appraisal', *Economica*.

Lucas, R. E. (1976) 'Econometric Policy Evaluation: A Critique'. In K. Brunner and A. H. Meltzer (eds), *The Phillips Curve and Labour Markets*. Carnegie Rochester Conferences in Public Policy, North-Holland, Amsterdam.

Lucas, R. E. (1977) 'Understanding Business Cycles'. In K. Brunner and A. H. Meltzer (eds), *Stabilization of the Domestic and International Economy*, Carnegie-Rochester Conference Series in Public Policy, North-Holland, Amsterdam.

Machlup, F. (1939) 'Period Analysis and Multiplier Theory', *Quarterly Journal of Economics*.

Mayer, T. (1984) Book review, *Journal of Monetary Economics*.

McCallum, B. T. (1984) 'Are Bond-financed Deficits Inflationary? A Ricardian Analysis', *Journal of Political Economics*.

McKinnon, R. I. (1969) 'Portfolio Balance and International Payments Adjustment'. In R. A. Mundell and A. Swoboda (eds), *Monetary Problems of the International Economy*, University of Chicago Press.

Meltzer, A. H. (1981) 'Keynes's General Theory: A Different Perspective', *Journal of Economic Literature*.

Minford, P. and Peel, D. (1983) *Rational Expectations and the New Macroeconomics*, Martin Robertson, Oxford.

Modigliani, F. (1944) 'Liquidity Preference and the Theory of Interest and Money', *Econometrica*. Reprinted in F. A. Lutz and L. W. Mints (eds), *Readings in Monetary Theory*, Blakiston, Philadelphia (1951).

Modigliani, F. (1963) 'The Monetary Mechanism and its Interaction with Real Phenomena', *Review of Economics and Statistics*.

Moggridge, D. (ed.) (1973) *The Collected Writings of John Maynard*

288 *Bibliography*

Keynes, Vol. XIV, Macmillan Basingstoke.

Moggridge, D. (ed.) (1980) *The Collected Writings of John Maynard Keynes*, Vol. XXVII, Macmillan, Basingstoke.

Morley, R. (1988) *The Macroeconomics of Open Economies*, Edward Elgar, Aldershot.

Ohlin, B. (1937) 'Some Notes on the Stockholm Theory of Savings and Investment', *Economic Journal*.

Parkin, M. and Bade, R. (1982) *Modern Macroeconomics*, Philip Allan, Deddington, Oxford.

Patinkin, D. (1956) *Money, Interest and Prices: An Integration of Monetary and Value Theory*, Row Peterson, Evanston, Illinois.

Patinkin, D. (1982) *Anticipations of the General Theory*, Basil Blackwell, Oxford.

Phelps, E. S. (1967) 'Phillips Curves, Expectations of Inflation and Optimal Unemployment over Time', *Economica*.

Phelps, E. S. and Taylor, J. B. (1977) 'Stabilising Powers of Monetary Policy under Rational Expectations', *Journal of Political Economy*.

Phillips, A. W. (1958) 'The Relationship between Unemployment and the Rate of Change of Money Wage Rates in the United Kingdom, 1861–1957', *Economica*.

Pigou, A. C. (1914) *Unemployment*, Home University Library, London.

Pigou, A. C. (1933) *The Theory of Unemployment*, Macmillan, London.

Pigou, A. C. (1943) 'The Classical Stationary State', *Economic Journal*.

Poole, W. (1970) 'Optimal Choice of Monetary Policy Instrument in a Simple Stochastic Macro-model', *Quarterly Journal of Economics*.

Reuber, G. L. (1964) 'The Objectives of Canadian Monetary Policy, 1949–61: Empirical "Trade-Offs" and the Reaction Function of the Authorities', *Journal of Political Economy*.

Robertson, D. H. (1915) *A Study of Industrial Fluctuation*, P. S. King and Son, London.

Robinson, J. (1971) *Economic Heresies*, Macmillan, Basingstoke.

Rowley, J. C. R. and Wilton, D. A. (1973) 'The Empirical Sensitivity of the Phillips Curve', *The American Economist*.

Samuelson, P. A. and Solow, R. M. (1960) 'Analytical Aspects of Anti-inflation Policy', *American Economic Review*.

Sargent, T. and Wallace, N. (1975) 'Rational Expectations, the Optimal Monetary Instrument and the Optimal Money Supply Rule', *Journal of Political Economy*.

Sawyer, M. C. (1982) *Macroeconomics in Question: the Keynesian-Monetarist Orthodoxies and the Kaleckian Alternative*, Wheatsheaf Press, Brighton.

Shackle, G. L. S. (1967) *The Years of High Theory*, Cambridge University Press.

Shapiro, E. (1982) *Macroeconomic Analysis* (5th edn), Harcourt Brace Jovanovich, New York.

Shieh, Y. N. (1980) 'A Note on Bond Finance and Stability in a Simple Income–Expenditure Model', *Public Finance/Finances Publiques*.

Silber, W. L. (1970) 'Fiscal Policy in *IS–LM* Analysis: A Correction', *Journal of Money, Credit and Banking*.

Solow, R. M. (1980) 'On Theories of Unemployment', *American Economic Review*.

Thirlwall, A. P. (1986) *Balance of Payments Theory and the United Kingdom Experience*, 3rd edn, Macmillan, Basingstoke.

Tinbergen, J. (1952) *On the Theory of Economic Policy*, North-Holland, Amsterdam.

Tobin, J. (1972) 'Friedman's Theoretical Framework', *Journal of Political Economy*.

Tobin, J. (1980) 'Are New Classical Models Plausible Enough to Guide Policy?', *Journal of Money, Credit and Banking*.

Weintraub, E. Roy (1979) *Microfoundations: The Compatibility of Microeconomics and Macroeconomics*, Cambridge University Press.

Winslow, T. (1989) 'Keynes on Rationality', mimeo, University of Toronto.

Index